ONONDAGA
IROQUOIS
PREHISTORY

A NEW YORK STATE STUDY

ONONDAGA IROQUOIS PREHISTORY

A Study in Settlement Archaeology

JAMES A. TUCK

SYRACUSE UNIVERSITY PRESS

JAMES A. TUCK received the Ph.D. from Syracuse
University. He is the author of many articles on
Northeastern prehistory and is archaeological con-
sultant to the Department of Provincial Affairs,
Government of Newfoundland and Labrador. Tuck
is associate professor of anthropology, Memorial
University of Newfoundland, St. John's, where he
is also associated with the Institute for Social and
Economic Research. His current field work in-
cludes investigating the archaeology of Northern
Labrador.

Manufactured in the United States of America

Contents

Plates

Figures

Tables

Preface

THIS BOOK summarizes excavations carried out in Onondaga County, central New York State, during the summers of 1965 through 1967 and subsequent study of collections made by other archaeologists, both amateur and professional, before and after that time. The title may, in part, be slightly misleading, for while the prehistory of the Onondaga nation of the Iroquois Confederacy is our principal concern, the historic period is considered in some detail to provide a basis for reconstructions of the archaeological evidence.

The study was originally designed to demonstrate on a local level that Iroquois culture as recorded by early European visitors was the product of a long *in situ* evolution in the area which now comprises upstate New York. Through an analysis of the fine design of ceramics and other artifacts and a settlement approach to Iroquoian prehistory, we were able not only to deliver the *coup de grâce* to any theory of a recent migration of the Onondaga people into central New York but to offer some positive suggestions as to the origin of the social and political structure that characterized not only the Onondaga but the entire Five Nations and many other Northeastern peoples at the time of European contact. The settlement approach considers as the basis of archaeological analysis and interpretation not the artifact but the settlements where artifacts and other evidence of human habitation are found.

Our investigations revealed evidence of at least three distinct communities in Onondaga County, two of which contributed directly to the development of the Onondaga nation. We were able to trace the course of the village removals and resettlements of both of these communities over several centuries—in one case for nearly seven hundred years. As a result we arrived at a model of Iroquoian prehistory which is

xi

very different from the branching model so often held to describe Iroquois cultural and political development.

It remains to be determined whether the kinds of events proposed here as having characterized the Onondaga over the past seven hundred years were occurring simultaneously elsewhere in Iroquoia. Other researchers now engaged in Iroquois studies may soon provide the answer to this question. In the meantime, however, the Onondaga's central position, both geographically and politically, among the Five Nations suggests that the Onondaga may well be exemplars of Iroquois cultural development, and until evidence to the contrary appears, the model proposed here presents a hypothesis worth testing in other areas of Iroquoia.

The chapters that follow present first a brief historical outline of Onondaga culture and a sketch of the major developments in Iroquois prehistory. Secondly, descriptions of our excavations at settlements spanning nearly the entire range of Onondaga pre- and proto-history are presented. The description of each site contains a brief account of its discovery, usually through land-clearing activities but occasionally by intentional survey, its location in relation to other sites and natural features, our testing and excavations, and descriptions of the artifacts and other evidences of human habitation. In most cases these are augmented by photos, drawings, or maps, with a few exceptions as noted, taken or prepared by the writer. The site descriptions are arranged in chronological order by cultural "phases" as described by William A. Ritchie, New York State Archaeologist. Sites are usually named for the landowner on whose premises they are located (e.g., the Schoff site) or for some distinguishing geographic feature (e.g., the Furnace Brook site).

Finally, we summarize our data and present our analyses and interpretations pertaining to the origin and development of Onondaga culture in the last chapter.

At this point I would like gratefully to acknowledge the financial support of the Wenner-Gren Foundation for Anthropological Research which financed the initial investigations at the Howlett Hill site; the Rosamond P. Gifford Charitable Organization which financed our excavations at the Furnace Brook and Cabin sites and made it possible to film a motion picture at the Furnace Brook site; the New York State Museum and Science Service and the Syracuse University Graduate School whose support allowed our research to proceed a third season into the Chamberlin, Schoff, Bloody Hill, Burke, and Cemetery sites; and finally to the Canada Council whose support allowed me to conclude these investigations with a study of material from protohistoric Onondaga sites now housed in the collections of Robert Hill of Rochester, New York, Claude Doxtator of Waterloo, New York, the Rochester Museum and Science Center, and the New York State Museum.

Thanks are due as well to the individuals whose assistance in many ways brought this project to fruition after more than three years of field research. These people include students and assistants, many of whom, despite the rigorous field work of settlement archaeology, have continued within the discipline, and the many collectors and landowners who extended us every courtesy throughout our investigations. Robert Ricklis led me to three of the sites discussed here and assisted in many of the early excavations. The assistance of Gordon DeAngelo, Robert Burdick, and Dr. John Calvert is deeply appreciated. Dr. Joseph Waters of the Department of Biology, Villanova University, helped in identifying faunal remains unearthed at all the stations described here; Mrs. Christine Poole, Miss Yvonne Bueler, and Mrs. Jeanette Gleeson typed the manuscript during several revisions; Mrs. Toby Ornstein assisted with the proofreading; David Moyer offered numerous helpful suggestions. My wife, Lynn, provided assistance and encouragement. Finally, Dr. William A. Ritchie deserves especial thanks for his continuing interest, advice, and encouragement throughout the project from beginning to end.

St. John's, Newfoundland
Spring 1971

ONONDAGA
IROQUOIS
PREHISTORY

CHAPTER 1

Historical Background

WHEN EUROPEANS first reached what is now central New York, in the mid-seventeenth century, they found themselves in the forest home of the Onondaga, who called themselves "the People on the Hills," at the center of the Five Nations with whom the French had alternately traded and fought for more than half a century. These early travelers described Onondaga as rich, beautiful, and productive, and its forests, fields, lakes, and streams provided a good living for all who dwelt or journeyed there.

The boundaries of this country were apparently well known to its aboriginal inhabitants but it was not until the mid-nineteenth century that they were explicitly described, by Lewis Henry Morgan, in *The League of the Iroquois* (1901:42–43): "On the boundary line between the Onondagas and the Oneidas, the most prominent point was the Deep Spring (Do-o-song'-wa) near Manlius, in the country of Onondaga . . . ; From the Deep Spring, the line ran due south into Pennsylvania, crossing the Susquehanna near its confluence with the Chenango. North of this spring the line was deflected to the west, leaving in Oneida territory the whole circuit of that lake. Crossing the She-u'ka, or Oneida outlet, a few miles below the lake, the line inclined again to the east, until it reached the meridian of the Deep Spring. From thence it ran due north, crossing the Black River at the site of Watertown, and the St. Lawrence to the eastward of the Thousand Islands." To the west the boundary was somewhat unclear, but "it commenced on Lake Ontario, near the mouth of the Oswego River, and on its west side, and passing between Cross and Otter Lakes, continued south into Pennsylvania, crossing the Susquehanna west of Owego."

Surrounded as they were by the Oneida and Mohawk to the east and the Cayuga and Seneca to the west the Onondaga were at the geo-

graphic as well as political center of the League of the Five Nations
who occupied a relatively small area between the banks of the Genesee
and Hudson Rivers but whose influence extended far beyond the boundaries of what is now New York State. As might be expected, the culture
of the Onondaga as it is today, and as it was described by explorers,
missionaries, and travelers during the early decades of European contact, differs little from that of the surrounding Five Nations tribes. In
many respects the Onondaga were similar to the Huron, Neutral, and
probably the Erie and Susquehannock—other Iroquoian speaking peoples of the Northeast. The description below provides a brief summary of
Onondaga culture upon which we must draw to flesh out the bare skeleton of a culture as it is reflected in the archaeological record, and also
demonstrates the similarity of Onondaga culture to other Iroquoians, suggesting that the surrounding peoples may have had a history very similar to the Onondaga.

In the midst of the wilderness which is now central New York, the
scattered towns of the Onondaga were found, usually two in number, a
pattern which we shall see had persisted through time for several
hundred years before the coming of the Europeans. Our excavations
take on new meaning when we read the early descriptions of these
walled "castles," for many of the features described by the Jesuits in the
seventeenth century fit perfectly with those whose remains are revealed
to us in the archaeological record. Although there are no surviving original descriptions of stockaded Onondaga towns (save Champlain's record
of his raid upon an unknown, possibly Onondaga town in the early seventeenth century) the descriptions of Huron villages recorded by the
Jesuits, and Morgan's (1901:315–20) and Parker's (1923:37–55) descriptions compiled from the nineteenth-century Iroquois, provide us with a
three-dimensional picture of the houses and other structures which we
are able to trace as post mold patterns in the ground.

These houses were framed with saplings and small trees to form an
arbor-like domed structure which was then covered with large shingles,
usually of elm bark. Doors were located at either end, and a central corridor through the house contained the cooking fires of its inhabitants.
On each side of these fires were the sleeping platforms or, in the words
of John Bartram, the "apartments," each presumably inhabited by a nuclear family of a man, a woman, and their children. The houses of the
Onondaga were apparently arranged in somewhat orderly rows—for Father Chaumonot (Chaumont) found the "streets cleaned" when he arrived at Onondaga in 1654 (*Jesuit Relations*, hereafter cited as *JR*,

42:87). Until the eighteenth century, the houses were surrounded by a wooden fortification composed of from one to three rows of tall upright saplings with the lower portions reinforced with withes or bark woven among the uprights. Frequently there were platforms or bastions from which the defenders of the fort could hurl stones or arrows or pour hot water on attackers (see Tooker 1964:41–42).

The Jesuits also reported visiting outlying cabins from time to time to perform religious duties and, on at least one occasion, to avoid the dream-guessing ritual (see pp. 8–9) taking place at Onondaga which frequently caused them considerable discomfort and embarrassment (*JR* 42:127, 157; 52:165; Beauchamp 1916:60).

Fishing villages were located at favored spots some distance from Onondaga, notably at the Oneida Lake outlet, and there is some indication in the eighteenth century that these locations were controlled, at least seasonally, by "a chief . . . and his people, who belong to him." One fishery is said to have *belonged* to a chief (Beauchamp 1916:182–85). Our finding of fish bones at the Cabin site, described in Chapter 2, quite far-removed from any large body of water, suggests that similar fishing villages were in use long before the coming of the Europeans. Between these villages and those of other nations there were many paths through the forest, the Iroquois apparently traveling as much by land as over the many waterways of New York State.

These villages, substantial as they may sound with their palisades and wood and bark houses, were not permanent settlements but were shifted periodically to new locations for various reasons which probably included the exhaustion of firewood, soil, and of local game supplies, and perhaps such things as disease, disrepair, and even such seemingly irrational motives as dreams. We have been able to trace the procession of these villages through many centuries, but nowhere in the archaeological record could we hope to find a description of an actual village removal such as that recorded by Father Lamberville in 1682:

> On my arrival, I found the Iroquois of this village occupied in transporting their corn, their effects, and their cabins to a place 2 leagues distant from their former residence, where they had dwelt for 19 years. They made this change in order to have firewood in convenient proximity, and to secure fields more fertile than those they were abandoning. This is not done without difficulty; for, inasmuch as carts are not used here, and the country is very hilly, the labor of the men and women, who carry their goods on their backs, is consequently harder and of longer duration. To supply

the lack of horses, the inhabitants of these forests render reciprocal
aid to one another, so that a single family will hire sometimes 80
or 100 persons; and they are, in turn, obliged to render the same
service to those who may request it from them, or they are freed
from that obligation by giving food to those whom they have employed. [*JR* 62:55–57]

Food remains, of both animal and plant foods, often comprised a
part of our archaeological discoveries at Iroquois towns. Wild plants utilized by the Onondaga and mentioned by early visitors include black-
berries, strawberries, grapes, plums, cranberries, mayapples, chestnuts,
walnuts, probably hickory nuts, and the "universal plant," a medicinal,
probably sassafras (*JR* 43:147, 257–59; 47:75). Domesticated plants include corn, beans, squash, and sunflowers (*JR* 43:183; 42:197), the seeds
of which were occasionally found in carbonized condition among the
camp refuse which we investigated. Tobacco is not directly represented,
but smoking pipes attest to its cultivation. Archaeologically, the methods of food preparation are practically unknown, but mention was made
by early explorers of "chestnut milk," presumably crushed or boiled
meats of these nuts mixed with water, boiled Indian corn (Beauchamp
1916:89), "sagamite," a dish described by the Jesuits as "clear water
whitened with a handful of Indian corn" (*JR* 47:189), fresh corn, baked
squash (*JR* 42:85; 43:183), and loaves of bread, presumably made from
corn or other vegetable products.

Animals which provided food for the Onondaga were those species
which, with few exceptions, are still to be found in Onondaga County,
as the summaries of faunal remains in the succeeding chapters will indicate. No domestic animals were customarily kept by the Onondaga,
though occasionally a bear cub might be kept penned and fattened for a
feast. In 1755 the Moravian missionary David Zeisberger built a small log
house for a bear cub belonging to his Indian hostess at Onondaga
(Beauchamp 1916:201). Other mammals eaten by the Onondaga which
were mentioned by seventeenth- and eighteenth-century journalists include elk, deer, wildcats, bear, and beaver (*JR* 42:87, 211; 43:139–41;
Beauchamp 1916:201). Birds were also exploited by the Onondaga, notably passenger pigeons which were caught in nets, especially around the
lakes where they flocked in great numbers in the springtime (*JR* 42:97;
43:153). Fish were taken by spearing, by drawing up through the ice in
winter, by means of weirs, and sturgeon were reported to have been
killed with hatchets. Other species taken included yellow perch, black
bass, "black perch, brill," catfish, salmon, pike, and eels which could be

speared by the hundreds by a single man in one evening (*JR* 42:71–73, 97; 43:147, 151, 261). Turtles are not mentioned as a source of food, but they may have been utilized. Rattlesnakes, however, were caught and eaten by the Onondaga. The flesh reportedly tasted like eels and the scales served as a remedy for toothache (*JR* 43:153).

These types of settlement and economic patterns are all fairly well represented in the archaeological record, many of them directly so. But these economic and technological aspects of Iroquois culture were not, and are not today, the cultural elements which made them distinctively Onondaga or Iroquois. Instead, a combination of these elements, most of which were shared by other northeastern peoples, with somewhat more distinctive (but not unique) political, social and religious systems, made them more or less distinctively "Iroquois." These systems are among the most difficult things to read from the archaeological record, but the description left us by early visitors to Onondaga and those reconstructed by present-day ethnologists enable us to project these systems backward into time with considerable confidence, especially when some thread of archaeological evidence exists upon which to base our projections. Our study of settlement patterns and community distributions, as well as a detailed study of material remains which serve to supplement this record, have allowed us to interpret our data with considerable confidence in terms of social and political developments which project the following description of Iroquois "non-material culture" into the prehistoric period, and may, in fact, offer some suggestions as to the origins and development of the Iroquois way of life, at least among the Onondaga.

The Iroquois Confederacy was originally composed of five nations which were drawn together in a league under the influence of Degana-widah, called the "Law Giver," and Hiawatha, a reformed cannibal who persuaded the terrible wizard, Atotarho, a chief of the Onondagas, to bring his people into confederation thus completing the "longhouse" which ran from the Mohawk to the Genesee Rivers. In return for joining the Confederacy the Onondaga were made "Keepers of the Wampum," a position which they continue to enjoy, and Atotarho was made the head chief of the League of the Five Nations, a position also held by an Onondaga sachem since the very beginning of the League.

The League was ruled over by fifty sachems, between eight and fourteen from each tribe of the Five Nations. They met periodically in council at Onondaga where they transacted the business of the League. These councils were generally the occasion for feasting, dancing, and other ceremonies and festivities. Many such councils are mentioned by the Jesuits and other early visitors to Iroquoia (see *JR* 43:167 ff; 44:215; 47:77; Colden 1922 1:127–38). More recent visitors to Onondaga have also witnessed the League council in action, and several good descriptions are available (see Morgan 1901:103–26).

Political organization within the tribes is not so well known as its more striking counterpart on the Confederacy level, but it apparently paralleled, on a smaller scale, the workings of the League. Morgan (1901:69–71) states that the sachems from each tribe ruled it in the same manner as the council of fifty ruled the League and that there were also "chiefs" of lower status whose titles were not hereditary who also had a voice in local affairs. In 1655 Father Chaumont addressed such a council at Onondaga which was composed of "30 Elders" (*JR* 42:93–95), a fact which implies an organization like that described much later by Morgan.

Other aspects of Iroquois social organization and ceremonialism also left little trace in the earth, but again, occasional unusual discoveries afford us a glimpse at these cultural systems. There remains little doubt that the Iroquois were organized into phratries or moieties, each of which was further divided into a number of exogamous clans. Inheritance within these clans was in the female line; the hereditary titles of the sachems were passed from a man to his younger brother or, more commonly, to his sister's son. Besides inheritance these moieties or phratries functioned principally on ceremonial occasions such as games and funerals. The idea that the Iroquois were matri*local* as well as matri*lineal* has recently been called into some question (see Richards 1967). Our data again reveal little direct evidence about social organization, but offer some interesting suggestions about residence patterns and community relations, as is shown in Chapter 7.

We occasionally found graves of the inhabitants of Onondaga in connection with our explorations and from them recovered a bit of information about burial practices at the time. Cemetery locations, burial position, and kinds and amount of grave goods are about all we can hope to reconstruct. However, from the literature on the ceremonies and ritual activities which accompanied death and burial among the seventeenth-century Onondaga we can draw a much more vivid picture of the mortuary ceremonialism which must have taken place when the bones were originally interred. Upon the approach of death an Onondaga customarily gave his death feast (*JR* 58:215), was surrounded by all his best possessions, and may even have selected the garments in which he wished to be buried. Immediately upon the death of the individual "frightful lamentations" were set up in the cabin in which the death had taken place (*JR* 43:267). In the case of tortured captives the people beat upon the bark of cabins to celebrate the death and to frighten away the soul of the deceased, but members of the Onondaga tribe were treated with considerably more respect. The Moravians mentioned that in 1753 the Onondaga put away all ornaments and dressed in rags during mourning and that a feast was held in the presence of the dead woman at noon (Beauchamp 1916:183), a practice which may also have occurred in earlier times. After the interment had taken place, the grave was filled with provisions for the sustenance of the soul of the departed, and a sacrifice was made by burning corn. The effects of the deceased were then distributed among those who had given presents of consolation. Occasionally reburial was practiced, one instance being recorded in which a mother had her son's body disinterred and redressed in new garments two or three times until only the bare bones remained which were then wrapped in a blanket and given to the woman (*JR* 43:267–69).

Little also remains in the ground of the Onondaga seasonal ceremonial cycle which included the Thanks to the Maple, Planting Festival, Strawberry Festival, Green Corn Festival, Harvest Festival, and New Year's Jubilee or Midwinter Festival (see Tooker 1970b). These festivals lasted either one day (Maple, Berry, and Planting Festivals), several days, or as long as a week, but the component parts of each were roughly similar. Preparations for each were made by a special class of officials, the "Keepers of the Faith," whose positions, in contrast to those of the political leaders, were not hereditary. They were selected by the "wise men and matrons out of their respective tribes" (Morgan 1901:185). The feasts were prepared, the date determined, the people summoned, and many of the speeches were made by the Keepers of the Faith. A speech of thanksgiving opened the Thanks to the Maple Festival, followed by other speeches which Morgan said "were in the nature of exhortations to duty." Dancing followed—not social dancing, which frequently also accompanied religious festivals—but the Great Feather Dance "performed by a select band, in full costume, and . . . reserved exclusively for religious councils, and for great occasions" (Morgan 1901:190). Following this, other dances were performed with the entire assembled group occasionally joining in. Tobacco was then burned, a final speech was made by one of the Keepers of the Faith, and the feast was concluded. The Planting and Berry Festivals differed only in slight details from the Maple Festival.

The Green Corn and Harvest Festivals each lasted four days. The first two days were absorbed by speeches of thanksgiving and dancing, including the Great Feather Dance, which were similar in most respects to those described above. The third day was the "Ah-do'-weh," a ceremony in which thanks were given for bounty received from the natural and spiritual world as well as for "acts of kindness, personal achievements, political events, in a word, all the affairs of the public and private life were open on this occasion to the indulgence of the grateful affections" (Morgan 1901:203). On the fourth day of the festival the Bowl Game was played between the two moieties. This was a game of chance with a very complex scoring system. Six peach stones, or those of other fruits, were blackened on one side and tossed from a bowl. Points were scored based upon the number which landed with the same face showing (see Blau 1967 for a detailed description of this game as it is played today at Onondaga).

The most important festival of the annual cycle was, and is today, the New Year's or Midwinter Festival. The details of this series of ceremonies are too extensive to enumerate completely here, but it is sufficient to say that it included in aboriginal times all of the elements mentioned previously with the addition of the White Dog Sacrifice and costumed performances by the Keepers of the Faith during which they visited each house to give thanks at the time of the New Year. Outdoor sports and games, and social dancing, usually accompanied each of these festivals but did not comprise part of the religious celebrations (see Tooker 1970b for a complete description and analysis of this important annual event).

Again we are offered suggestions of these ceremonials in the archaeological record by such indirect evidence as the fact that the economy of the prehistoric Iroquois was identical to that of the Onondaga who performed the ceremonies mentioned above which suggests to us that the stimulus or the need for such ceremonies—for example, to secure a sufficient supply of food—was present in the prehistoric period, and the ceremonial cycle presumably had its roots there. Also, many of our collections contain materials often specifically connected in one way or another with these ceremonies—such as bangles of deer bone which decorated the costumes of the dancers and turtle shell rattle parts presumably used to provide music for the festivals, etc.

We also find occasional evidence of other Iroquois ritualism, for instance the possible dream bundle from the Cabin site (see pp. 40–41), which brings to mind the strong part dreams played in the life of the Onondaga. Dreams were interpreted as "wishes of the soul," and every attempt was made to satisfy a dream lest some harm befall the dreamer (Wallace 1958). The Jesuits repeatedly mentioned the apparent dishar-mony caused by this practice, and regarded dreams as a great impedi-ment to the spread of Christianity (*JR* 52:153–55). Many of the Onon-daga dreamed they should obtain articles belonging to the Jesuits, including the crucifix and the robes of the fathers (*JR* 42:151–53; 47:183). Some went so far as to have themselves tortured in response to dreams (see *JR* 47:179–81).

Curing societies also formed an important part of Onondaga culture, particularly the well-known False Face Society, many of whose mask styles and other features may have been typically Iroquoian. This com-pany is in existence today, and apparently has been from prehistoric times as suggested by the presence of miniature maskettes which resem-ble the historically known false faces. Perhaps the best description of one of the members of this company and his performance is that wit-nessed at Onondaga in 1743 by John Bartram (1751:43–44):

> At night, soon after we were laid down to sleep, and our fire almost burnt out, we were entertained by a comical fellow, dis-guised in as odd a dress as Indian folly could invent; he had on a clumsy vizard of wood colour'd black, with a nose 4 or 5 inches long, a grining mouth set awry, furnished with long teeth, round the eyes circles of bright brass, surrounded a larger circle of white paint, from his forehead hung long tresses of buffalo hair, and from the catch part of his head ropes made of the plaited husks of In-dian corn; I cannot recollect the whole of his dress, but that it was equally uncouth: he carried in one hand a large staff, in the other a calabash with small stones in it, for a rattle, and this he rubbed up and down on his staff; he would, sometimes, hold up his head and make a hideous noise like the braying of an ass; he came in at the further end, and he made this noise at first, whether it was be-cause he would not surprise us too suddenly I can't say; I asked Conrad Weiser, who as well as myself lay next to the alley, what noise that was? and Shickalamy the Indian, our companion, who I supposed, thought me somewhat scared, called out, lye still John, I never heard him speak so much plain English before. The jack pudding presently came up to us and an Indian boy came with him and kindled our fire, that we might see his glittering eyes and antick postures as he hobbled round the fire, sometimes he would turn the buffaloes hair on one side that we might take better view of his ill-favoured phyz, when he had tired himself, which was sometime after he had well tired us, the boy that attended him

struck 2 or 3 smart blows on the floor, at which the hobgoblin
seemed surprised and on repeating them he jumped out doors and
disappeared.

While not a typical performance of a member of the false face com-
pany whose primary function it was to cure and prevent disease, Bartram's description of the "hobgoblin" contains all the elements of the
costume still in use today—the mask, old clothes, staff, and rattle, in
this case of a gourd, whereas turtle-shell rattles are favored today—
many of which are occasionally represented in the archaeological record.

Finally, Iroquois warfare and the ceremonialism connected with it
are well represented in both the archaeological and historic records.
The former contains evidence of warfare in the form of palisaded villages located upon defensible hilltops, and in at least one case by the remains of what appears to have been a cannibalistic feast. The historic
record is filled with accounts of Iroquois warfare which was prosecuted
as far from Iroquoia as the country of the Abnaki in Maine, near Virginia to the south, and westward to the territories of the Ox Nation
(Sioux) and other midwestern peoples (JR 47:141–53). These wars seem
originally to have been of a different ilk from our wars today and more
probably assumed the form of a deadly game played by the Iroquois to
"shed blood and distinguish themselves as murderers" (JR 43:263–65),
practices which, bloodthirsty as they sound, were very much at home
among many peoples of the Northeast. Preparations for war involved the
boiling of a "war kettle," which in at least one case lasted from fall until
the following February when a feast took place at which all the partici-
pants "sang, danced, made grimaces, and declared their determination
to go to war." To prove their bravery they "threw live coals and hot
ashes at one another, exchanged heavy blows, and burned each other"
(JR 42:171).

When members of the war party returned they often brought with
them captives whose care was entrusted to those who had lost a relative
in the recently concluded warfare. At the hands of these people the vic-
tims were frequently tortured to death and often were ceremonially
eaten by members of the Onondaga and other Iroquois nations. The Jesuit Relations abound with descriptions of such proceedings, such treatment being accorded equally to both Europeans and Indians (see
JR 62:59–91).

Despite the excellent historical documents which have preserved so much of the Iroquois culture for us, and despite the ever-increasing so-phistication of ethnological analyses of Iroquois culture based upon his-torical and contemporary sources, there are still many unanswered ques-tions surrounding the Iroquois, their culture, and their history. Chief among these questions are those which inquire as to where the Iroquois originated, when they first arrived in New York State, and what factors were important in the development of that more or less distinctive con-stellation of cultural traits, summarized briefly on the preceding pages, which distinguished the Iroquois.

The problem of Iroquois origins has been debated by historians and anthropologists—amateur and professional alike—for several hundred years. The course of these theoretical developments has been outlined by several writers (see especially Ritchie 1961b), so a brief summary at this point will serve to provide a framework into which the concepts de-veloped in this book can be fitted. Theories attempting to explain the or-igin and subsequent development of Iroquois culture can be divided into two migration hypotheses and the more recent *in situ* theory.

The earlier of the two migration theories is known as the "northern hypothesis." It postulated that the Iroquois people and culture origi-nated somewhere north of their present homeland, probably in the St. Lawrence Valley, a possibility not entirely without historical basis. Car-tier, in 1534, encountered at least one, and probably two, groups of pre-sumed Iroquoian speakers in the St. Lawrence Valley at the villages of Hochelaga and Stadacona, near the present-day cities of Montreal and Quebec, respectively, and left a description of the former (Biggar 1924:152–61) which coincides nicely with the description of other Iro-quoian towns provided by other early writers and archaeologists. More-over, vocabularies collected by Cartier were later shown to be Iroquoian (Cuoq 1869). These observations leave little doubt that there was an Ir-oquoian population in the St. Lawrence as recently as the early sixteenth century.

The theory that a migration from this area took place between the visit of Cartier and the beginning of the seventeenth century is sug-gested by the record of Champlain's visit in 1603. He found the area un-inhabited, though the Iroquois were in a struggle with an Algonkian group for its control (from Trigger 1967a:205). These two historical re-cords (Cartier's and Champlain's) suggested to many investigators that an actual migration accounted for the historic positions of some or all of the Iroquois tribes. Additional support for a northern origin of the Iro-quois early appeared in a persistent tradition first recorded by Nicholas

Perrot sometime between 1680 and 1718 (Blair 1911:1, 42–43). No source was given for this tradition, which holds that the Iroquois originally inhabited an area near the present city of Montreal, Canada, were driven from there by hostile Adirondacks, and settled in the areas in New York where they were encountered by seventeenth-century explorers. Somewhat later Lafitau also wrote (1724:1, 101) of this possibility when he recorded a Mohawk tradition that that group had once lived near present-day Quebec City. Cadwallader Colden, in his *History of the Iroquois* (1922), repeated Perrot's tale almost exactly, although he gave no source for his material, an unfortunate characteristic of most early works.

In the next century, migration hypotheses were kept alive through repetitions of these earlier legends. Morgan, though he tried long and hard to discover something about Iroquois origins from the people themselves, was unsuccessful and was forced to rely on Lafitau (Trigger, personal communication). Morgan's basic story was the same as that of earlier writers, though he embellished it somewhat by adding that it was in the St. Lawrence Valley that the Iroquois "learned husbandry and became enured to the hardships of the chase and warfare" (Morgan 1901:5–6). It is worth noting that Morgan seems to be the first writer to show concern for the development of Iroquois *culture* (i.e., "husbandry . . . warfare and the chase") as well as with prehistoric and historic tribal movements.

Much work was stimulated by this hypothesis, a good deal of it before the beginning of the twentieth century. In 1860 and 1861 William Dawson described the remains of an Indian village or encampment which had been discovered near the McGill University campus in Montreal. The material recovered from his excavations at this site included early trade goods from about the time of Cartier (Dawson 1860, 1861). Dawson originally pronounced this to be an Algonkian site but later, when Abbé Jean-André Cuoq showed that the Cartier vocabularies were unquestionably Iroquoian, Dawson changed his mind and pointed out similarities between his "Hochelage" and the Erie, an Iroquoian group which had lived south of the lake by that name. Later the material excavated at the McGill campus site was examined by other scholars and pronounced to be Huron, Tuscarora, Petun, Seneca, or Mohawk (Trigger 1967a:208). Although each of these proposals has had some effect upon the course of development of Iroquois prehistory, most can now be shown to be the result of uncritical use of the very limited data available at the time.

Linguists, too, became interested in the Iroquois during the latter half of the nineteenth century. Father Cuoq, mentioned above, demonstrated that the Cartier vocabularies were unquestionably Iroquoian and further related them specifically to Mohawk. Other investigators made much of Cuoq's discovery, some going so far as to suggest that all of the Iroquois had originated in the St. Lawrence Valley (Hale 1884:10–11).

About the turn of the century, the northern hypothesis of Iroquois origins began to lose popularity in favor of a theory which proposed a southern origin for the Iroquois. The northern hypothesis was never completely discarded, however, being at first combined with the southern theory and remaining until very recently to account for the origins of the Onondaga and/or Oneida. This southern hypothesis first appeared in Herbert Lloyd's notes in the 1901 edition of Morgan's *League of the Iroquois*. Lloyd, in a statement which he appears to attribute to Morgan, says that the Iroquois were originally derived from Puget Sound, where they lived on fish and had no knowledge of agriculture. According to this theory, the Iroquois then moved eastward into the Mississippi Valley where they learned to practice agriculture (in contrast to Morgan's theory which said that they had learned this in the St. Lawrence Valley). It was also in the Mississippi Valley, according to Lloyd, that the Iroquois learned to live in settled villages. At this juncture in Iroquois prehistory the Cherokee, a southern group of Iroquoians, were supposed to have left the main band and taken up residence in the Southeast. The group remaining in the Mississippi Valley then split into two parts. One part, the proto-Huron-Onondaga-Oneida-Mohawk, moved north of Lakes Erie and Ontario to settle in the St. Lawrence Valley from where a secondary dispersal proceeded about as in the northern hypothesis. The second group, which, according to this theory ultimately became the historic Erie, Seneca, and Cayuga, gradually drifted northeastward from the Mississippi, passed south of Lakes Erie and Ontario, and settled in the lands where they were first encountered by Europeans. This hypothesis, as well as Lloyd's explicit rejection of both the northern hypothesis and a southeastern origin for the Iroquois, set the tone of Iroquois studies for the next fifty years.

Arthur C. Parker, basing his interpretation upon the archaeological data which were then becoming available, partly through his own efforts, arrived at essentially the same conclusions as had Lloyd. Parker added, however, that the Iroquois tribes overcame the "Mound Builders" in Ohio and absorbed them into their tribes. The lack of Mound Builder artifacts in Iroquois assemblages is accounted for by the extreme animosity of the Iroquois toward their defeated enemies—an animosity which resulted in the destruction of much of their "material culture" and a refusal to adopt most of what remained (Parker 1916:503–507).

During the 1930s and 1940s several studies of importance to Iroquois prehistory appeared, not all of them produced by archaeologists. In 1939, Regina Flannery pointed out in some detail that Iroquois culture was not unique in the Northeast and was, in fact, quite similar to that of the surrounding Algonkian tribes. In 1940, William N. Fenton's paper on the historic position of Iroquois tribes appeared. Considering primarily ethno-historic data, Fenton carefully presented the facts pertaining to Iroquois movements since Cartier's visit in 1534. Because Fenton limited his work to historically documented evidence and refrained from making any premature conclusions about the ultimate origin of Iroquois culture (though the northern origin of the Onondaga-Oneida was still accepted) his work has provided the basis for subsequent studies of Iroquois population shifts, especially those employing the direct historic approach.

In 1943, James B. Griffin began to question, from several points of view, some of the earlier migration hypotheses. He agreed with Flannery that Iroquois culture was not unique in the Northeast, and further speculated that the apparent distinctiveness of the Iroquois might be due not to actual cultural differences, but to their martial and political strength and position as a buffer between the Dutch and British which allowed them to maintain their culture while other native peoples were being destroyed by white contact. Looking then to other areas of anthropology to support the possibility that the Iroquois were not as distinctive as supposed, Griffin found further evidence to suggest that the Iroquois were not relatively recent arrivals in the Northeast. Linguistics, he said, showed the Iroquois-Cherokee divergence was actually much earlier than formerly thought. Physical anthropology had demonstrated that the Iroquois were skeletally very similar to the surrounding Algonkian peoples. Finally, he pointed out that the cultures thought to be ancestral to Iroquois were now known to be contemporary with them.

In 1944 William A. Ritchie published similar findings which were based on over fifteen years of field research in New York State. Specifically, Ritchie began to see some very strong resemblances between Iroquois and an "Algonkian" culture which he had defined and named the "Owasco" aspect or culture.

This "new" archaeological culture, described on the basis of Ritchie's excavations at more than thirty stations, was characterized by him as a culture whose camp, village, and workshop sites were often situated on hilltops a mile or more from navigable water were often palisaded, and had been found from the Genesee River in western New York to the Hudson and Lake Champlain Valleys on the east, and southward into New Jersey and Pennsylvania through the courses of the Delaware and Susquehanna Rivers. Further traits were enumerated in some detail and included a weak polished stone industry, a relatively small inventory of chipped stone work of high quality, a well diversified bone and antler component, and an advanced ceramic complex, the latter embracing smoking pipes, almost exclusively of the obtuse angle elbow type, and grit-tempered pottery vessels, surface-malleated with cord or fabric, of two general forms. The more recent of those two forms, to which we will pay particular attention in this report, "while somewhat elongated, is a semiglobular or globular, round bottomed receptacle, with a marked neck constriction, straight to excessive degree of rim eversion and not infrequently an incipient to bold collar." Designs on such ceramics are said to consist of "simple rectilinear lines, often combined with the herringbone, chevron, rhomboid, or plait composed of a vertical or oblique group of short parallel lines."

While noting some ceramic similarities between these Owasco vessels and those of the Iroquois, as well as similarities in projectile points, celts, faceted pebble hammerstones, sandstone discs, and incised bone, Ritchie attributed these similarities to culture contact rather than a generic relationship between Owasco and Iroquois. Later in the same work, however, he pointed out that Iroquois-Owasco relationships required further investigation.

Despite these hints that the Iroquois may have been related to earlier cultures in New York and despite the fact that no precursors for the Iroquois could be found outside the area of their historic habitation, both Ritchie and Griffin continued to be influenced by earlier migration hypotheses. Griffin (1943:364) saw a southern origin for Iroquois, in Hopewell, an elaborate culture of the Midwest during several centuries B.C. and A.D., and stated that "legend, history, and archaeology coincide in confirming that the Iroquois were driven from the St. Lawrence to New York in the late sixteenth century." Ritchie, too, continued to accept the migration hypothesis as correct, though, as he later said in 1961, it was because evidence for a theory of local development in New York was too flimsy, a situation which was certainly the case.

In 1952, a major theoretical change in Iroquois prehistory was begun which effected a revival in the study of Iroquois archaeology. This was the *in situ* theory proposed by Richard S. MacNeish, who based his conclusions upon a study of Iroquois pottery types, in addition to brief consideration of those lines of evidence proposed by Ritchie and Griffin. Perhaps MacNeish's own "tentative historical reconstruction" expresses most succinctly the conclusions at which he arrived from his study of Iroquois ceramics (1952:89):

    1. The first culture that can possibly be connected with historic remains is Point Peninsula [a pre-Owasco "Middle Woodland" culture] which, with little regional variation, was spread over southern and eastern Ontario and northwestern and central New York. This homogeneous widespread Point Peninsula culture may be considered proto-Iroquois.

    2. Gradually four regional variants with an Owasco, or Owascoid, type of material culture developed from Point Peninsula. These developments may represent the first differentiations of the proto-Iroquois into tribal and proto-tribal units. The easternmost regional variant (an Owasco Culture represented by the Wickham, Castle Creek, and Bainbridge sites) is probably ancestral to Mohawk, while the related north-central Owasco variant (represented at the Pillar Point and Calkins Farm sites) may be ancestral to the Onondaga-Oneida. In western New York the Levanna to Canandaigua Owasco sequence may have given rise to Cayuga and Seneca; while in the Ontario Peninsula area there is an Owasco variant (represented in the lowest levels of Middleport, Kreiger, and Goessens sites) which is ancestral to the material cultural units of the Neutral-Erie and Huron.

    3. There is a general tendency for these Owascoid variants to develop an Iroquoian type of material culture and to differ further in their material cultures. These further differentiations of the Iroquois general culture type represent the cultural assemblages of specific Iroquois tribes. Thus the Mohawks continued their development from an Owasco base, while the Onondaga-Oneida did the same until almost historic times when they split into two tribal units. The Seneca and Cayuga (and possibly Susquehannock) seem to have separated from each other in late Owasco times just before their development of an Iroquoian type of material culture. The Huron and Neutral-Erie separated somewhat later. This general reconstruction has been labelled the *"In Situ"* theory of Iroquois prehistory.

Evidence confirming MacNeish's hypothesis was not long in coming. In 1958 (and again in 1963) New York State Museum parties under William A. Ritchie and Robert E. Funk carried out excavations at the Kelso site, discussed in Chapter 3 of this volume. The earlier of these investigations and further explorations of the transitional Owasco-Iroquois period in eastern New York between 1952 and 1960 allowed Ritchie (1961b:30) to write that the *in situ* theory had "been accepted as a working hypothesis by the majority of archaeologists in the Iroquois field."

Other investigators also demonstrated the general validity of the *in situ* hypothesis in various sub-areas of Iroquoia. Donald Lenig's study (1965) of the Oak Hill horizon (now *phase,* see Ritchie 1965:302; also pp. 47–48 in this volume), the transitional Owasco-Iroquois stage in eastern New York, showed clearly some lines of development of Mohawk "material culture." James V. Wright, in his monograph (1966) on the Ontario Iroquois, has also demonstrated on a very broad horizon that the Iroquois tradition has considerable time depth in the Northeast. He traces the Ontario branch of Iroquois culture back to the year A.D. 1000 to the Glen Meyer and Pickering branches of the early Iroquois tradition in that area.

This, then, was the state of attitudes toward Iroquois prehistory in the mid-1960s. Migration hypotheses were on the wane while evidence for an *in situ* development of Iroquois culture was steadily increasing. Ritchie's continued excavations in New York State had revealed increasingly complete pictures of the archaeological manifestations of Iroquois and Owasco cultures. His studies had proceeded to a point where each could be divided into a number of discrete phases, distinguished by "a recurring complex of distinctive archaeological traits, sufficiently different from any other complex to suggest that it represents the product of a single cultural group, pertaining to a limited territory and to a relatively brief period of time" (Ritchie 1965:xvi).

Nevertheless, the question of Iroquois origins was far from settled. Despite the growing body of data supporting the *in situ* hypothesis, the older migration theories were still retained in some quarters. Even among the supporters of the *in situ* theory there remained elements of doubt about many of the changes and continuities in "material culture" upon which the connections between Owasco and Iroquois were based. Comparisons between sites of one phase from one tribal sub-area with those of the succeeding phase from another sub-area often revealed startling discontinuities in traits which, by the *in situ* hypothesis, should have been continuous. The absolute chronologies for some of the phases defined by Ritchie were also somewhat unclear. The validity of the "branching" or "dendritic" model of Iroquois development proposed by

MacNeish, which implied that the Five Nations resulted from progressive divisions of a single parent stock during the early second millenium A.D., remained to be tested by more intensive researches in restricted areas of Iroquoia. Finally, the origin of the Onondaga nation, the central tribe of the League, was still a matter of doubt, since some evidence, mostly non-archaeological, pointed to a northern origin (in the St. Lawrence Valley), while excavations of early Iroquois sites in central New York (especially the Kelso site) suggested the presence of Iroquois culture in Onondaga before the supposed exodus from Jefferson County and the St. Lawrence Valley.

In an attempt to solve some of these problems the present study was designed to investigate in detail a series of prehistoric Iroquois remains in the Onondaga sub-area. The focus of this study is the settlement—"artifacts, . . . other evidences of human occupation, and . . . their depositional context" (Chang 1967:41)—rather than exclusively ceramics, smoking pipes, or any part or all of an artifact complex. An attempt was made to isolate socially and politically meaningful clusters of settlements, and to trace these through time, which we hoped, in the words of Bruce G. Trigger, would "lead to an improved understanding of the social and political aspects of Iroquoian prehistory."

It was further assumed that each settlement represents the remains of a single community which dwelt there at a certain point in time. If this is the case, and there is no reason to doubt that it is, then it follows that we might be able to trace individual communities as they moved their villages from one place to another in typical Iroquois fashion (see p. 217). In this respect the artifacts left behind by the members of each community are very important, for the artifacts reflect the minor variations in ways of doing things (making pottery, pipes, or tools, building houses, etc.) which enable us to distinguish the products of one community from those of another. Ceramics, which constitute the majority of artifacts from most sites, are especially useful in this respect, and a careful analysis of the individual stylistic attributes incorporated into the manufacture of pottery (see Appendix A) revealed at least one clear-cut example of a distinctive ceramic microtradition among the potters of one community which helped us to follow its village removals and resettlements over several hundred years.

In the pages which follow, the results of our investigations are first summarized, in chronological order, in accordance with the system of culture phases as described by Ritchie (1965; 1969), beginning with the Castle Creek phase of Owasco culture and finishing with the historic Iroquois period. The salient and distinguishing general characteristics of each phase, as outlined by previous authors, will be given; then the sites we investigated which pertain to each phase will be discussed, the artifact samples described, and similarities with or divergences from the general pattern for that phase mentioned.

Specifically, the sites described include: *Castle Creek Owasco sites* (A.D. 1200–1300)—Chamberlin (Figure 1, no. 1) and Cabin (Figure 1, no. 3); *Oak Hill phase Iroquois sites* (1300–1400)—Kelso (Figure 1, no. 2), Furnace Brook (Figure 1, no. 4), Howlett Hill (Figure 1, no. 5), and Coye II (Figure 1, no. 7); *Chance phase Iroquois sites* (1400–1500)—Schoff (Figure 1, no. 6), Bloody Hill (Figure 1, no. 8), Keough (Figure 1, no. 9), Christopher (Figure 1, no. 10), Burke (Figure 1, no. 11); *Garoga phase Iroquois sites* (1500–c. 1575)—Cemetery (Figure 1, no. 12) Nursery (Figure 1, no. 13), Barnes (Figure 1, no. 14), McNab (Figure 1, no. 15), Temperance House (Figure 1, no. 16), Atwell (Figure 1, no. 17); *Protohistoric Onondaga sites* (c. 1575–1654)—Quirk (Figure 1, no. 18), Chase (Figure 1, no. 19), Dwyer (Figure 1, no. 20), Sheldon (Figure 1, no. 21); *Historic Onondaga sites* (1654–c. 1800)—Pompey Center (Figure 1, no. 22), Carley (Figure 1, no. 23), Indian Castle (Figure 1, no. 24), Indian Hill (Figure 1, no. 25), Weston (Figure 1, no. 26), Jamesville Pen (Figure 1, no. 27), Coye (Figure 1, no. 7), Valley Oaks (Figure 1, no. 28); *Onondaga Reservation* (c. 1800–present)—Figure 1, no. 29.

Finally, our results are summarized in the last chapter, which shows that the careful excavations and analyses mentioned above and described in detail in Chapters 2–6 have revealed a series of Owasco and Iroquois village sites pertaining to at least three communities which lived contemporaneously in central New York during the late Owasco and early Iroquois periods. Each of these early phases has been radiocarbon dated, thus providing an absolute chronology for the years between A.D. 1250 and 1500. Not only have our investigations demonstrated beyond cavil that the "proto-Onondaga" were resident in central New York long before the sixteenth-century disappearance of the St. Lawrence Iroquois, but further that the St. Lawrence Iroquois contributed little, if anything, to the social, cultural, or political development of the Onondaga Nation.

Moreover, we shall see that there was nothing very mysterious about the development of Onondaga culture, and presumably all Iroquois culture as well, and that the Onondaga were simply one manifestation of a pattern of cultural development—including agriculture, stockaded villages, warfare, certain ceramic and other technological traits, and even

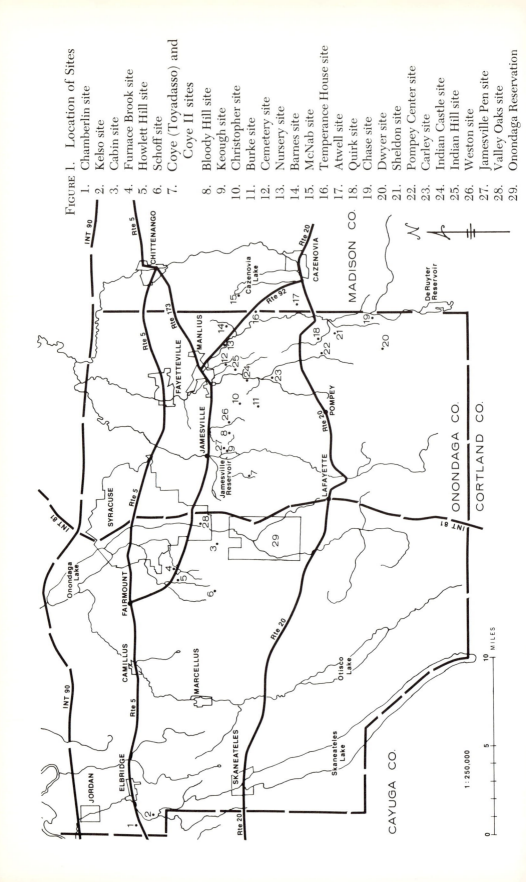

FIGURE 1. Location of Sites

1. Chamberlin site
2. Kelso site
3. Cabin site
4. Furnace Brook site
5. Howlett Hill site
6. Schoff site
7. Coye (Toyadasso) and Coye II sites
8. Bloody Hill site
9. Keough site
10. Christopher site
11. Burke site
12. Cemetery site
13. Nursery site
14. Barnes site
15. McNab site
16. Temperance House site
17. Atwell site
18. Quirk site
19. Chase site
20. Dwyer site
21. Sheldon site
22. Pompey Center site
23. Carley site
24. Indian Castle site
25. Indian Hill site
26. Weston site
27. Jamesville Pen site
28. Valley Oaks site
29. Onondaga Reservation

tribal confederations—which was becoming widespread over the Northeast at the time of European exploration and colonization and whose roots lie much farther back in time than any migrationary theory will allow. Hence all but an *in situ* hypothesis of Iroquois origins must be finally set aside.

CHAPTER 2

The Castle Creek Phase

The Castle Creek phase takes its name from a hilltop site in Broome County, New York, excavated in 1931 and 1933 by William A. Ritchie, then of the Rochester Municipal Museum. What at first appeared to be an Owasco-Iroquois contact site was soon determined to be a distinct "focus" of the Owasco "aspect" in the terminology of the mid-1940s (Ritchie 1944). In his recent synthesis of New York prehistory, Ritchie retained the concept of a "late, efflorescent, or Castle Creek phase" of Owasco culture, but with the warning that "as the culture represents a developmental continuum through time and space, it becomes exceedingly difficult, if not impossible, narrowly and specifically to define and characterize separable and distinctive phases" (Ritchie 1965; 1969:273). This caveat cannot be overemphasized for it is extremely important that the flow of cultural development be constantly borne in mind.

The defining characteristics of this phase, while clearly indicating its earlier Owasco heritage, foretell as well many of the patterns of Iroquois culture which are to follow. Subsistence during the Castle Creek phase included a well-established mixed horticultural base consisting primarily of corn, beans, and squash, but hunting, fishing, and collecting wild vegetable foods remained important. Settlements were located upon defensible hilltops away from waterways as our own data abundantly confirm. House types were not previously known in detail, but our excavations provide some important data on this topic.

The principal defining characteristics of the Castle Creek phase are "material cultural," with ceramics perhaps the most important. Projectile points, following a widespread trend in the Northeast, are both equilateral and isosceles in form with the trend toward the latter. Pottery of the Castle Creek phase consisted of rounded vessels with a well-differentiated rim area, often collared and castellated. Decoration consisted of simple linear motifs, confined, for the most part, to the rims, collars, necks, and occasionally shoulders of the vessels. Most decoration was applied by pressing the edge of a cord-wrapped paddle into the still-wet clay, but incising was not uncommon, especially on vessel necks. Smoking pipes, too, were distinctive during the Castle Creek phase and included a variety of bowl forms—barrel shaped, acorn, and vasiform—decorated by incising, fine cord impressing, *pointille* work, and frequently by molding designs into the clay.

Chronology for this phase is somewhat unclear, because the C-14 dates from Castle Creek are mutually contradictive (A.D. 1196±200 and A.D. 1435±200) with the date from a second Castle Creek station in eastern New York—the Nahrwold No. 1 site, A.D. 1310±75—falling almost precisely between the two. Our own dates, both from a Castle Creek phase site and from succeeding cultural stages, have helped to date very closely the terminal Owasco phase in central New York.

This, very briefly and omitting much detail, is a capsule description of Castle Creek Owasco culture. Our own excavations at two Castle Creek phase sites discussed below provide much detail which need not be repeated here. For a more complete description of the Castle Creek phase and Owasco culture as a whole the reader is referred to Ritchie's *Archaeology of New York State,* pp. 272–300.

In the following discussion of excavations at the Chamberlin and Cabin sites, the settlement data including location, defenses, houses, and other structures are described, and the artifact samples from both are discussed, especially with respect to those characteristics which are most important to our reconstruction of Iroquois culture history.

THE CHAMBERLIN SITE

The Chamberlin Site (Bwv. 15–3) ° is located in the Township of Elbridge, New York, on the extreme western edge of Onondaga County (see Figure 1), on land owned by John and Richard Chamberlin, who kindly allowed us to excavate a portion of the site during the summer of 1967. The site occupies the southern end of a long north-south drumlin.

° Site designations are made by the New York State Archaeological Association system. The first three letters abbreviate a specific United States Geodetic Survey 1:50,000 map. Those referred to in this report are: Baldwinsville (Bwv), Tully (Tly), and Cazenovia (Cza). The next digit(s) are assigned to each site within the bounds of a map in the order they are reported to the N.Y.S.A.A. The final digit refers to the quadrant of the map in which the site is to be found, numbering from left to right and top to bottom.

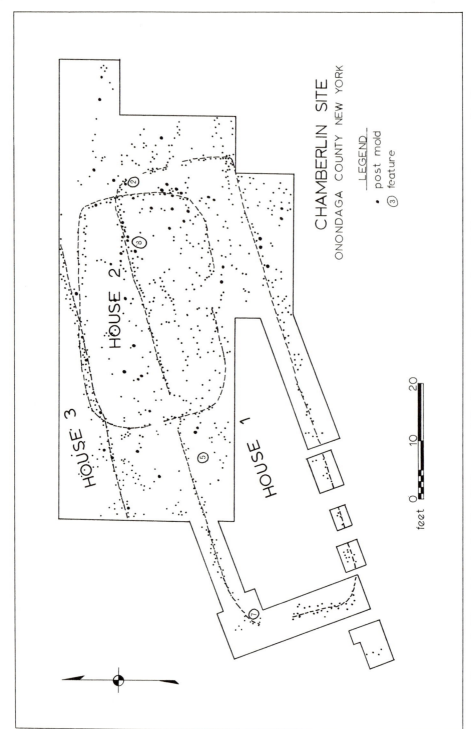

FIGURE 2. Excavations at the Chamberlin site, 1967, showing interpretation of post mold patterns as suggested in the text.

To the north of the site is a now-dry stream bed which may have served as a water source in aboriginal times, as may have a small spring to the southeast of the village. The sides of the hill upon which the village was located are not especially steep, but its height and the excellent visibility from the hilltop doubtless provided some measure of natural defensive advantage (see Plate 1).

The soil within the area of settlement is a dark, sandy loam from ten to fourteen inches deep. It contains occasional artifacts, flint chips, bone scraps, charcoal, and other evidence of Indian encampment. The soil surrounding the village area is generally similar, although somewhat more rocky and lacking the characteristic dark color of "Indian dirt" which results from the decay of village refuse that accumulated while the site was occupied.

This site has apparently been known locally since the early nineteenth century and is frequently mentioned in early records of Onondaga County. Arthur C. Parker, drawing upon some of these earlier accounts, described the site as having consisted of an earth ring, "elliptic," in shape "the longest diameter being north and south, enclosing about 2¾ acres . . . a gate on the east as well as the west" (Parker 1922:649), an estimation of village size which our excavations suggest is about twice the actual size of 1½–1¾ acres.

In 1960 the site was investigated briefly by James B. Richardson, of Syracuse University, who made a small collection of pottery and other artifacts from the village surface. Later that same year a small party from the New York State Museum, under the direction of William A. Ritchie, conducted a further survey of the site and excavated a large cooking pit which they discovered on the hilltop (Ritchie, personal communication). During the summer of 1966 the writer visited the site, which had then been freshly plowed. Viewed from the top of the hill the limits of the village were clearly discernible to the east, south, and west in the newly turned earth. The limits of the dark soil undoubtedly marked the location of the earth ring mentioned (but not seen) by Parker.

During these preliminary investigations we discovered a small patch of intensely black soil containing considerable refuse on the southern edge of the village area. Since the field was soon to be seeded and it was not then certain whether we would be permitted to return the following year, this small area was excavated. The dark soil proved to be a large cooking pit, very similar to that excavated by the New York State Museum. This feature (Feature 1) is described completely below.

During the last three weeks of August, 1967, a Syracuse University

PLATE 1. Looking from the east toward the drumlin on which the Chamberlin site is located.

PLATE 2. Small hearth located near the wall of House 1 at the Chamberlin site.

PLATE 3. Section through Feature 1 at the Chamberlin site showing dark fill and burned stone and a line of post molds which intersects the feature.

field party under my direction returned to the Chamberlin site to carry out further investigations which we hoped would provide a reasonable sample of artifacts and some settlement data from the Castle Creek phase of Owasco culture. House types were especially sought after for convincing house patterns were almost entirely lacking for the terminal stages of Owasco culture.

Settlement Data

Since numerous post molds were encountered in an initial exploratory trench, we decided to continue excavations to the south because this seemed most likely to be the area where house remains could be most easily uncovered. Time did not permit a search for the palisade and earth ring which once apparently existed at the Chamberlin site, but another interesting clue to settlement pattern was provided by a brief surface inspection of nearby hilltops. On the hill immediately east of the main village, and only several hundred yards away, we found a chipped disc, flint chips, and a few potsherds different in no way from those in the main village. This indicated that there might have been outlying houses surrounding the central encampment, a situation paralleled by our findings at the Cabin site which is of similar age and cultural affiliations.

House 1, which ran roughly east-west, or against the long axis of the hill and the village, was indicated by a very irregular row of post molds which outlined the structure. Apparently this house was approximately eighty-five feet long and between twenty-two and twenty-three feet wide (Figure 2). The posts which comprised its outer walls averaged very close to three inches in diameter and were sunk in the soft, sandy subsoil to a depth of eight to twelve inches. Exceptions to this were larger posts, averaging eight inches in diameter, which were spaced somewhat irregularly along the exterior walls. These probably provided additional support for the low vertical side walls which supported an arbor-like roof of arched saplings. The ends of this house, as in others to be described, were slightly flattened although with distinctly rounded corners. Numerous extraneous post molds belonging to unidentified structures partially obscured the ends of House 1 as well as of other houses. For this reason doors were indistinct, although a gap in the western end and another in the northern wall of House 1 may indicate entranceways. The existence of a side door is more characteristic of Owasco houses than it is of later Iroquois. In fact, one small house at the earlier Owasco Maxon-Derby site had doors in the side and in the end as did House 1 at

Chamberlin (Ritchie 1965:282). Internal structure is also somewhat unclear in this house, but the presence of numerous large post molds, apparently placed in holes dug to receive them, indicates some type of internal support. Besides supporting the roof, these posts may have held
bench-beds as they did in historic Iroquois times.

House 2, which partly intersected House 1, was not as clearly defined
as the former structure. The most reasonable reconstruction would place
the length at about fifty feet and the width between twenty-three and
twenty-four feet. Exterior construction and shape are essentially the
same as in House 1; doors again seem to be located in both the end and
on the north side, though the welter of post molds near the west end of
the house renders this more than a little questionable. Interior structure
in House 2 is considerably more clearly indicated than in House 1.
There seems to have been an irregular row of large support posts about
five to seven feet inside the north wall of this structure and roughly parallel with it. That this row of posts is found along only one wall is significant in that this is typically a feature of Owasco houses in contrast to
later Iroquois dwellings which had supports lining both walls.

House 3, another probable house structure, is indicated by the single
row of post molds which extends east-west for nearly 50 feet north of
House 1 and nearly parallel with it. Although our excavations were unable to proceed farther north to expose more of this structure, it seems
very likely that these molds represent a portion of a house of dimensions
about equal to those of House 1 and probably contemporary with it.
This type of village planning is evident at most Iroquois sites which we
have excavated to date. Post molds in this wall are similar in all respects to those in the walls of the other two houses described.

Although there is no evidence to indicate the relative temporal positions of House 2 and the supposedly coexistent Houses 1 and 3, it is
tempting to speculate that the smaller house was built first and later replaced by the larger houses which are, in some respects, especially their
length, more like Iroquois houses. It must be pointed out, however, that
houses at any one site, regardless of the period of cultural development,
tend to be of greatly varying lengths (see the Howlett Hill site, Figure
4).

Features

Aside from Feature 1, a large outdoor roasting pit, all features were
located within the houses and consisted of large post molds and small
hearths. No storage pits, typical of sites of this period in eastern New

York (Ritchie 1944:50, 52), were discovered. This must indicate some cultural preference on the part of the Chamberlin people, because the topsoil and subsoil are both of a soft, sandy texture which provides easy digging and would have made well-drained storage pits for vegetable foods. Thus there must have been some other means of storing these food products. Discoveries of small round structures at Kelso, Furnace Brook, and Howlett Hill suggest that aboveground granaries were used for this purpose.

The post molds, all pertaining to internal support posts, are shown unnumbered by the larger post mold symbols on Figure 2. To maintain a consistent record of the material found within them they were given feature numbers in the field. All were roughly eight inches in diameter, ranged up to sixteen inches deep, and were frequently flat bottomed, indicating that they were dug to receive the poles. Stones were frequently found at the edges of these features where they had apparently been wedged in an effort to stabilize the post.

The four hearths (Features 2, 5, 7, 8) all appear to have belonged to House 1 because they are aligned with, and very close to, the north wall of that structure (see Figure 2). This arrangement of hearths within the dwelling is much more typical of Owasco houses than of Iroquois. It is, in fact, precisely the pattern discovered at the nearby Maxon-Derby site (Ritchie 1965:282). These hearths are all roughly round, ranging in diameter from about seventeen inches to two and a half feet, and from two and a half to twelve inches deep measured from the base of the plow zone (Plate 2). This depth, added to the ten or more inches of tilth zone, would have given the hearths an original depth of some twelve to twenty-four inches, certainly sufficient to protect the nearby house walls from fire.

The large cooking pit mentioned above as having been excavated in the fall of 1966 was the most important single feature excavated at the Chamberlin site, for it provided us with enough wood charcoal for a radiocarbon date. The feature was roughly oval in horizontal section, measuring five by three feet, and was slightly over one foot deep (see Plate 3). Through the center of the pit ran a line of post molds which were very similar to those later discovered in the walls of the houses described above. The fill was a uniformly dark humus containing considerable ash, fire-broken stone, and numerous large chunks of wood charcoal. Near the bottom was a large concentration of this charcoal in the form of carbonized logs up to five inches in diameter which provided the basis for our radiocarbon determination. Artifacts found within this

PLATE 4. Ceramics from the Chamberlin site. 1 and 2, exterior and interior of uncollared rim sherds; 3 and 5, neck sherds decorated with herringbone motif; 4, neck sherd decorated with oblique cord-wrapped paddle impressions; 6 and 7, right and left oblique decorated sub-neck sherds, both with check-stamped body surfaces.

feature included numerous potsherds, both check-stamped body sherds and corded neck sherds, and a broken ovate knife as well as a small fragment of a smoking pipe stem. Food remains included a few scraps of unidentifiable animal bone, some calcined, a few small fish bones, and vegetable remains including a bean, a walnut meat, and a plum pit, all carbonized. The rather large size of this feature and its location on the edge of the village bring to mind the cooking pits excavated at the Kelso site and mentioned by Ritchie (1965:309) as being probably ceremonial. The fill is not the same, however, and the relationship between the two types of features is still uncertain.

Artifacts

Material remains from the Chamberlin site are extremely scarce. Our excavations produced little more than a handful of potsherds and almost nothing in the way of other remains. The owner of the property has a sizeable collection of projectile points said to have been found in the field where our excavations were conducted. However, since it includes Archaic, Early, and Middle Woodland forms spanning some four to five thousand years in addition to some points obviously produced by the Castle Creek phase occupants of the Chamberlin site, this collection was not utilized in the analyses described here.

Ceramics from the Chamberlin site are few in number, hence conclusions drawn from their study are of low statistical reliability. The distinguishing characteristics, listed here in the order followed throughout this report, are as follows (the terminology for ceramic attributes utilized will be found in Appendix A): (1) five (100 percent) plain lip rim profiles; (2) all uppermost interior surfaces decorated with oblique cord-wrapped paddle impressions; (3) all vessel lips decorated in the same motif and technique; (4) exterior lip edges not decorated; (5), (6), and (7) do not apply as no collared vessels were found; (8) "sub-lip" areas are decorated in every case; (9) herringbone (50 percent) and horizontal plaits (28 percent) decorating most vessel necks, almost exclusively (96 percent) done in cord-wrapped paddle impressions; (10) all sub-neck areas decorated with oblique cord-wrapped paddle impressions; (11) no decorated vessel shoulders; and (12) body surface treatment 95 percent check-stamped, 4 percent smoothed-over check-stamped, and 0.6 percent corded.

A single round pipestem found in Feature 1 and a pipe bowl typical of the late Owasco period found earlier by Ritchie (personal communication) are the only smoking pipe fragments recovered at the Chamberlin site. Chipped stone tools are equally scarce—our party recovered only debitage and rejectage, though Chamberlin's collection contains numerous broad triangular arrowpoints, some with indented bases, which probably were in use at the same time as the other artifacts we unearthed. Rough stone tools are only slightly more common, and our efforts were rewarded by the discovery of three battered cobble hammerstones, and fragments of several flat chipped stone discs which may have served as hoes. No bone modified by human workmanship was unearthed during our excavations at the Chamberlin site.

Food Remains

The diet of the people who dwelt at the Chamberlin site is indicated by both animal and vegetable remains. Animal bone was particularly scarce, owing to poor preservation in the acid soil, but deer, bird, and some fish were represented. Freshwater mussels, however, which produce their own basic environment, are particularly well represented at this site. Feature 1 produced a walnut and a plum pit, as well as a few beans, the only cultigen recovered from this site. Doubtless corn was also cultivated since it accompanies beans at many other late Woodland sites, and the people probably made use of most available food resources from the surrounding forests and waters.

Chronology

The limited artifactual material from the Chamberlin site indicates an occupation typical of the Castle Creek phase, the absolute chronology of which remains in some doubt. A single radiocarbon determination, run on wood charcoal from Feature 1, helps to clarify this situation. Our date of A.D. 1290±60 (Y-1817),* which is nearly identical to that from the Nahrwold No. 1 site, suggests strongly that the Castle Creek phase existed during the thirteenth century, a suggestion subsequently borne out by a series of dates from slightly later stations.

THE CABIN SITE

The Cabin site (Tly 1-1), discovered by Robert Ricklis, was named by him because the ruins of an abandoned cabin, presumably the residence of some early settler, are located nearby. Ricklis has published a prelim-

---

*This symbol designates the laboratory which analyzed the sample, in this case the Yale Radiocarbon Laboratory, and the sample number assigned by that institution.

inary report on his excavations at the site (1965), the collection and data
from which he subsequently donated to Syracuse University.

The site is located on the properties of two individuals, one of whom,
Norman McGowan, allowed us to excavate there during the fall of 1965
and the following summer. The same field party which excavated the
Furnace Brook site visited the Cabin site regularly during the course of
our excavations at that larger site. These excavations resulted in the recovery of the largest collection of artifacts included in this study.

Settlement Data

The site occupies a small hilltop on the edge of a steep, in places almost precipitous, drop formerly occupied by the outlet to an old glacial
lake. The land today drops off to the floor of the Onondaga Valley
where it becomes relatively level and is productive farm land. This valley was once subject to periodic flooding, but flood control dams on the
Onondaga Indian Reservation have now alleviated this problem. The
main concentration of refuse which delimits a living area of slightly less
than one-half acre is located just over the crest, to the south, of the
highest point of land along this hillside. There are, however, two other
small concentrations of refuse which may very well mark the locations
of outlying houses in a somewhat dispersed settlement, a situation parallel to that described previously at the Chamberlin site. The material
from these small concentrations of refuse, though consisting of but a few
potsherds, chips, and a celt (or axe) fragment, is in no way different
from the material recovered in the main area of occupation or the
dumps which pertain to it. These data comprise almost the sum of our
knowledge of the settlement pattern at this site as we were refused permission to excavate the hilltop. A single five-foot trench was extended
over the lip of the steep hillside onto a small portion of the hilltop
owned by McGowan. This trench exposed several post molds which apparently pertained to the rounded end of a small east-west oriented
house although this is very questionable because of the limited nature of
our excavations. No evidence of a stockade was discovered on the east
side of the site but such a structure may well have existed on the remaining, less easily defended perimeter of the village.

Our excavations were concentrated in two areas of the steep eastern
hillside which contained extensive middens. Thirty-three five-foot
squares were explored; a total of some 825 square feet. The uppermost
layer of soil was a rich humus varying from dark brown to intense
black and ranging in depth from less than two inches to more than a

PLATE 5. Ceramics from the Cabin site. 1 and 2, uncollared rim sherds; 3–5, collared rim sherds; 6 and 7, everted-lip rim sherds; 2–6 are decorated with cord-wrapped paddle, 1 with trailed lines, and 7 with linear-stamp impressions.

foot. Throughout this layer and occasionally into the lighter sandy-clay subsoil were found great quantities of refuse of all kinds, including pottery, smoking pipes, stone and bone tools, and a great many unmodified animal bones as well as some vegetal remains, all of which are described below. There was no difference, either qualitative or quantitative, between artifacts from different depths within the midden or from different parts of the midden deposit. The entire deposit, therefore, doubtless represents an accumulation of refuse from a single occupation. From the amount of refuse a fairly long occupation is suggested, perhaps in the neighborhood of fifty or more years.

Artifacts

Material remains from the Cabin site comprise the largest sample from any site reported here. Nearly ten thousand individual specimens of pottery, smoking pipes, worked bone, and chipped and polished stone were recovered, cataloged, and analyzed.

Ceramics from the Cabin site included over eight thousand individual sherds. A precise breakdown of the sample is presented in the original report but the significant characteristics are (see Appendix A for a description of ceramic attributes): (1) a plurality (44 percent) of plain lip rim profiles, with 31 percent everted lip types, the first appearance of channeled low-collar rim profiles (16 percent), and a smattering of most other varieties; (2) uppermost vessel interior decorated in 75 percent of all cases, principally with oblique cord-wrapped paddle impressions; (3) over 99 percent of all vessel lips decorated with longitudinal (about 25 percent), straight or oblique lines (70 percent), or combinations of the two executed in cord-wrapped paddle impressions; (4) only 9 percent decorated-exterior lip edges; (5) collar motifs consisting of horizontal lines (66 percent), oblique lines between horizontal lines (12 percent), oblique or vertical lines (10 percent), horizontal lines between oblique lines (5 percent), and less than 2 percent each of various other motifs, almost all (90 percent) decorations applied with a cord-wrapped paddle edge; (6) a surprisingly high percentage (38 percent) of decorated collar bases, typically a late Iroquois trait, probably actually a "spillover" from the collar decoration, all save one done with a cord-wrapped paddle edge; (7) the neck surface immediately below the collar (the sub-collar area) distinctively decorated in 83 percent of the cases, mostly with oblique lines executed in cord-wrapped paddle impressions; (8) sub-lip areas, analogous to the above, decorated in 88 percent of the cases, principally with oblique lines executed in the cord-wrapped paddle technique; (9) a va-

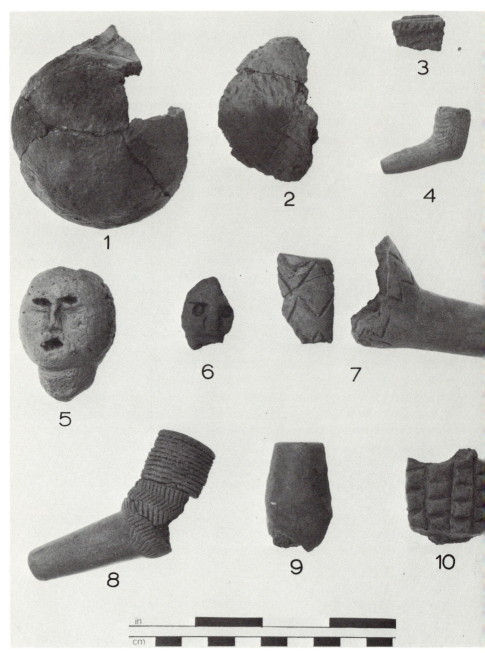

PLATE 6. Artifacts from the Cabin site. 1–3, fragments of miniature vessels; 4, miniature smoking pipe; 5 and 6, human-face effigies, 6 probably from a smoking pipe
bowl; 7, fragments of a smoking pipe decorated probably with fingernail linear-
stamp impressions; 8, smoking pipe decorated with fine cord-wrapped paddle impressions; 9, plain barrel-shaped pipe bowl; 10, fragment of corn-ear pipe bowl.

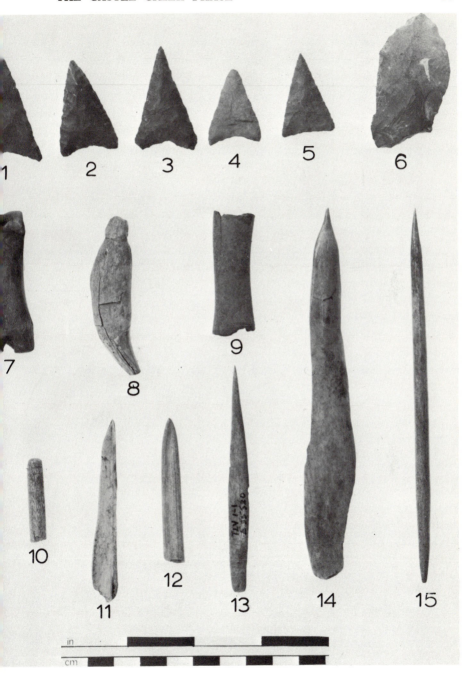

PLATE 7. Artifacts from the Cabin site. 1–5, triangular arrowpoints; 6, leaf-shaped knife; 7, deer phalanx bangle; 8, bear canine grooved for suspension; 9, tubular bird-bone bead; 10, head of bone pin; 11–14, bone awls; 15, bone leister point.

riety of neck motifs including herringbone (25 percent) vertical or oblique plaited (28 percent), opposed lines (17 percent), horizontal plaited (10 percent), and many other styles of lower frequency executed in either cord-wrapped paddle edge impressions (50 percent) or incising (46 percent); (10) sub-neck areas decorated in 87 percent of cases, chiefly with short oblique lines impressed with a cord-wrapped paddle-edge; (11) no decorated vessel shoulders; (12) body surface treatments are 96 percent check-stamped, 4 percent corded, and minute percentages smoothed-over check-stamped, fabric impressed, and smoothed; (13) average collar height 13.01 mm.

In addition to the ceramics described above portions of several miniature pottery vessels were found at the Cabin site, the most significant of these being the three small pots found together and in association with the miniature smoking pipe described below. Two of these small vessels have cord-malleated bodies, while the third appears to have a check-stamped exterior surface. All are of very hard, relatively fine paste and are well-fired. None of the interiors retains any sign of use. One specimen has the neck and sub-neck areas decorated with a fine cord-wrapped paddle while another is represented by a low-collared rim decorated with horizontal corded lines. The third specimen consists of only a corded body section. Several of these are illustrated on Plate 6, nos. 1–3.

In attempting to assign a function to these small pots several possibilities occur. They are often considered "toy pots," made either by children practicing the art of pottery-making or by adults for the amusement of children. The former possibility seems remote because these specimens are extremely well made (as is the small pipe); they are not made around a finger or thumb as are many other small pots from other Iroquois sites, and they are decorated with all the skill employed in the manufacture of full-sized pottery vessels. That they are a set of toys made by an adult is, of course, very likely, but another more interesting possibility was suggested by William N. Fenton. This is the possibility that these vessels represent some sort of ceremonial paraphernalia. Among the Huron and Iroquois during the seventeenth century, dreams played an important role in the life of an individual and in society in general. Dreams were often interpreted as wishes of the soul which had to be satisfied lest some misfortune, even death, befall the dreamer (Wallace 1958; Tooker 1964:86–114). Often the dreamer's desire was presented to the community in the form of a riddle which was then guessed in a ritual known as the dream-guessing rite. Occasionally the riddle was not guessed verbally, but objects thought to represent the desire of the soul were presented to the dreamer (Tooker 1964:110–14). A set of objects from an early historic Iroquois grave in western New York has been interpreted as representing such a collection of guesses or a "dream bundle" (White 1967:15; Tooker 1967:16; Tooker and White 1968). It seems not impossible that this collection of miniature objects represents a similar bundle. If so, this is a very early representation of an Iroquois ritual among people with a predominantly Owasco "material culture."

Another unusual artifact from the Cabin site is the unique pottery human-face effigy recovered from the hillside midden, pictured on Plate 6, no. 5. This, with the human-face effigy pipe described below, may provide some clue to another Iroquois trait already present at this early time, the masking complex which the Iroquois retain to this day. It is not supposed that the masking complex, if indeed it existed at this time, was developed nearly to the point it reached at later times, but this does offer an early clue to the beginnings of such a complex—the earliest being a similar maskette, in antler, from the early Owasco Snell site in eastern New York (Ritchie, Lenig, and Miller 1953:16).

Smoking pipe fragments from this site include portions of the bowls of fifteen specimens, mostly extremely small fragments, but several are reconstructible (Plate 6, nos. 6–10). Of these fragments thirteen can be assigned with reasonable certainty to one of the categories described on pp. 239–43. Seven, or 54 percent, are of the barrel-shaped bowl variety, and there are one each of the conical bowl, corn effigy, collared, vasiform, human-face effigy, and vertical barred styles.

In addition to these classifiable specimens there is a single fragment of the flaring rim of a small thin-walled pipe. Decorative motifs conform to those described for these varieties on pp. 239–43 as do techniques of execution of these various motifs.

The miniature pipe discussed above as a probable component of a dream bundle seems to be a unique specimen. It measures only 2.9 cm. in length, and the bowl is 1.8 cm. high. Decoration consists of several bands of a herringbone design running vertically on the bowl and interrupted by bands of straight vertical lines on the side of the bowl away from the smoker and on the side to the smoker's left (Plate 6, No. 4). The entire design was executed by impressing a fine cord-wrapped paddle into the half-dry clay. The interior shows no sign of having been smoked, though the stem is completely perforated and the pipe seems in every way to be functional.

Eleven whole or fragmentary pipe stems were found in the midden at the Cabin site. All are round in cross section, and all seem to pertain to relatively short, thick, and rather sharply tapered stems. None was provided with any type of specially prepared mouthpiece.

Chipped stone includes projectile points, a few retouched flakes, and a surprisingly small amount of rejectage and debitage in relation to the large number of other artifacts which were present in the middens.

The sample of projectile points (Plate 7, nos. 1–5) from the Cabin site, all triangular arrowpoints, is characterized by the presence of many early forms and by extreme variability. Some would be at home in early Owasco assemblages while others would not be out of place in collections from late prehistoric Iroquois sites. Early styles have convex sides and an indented or concave base which fall into Ritchie's Levanna type (Ritchie 1961a:32, 87), as do the points with straight sides and concave bases (attributes foreshadowing later Iroquois arrowpoints), but whose proportions tend toward equilateral rather than isosceles triangles. Relatively long and narrow forms are present, but these are the exception rather than the rule. The average length of all completed specimens is 3.48 cm., average width is 2.20 cm., and the length-width ratio is 1.58 to 1.

A single leaf-shaped knife (Plate 7, no. 6), probably related to later Iroquois ovate knives, and three utilized flakes comprise the remainder of the chipped-stone assemblage from the Cabin site.

Only five fragments or complete tools of rough and polished stone were recovered from the Cabin site middens. This may be because our excavations were centered on refuse deposits rather than in the living area. From our excavations at other sites it seems clear that these tools were either reused in one form or another, thereby remaining a part of the owner's tool kit, or that they were simply discarded within the village confines, and occasionally were used to line a hearth. A small, fragmentary celt of close-grained igneous rock, a thin possible notched pebble net sinker, a small fragment of a probable chipped stone disc, a well preserved and heavily utilized combination hammer stone with battered edges and deep pits on both flat faces, and a similar tool with one flat surface showing evidence of use as a muller comprise the entire assemblage from the Cabin site.

Modified bone tools and weapons were much more common. Awls (Plate 7, nos. 11, 13, 14) constitute the vast majority of specimens and were of three varieties, depending in part upon the amount of use each had received. The first (fifteen examples) are simple bone splinters 4 to 15 cm. long with a point at one end and no further modification; the second style (thirteen examples) is similar in all respects except that the edges, and more rarely the bases, are ground and/or polished; the third variety (ten examples), also of about the same dimensions as the first, is distinctive in that it either used the articulating surface of the raw material as a base or, alternatively, had a carefully cut and polished base. The two former varieties are manufactured from splinters of mammal or bird long bones. Among the latter a probable deer tibia, deer metapodial, deer rib, and the dorsal spine of a large catfish can be recognized.

Two leister (fish spear) points nearly round in cross section and bipointed—blunt at one end and very sharp at the other—were also recovered. The intact specimen measures 14 cm. in length. A single, badly eroded, unilaterally double-barbed bone point, 9 cm. long, may also have been an item of fishing gear.

A bone flaker made from a thick section of split bear (?) bone, battered at both ends from use, and a broken deer mandible showing wear patterns suggesting use as a scraper—perhaps to remove dried corn from the cob—complete the utilitarian bone material recovered from the Cabin site. As an interesting aside, the bone from which the flaker was made shows evidence of a probable arrow wound, now partially recalcified, in the form of an oval perforation, tapering to a sharp point, into which fit perfectly many chert points from the Cabin site.

Bone ornaments from this station include two deer phalanx cones, probably bangles, with the proximal articulating surface removed and a small hole drilled for suspension in the distal end (Plate 7, no. 7). The head of a bone pin, round in cross section, the head decorated with nearly invisible lines (Plate 7, no. 10), is similar to, though less elaborately ornamented than, specimens from the type site of the Castle Creek phase (Ritchie 1944:65). Two tubular bird-bone beads, one unfinished (Plate 7, no. 9), and the other a fragment of a much larger specimen, and a bear canine grooved for suspension (Plate 7, no. 8) are the only other decorative bone objects found during our excavations.

Food Remains

The only vegetable remains from the middens at Cabin are a carbonized eight-row corn cob and a few kernels of corn. There are no beans, squash, sunflowers, or other food remains, either wild or cultivated, though all were doubtless utilized by the members of this community.

As analyzed by Joseph Waters of Villanova University, the faunal remains from the Cabin site attest to the dependence of the late Owasco people upon the Virginia deer for the major part of the red meat in their diet. The summary in Table 1 indicates quite reliably the species exploited by the people of the Cabin site, though several species (i.e., skunk and meadow vole) were probably not eaten, and other unidentifiable fragments of fish and bird bone suggest a slightly greater reliance on these food sources than is indicated in the table.

TABLE 1. FAUNAL REMAINS FROM THE CABIN SITE

Species	No. pieces	Remarks
MAMMALS		
white-tailed deer (*Odocoileus virginianus*)	1,043	at least: 30 adults, two adult males, two 1–2 years old, two 2–3 years old, one over 3 years.
dog (*Canis familiaris*)	2	one adult
raccoon (*Procyon lotor*)	3	two adults
black bear (*Ursus americanus*)	7	at least two adults
red fox (*Vulpes fulva*)	1	one adult
striped skunk (*Mephitis mephitis*)	1	one adult
woodchuck (*Marmota monax*)	4	two adults
meadow vole (*Microtus pennsylvanicus*)	3	one adult
muskrat (*Ondatra zibethicus*)	7	two adults
beaver (*Castor canadensis*)	8	one adult
eastern gray squirrel (*Sciurus carolinensis*)	9	at least six adults
chipmunk (*Tamias striatus*)	3	two adults
red squirrel (*Tamiasciurus hudsonicus*)	1	one adult
BIRD		
Only identifiable species is passenger pigeon (*Ectopistes migratorius*)		
REPTILE		
probable map turtle (*Grapternys geographica*)	12	one adult
FISH		
sucker (*Moxostoma sp.*)	4	
SHELLFISH		
freshwater clam	1	

Chronology

Unhappily, no features were found beneath or near the hillside middens, and no reliable samples of charcoal were recovered from among the refuse. Therefore no radiocarbon determination is available for the Cabin site. Both the material remains, however, suggesting a date not much different from the Chamberlin site, and a date of A.D. 1300 obtained from the succeeding Furnace Brook site (see p. 71) indicate an occupation during the latter half of the thirteenth century.

Summary

In this chapter we have looked at two sites dating from the late 1200s excavated during the summers of 1966 and 1967. Although the data from each are far from complete, they complement each other to a great degree. Considering data from both sites, the earlier Owasco ancestry of the Castle Creek phase is clearly indicated—by small houses with side doors and hearths along one wall, by broad triangular arrowpoints, and by uncollared ceramics, decorated primarily with cord-wrapped paddle impressions—while traits foreshadowing later Iroquois culture are equally apparent. The latter include fortified hilltop villages, rectangular houses, a few relatively long and narrow projectile points, collared ceramics, and the appearance of many typically Iroquois design motifs and techniques.

Considered individually the two sites offer little basis for direct comparison, but the distance between them (over fifteen miles) suggests that they are not the product of the same community, for that distance is much greater than a typical Iroquoian village removal (see pp. 3–4). The settlement patterns may also have been slightly different for a smaller central village, and more outlying houses are suggested by our meagre data from the Cabin site. Finally the artifacts suggest some "micro-cultural" differences (i.e. small cultural distinctions not reflecting any great difference in the total way of life) between the two groups, especially in the technique of decorating vessel necks which were almost exclusively cord-wrapped paddle impressed at the Chamberlin but were incised in about 45 percent of the cases at the Cabin site. While not significant at this point, the trend itself becomes of greater importance later, when we are able to show its persistence over more than a century.

The chronology for the Castle Creek phase is on a somewhat firmer footing as a result of our dating of the Chamberlin site. Our date of A.D. 1290 nearly duplicates that from the Nahrwold No. 1 site and falls very close to the average of the two Castle Creek site dates.

While in many respects a pre-Iroquois or Owasco phase, the Castle Creek sites described here foreshadow the succeeding Oak Hill phase in as many respects. Settled hilltop villages of horticulturalists, probably palisaded, and containing proto-Iroquois longhouses and many attributes of the artifacts, clearly form a basis for developments in the next described period of Iroquois culture.

CHAPTER 3

The Oak Hill Phase

IN THE PRECEDING CHAPTER two important stations which define the terminal Owasco Castle Creek phase in central New York were described and discussed. There we saw many indications of Iroquois culture—stockaded hilltop villages, proto-longhouses, and cultivation of vegetable foods—which become increasingly more like Iroquois and less like their Owasco progenitors during the fourteenth-century Oak Hill phase.

The Oak Hill phase, considered for a number of years to be the nascent stage of Iroquois cultural development, received the most intensive treatment of any phase in this study. Two sites were explored by field parties under my direction; a third was equally thoroughly explored by the New York State Museum; and still another is known from a small amount of material collected before World War II by a local amateur archaeologist, Stanley Gifford.

As can be gathered from the descriptions which follow, all four are clearly within the cultural bounds of the Oak Hill phase as defined by Donald Lenig (1965) and William A. Ritchie (1965:302–305), though significant differences are apparent at each of the better-known components.

Settlements appear to have been small in the Mohawk Valley where the type station is located (Lenig 1965:40), although their locations away from major waterways is entirely in keeping with earlier practices. The principal diagnostic of the Oak Hill phase is a ceramic and smoking pipe complex defined thus by Ritchie, who based part of this definition on Lenig's 1965 monograph: ceramics consist of "a high predominance of corded-collar vessels, mainly of the Owasco corded-collar type [horizontal cord impressions on a low collar, see Plate 5, no. 5] and its derivative type, Oak Hill corded [opposed lines on a somewhat higher collar, see Plate 18, no. 10], a pottery spectrum much constricted from the

47

just-preceding ancestral late Castle Creek phase. Conversely, Oak Hill
pipe styles show an expanded stylistic range, including . . . straight-
sided, slight to moderately flaring, and barrel-shaped bowls. Decoration,
done by incising and punctation, . . . consists of plaits composed of parallel horizontal, oblique or vertical lines and dots; chevron herringbone
and rectangular designs. Modeled on the bowl and stem of a few specimens are effigies of the tree frog and salamander, reminiscent of Owasco
pipes" (Ritchie 1969:302–303).

In the Mohawk Valley the Oak Hill phase seems to have lasted from
A.D. 1200 to 1350 (Lenig 1965:63), although our data from Onondaga
suggest a somewhat different chronological placement for this early Iroquois phase.

The continuities between the Oak Hill phase and the Chamberlin
and Cabin sites of the preceding Castle Creek are probably already
partly apparent. The descriptions which follow emphasize these continuities and afford us the first real clue as to the dispersal of several distinct
communities within the boundaries of what later became Onondaga (see
p. 92).

The Furnace Brook Site

The Furnace Brook site (Syr 12-3), where a field party from Syracuse
University and another party composed of high school students from
several nearby towns spent the entire 1966 field season, was the most
ambitious undertaking of this project. At times over forty people were
employed at the site, which produced a large sample of material remains and the most complete settlement pattern of any site which we
excavated.

The site is located on Rte. 173 in the town of Onondaga, New York,
on land owned by Frank Degnan, of Syracuse, and leased to John
Dauenhauer, both of whom gave permission for our extensive explorations. The village lies about three miles north of the Cabin site and less
than a mile east of the Howlett Hill site (see Figure 1). It occupies a
portion of a long level bench and is located about seven hundred feet
west of where this bench is cut by the small stream from which the site
takes its name.

Soil on the living area and surrounding fields is a Palatine silt-loam
overlaying a clay subsoil which contains numerous and extensive limestone outcrops, some of which protrude through the topsoil and have
been broken by weather and plowing into thousands of fragments which

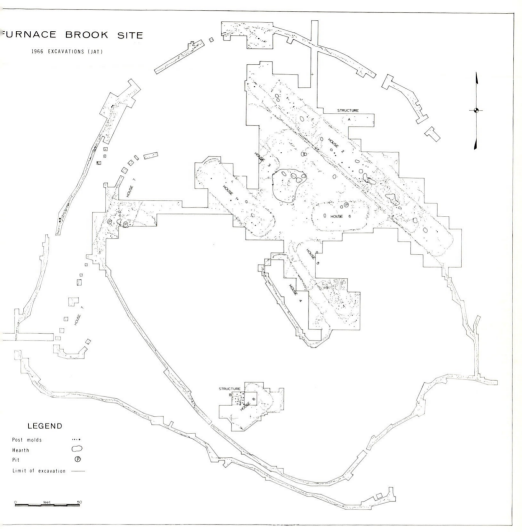

FURNACE BROOK SITE

1966 EXCAVATIONS (JAT)

LEGEND

Post molds   ····•
Hearth   ◯
Pit   ℗
Limit of excavation ———

0   feet   50

FIGURE 3. Excavations at the Furnace Brook site, 1966, showing palisade lines, houses, and other structural features, including hearths whose limits are shown by the solid line, and deep circular storage pits designated by the letter P.

litter this and the surrounding fields. The land upon which the village was built undulates only slightly, but there is a pronounced rise some fifteen hundred feet to the south and a fairly steep drop at the northern edge of the site, the latter probably providing some measure of defensive advantage.

The site was discovered by Robert Ricklis and the writer while on a survey of the area during the spring of 1965, when we were engaged in excavating the Howlett Hill site. Although the field had not been cultivated for several years the ground was littered with chips, points, potsherds, and other artifacts which gave evidence of an extensive occupation. The following spring we returned to the site and with the help of several volunteers put a five-foot-wide trench from the brow of the hill on the north some one hundred and fifty feet southward across the main part of the site where artifacts had been found. Numerous post molds and many artifacts were discovered in this trench, indicating that this site would provide good settlement data as well as a good sample of artifacts, the latter lacking at the Howlett Hill site.

During the summer of 1966 the field parties worked for eight weeks, after which a smaller party continued for several more weeks. During the course of these excavations more than thirty-five thousand square feet of subsoil were explored with shovels and trowels in a search for post molds and other features. Power equipment was used only to remove backdirt which had already been shoveled out and troweled—or sifted if it seemed productive of artifacts.

Settlement Data

Our excavations disclosed ample evidence of dwellings as well as a somewhat confusing pattern of defensive structures. The palisade, or palisades, enclosed an area measuring about three hundred feet by three hundred and forty feet or covering about two and one-half acres. As can be seen from the map shown in Figure 3, these several stockades present some problem in analysis. Two possible explanations for the multiple stockade lines present themselves. The first possibility is that there were two overlapping villages, a situation found at the Kelso site (Ritchie 1965:304–306; 1967:71). If this were true it is quite clear from the artifacts that there was no appreciable cultural or chronological difference between the two settlements. This would mean that the second village was merely a rebuilding of the first at the same location, *without* any temporal gap between. In this case the community would have been homeless for a short time during the rebuilding phase, unless they

PLATE 8. A possible gateway in inner stockade at the Furnace Brook site.

PLATE 9. Line of large post molds defining the outer stockade at the Furnace Brook site.

PLATE 10. Aerial view of excavations at the Furnace Brook site showing House 6 to the left of center and three building phases of House 2 in right half of photograph.

PLATE 12. Feature 57D at the Furnace Brook site, one of several small hearths composing the outdoor cooking area, Feature 57.

PLATE 13. Ceramics from the Furnace Brook site. 1–3, collared rim sherds; 4–7, collared rim sherds, 7 decorated by linear-stamp technique; 8, neck sherd decorated
with vertical plaits and a right oblique sub-neck decoration; 9 and 10, incised neck
sherds.

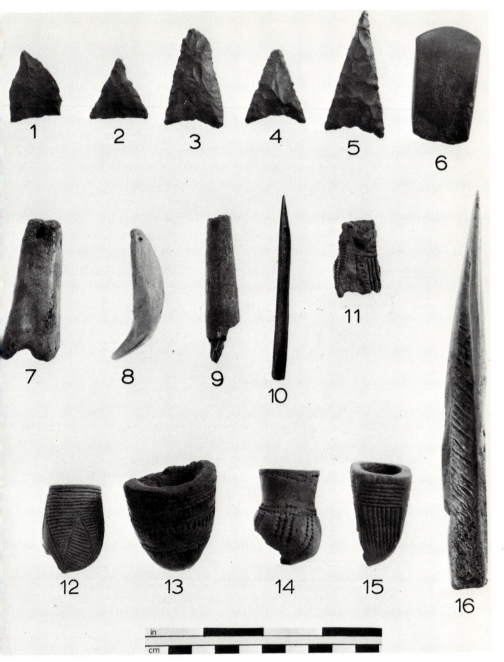

PLATE 14. Artifacts from the Furnace Brook site. 1–5, triangular arrowpoints; 6, small celt or chisel; 7, perforated elk phalange decorated with fine incised lines; 8, probable bear canine partially perforated; 9, smoothed antler tine; 10, bird-bone splinter awl; 11, fragment of smoking pipe bowl adorned with a probable lizard; 12, barrel-shaped pipe bowl decorated with fine cord-wrapped paddle impressions; 13, conical pipe bowl decorated in same technique as preceding specimen; 14, vasiform pipe bowl; 15, square pipe bowl; 16, large bone awl or bark perforator.

moved to a temporary village during this process, a suggestion which seems highly unlikely because it is at variance with historic records of Iroquois village removals. Another argument against this proposal is that there is but one case of overlapping houses in this village (House 2, see Figure 3), and this complex apparently represents several successive enlargements of the same structure.

The second explanation for these palisades is that they actually represent several expansions of the village in the eighty to one hundred years during which it was occupied. Some evidence indicates that this is the most reasonable conclusion. The first suggestion comes from the post molds in the stockades. The molds which comprise the *inside*, and presumably the earliest stockade, were uniformly three to five inches in diameter, only occasionally slightly smaller or larger and ranged roughly from eight to ten inches in depth below the surface of the subsoil. This palisade varied from one to three parallel walls around most of the site but generally consisted of but a single wall (see Plate 8). The molds on the southern, and especially the southwestern portion of the *outer* stockade indicated a structure of a somewhat different character. These molds were of two diameters—either relatively large (six to eight inches) or quite small (two and one-half to three and one-half inches)— and were placed in the ground so that the larger posts were frequently nearly touching. In those places where two adjacent large post molds were not found we discovered that two or three smaller posts had been placed in the ground between the larger posts to fill the gap (see Plate 9). It may be that a similar pattern prevailed in the northern portion of this stockade, but the soil was generally underlain by a dense layer of crumbling limestone which not only made post molds difficult to locate but in most cases actually determined the precise location of the posts and the depth to which they could be sunk in the ground, thereby limiting the pattern and dimensions of posts which remained for us to find.

The house remains discovered also point to the possibility that the village was not destroyed and completely rebuilt but that a slow population growth necessitated several village expansions. With the exception of House 2 and its several rebuilding phases, no houses overlap one another. This is quite remarkable in a town occupied as long as was Furnace Brook, and seems almost impossible had there been an entire rebuilding. Houses 1, 2, 3, 4, and 5 are almost perfectly parallel with one another; House 6 is somewhat out of line, but is not crossed by any other structure. House 7, on the western edge of the village, is not parallel with the rest but seems to have been fitted just within the southwest-

ern palisade extension, giving the impression that the palisade was enlarged to encompass the structure.

On summarizing the evidence it becomes apparent that this latter explanation, that of progressive village enlargments, is the most likely and
that the Furnace Brook site represents a long occupation, during which
considerable population growth took place. Whether this population
growth was due to a natural increase or represents some population in
flux from outside is a questionable point, but in view of the outlying
houses suggested by our explorations at the Cabin site (see p. 35), the
latter possibility takes on greater credence. Individual structures are described briefly below and illustrated in Figure 3.

House 1 was located in the central part of the village, somewhat to
the west of the center. This house measured seventy-five feet by twenty-
three feet and had relatively straight walls and rounded ends. One interesting feature of the ends of this and several other houses was the presence of a second, somewhat smaller row of post molds two to four feet
inside the main wall posts at both ends of the house. These posts measured between one and two inches in diameter in comparison to the
main walls in which the post molds measured between two and four
inches, averaging somewhat over three inches. The wall posts had been
set eight to ten inches into the ground, but occasional posts spaced irregularly along the walls and at the corners of the house were considerably larger (eight to ten inches) and had been set up to eighteen inches
below the surface of the subsoil. The smaller interior end walls were not
set as deeply into the ground as were the other posts forming the walls.
Their small size and shallow depth gave the impression of their not
being structural but of having served some other purpose, perhaps as in-
sulation or some type of storage shed at the ends of the house. The
doors of this house are located in the ends in typical Iroquois fashion
and measure very close to two and one-half feet wide.

Interior structure is not too clearly indicated, but the presence of
several large molds, mostly seven to eight feet inside either wall, probably indicates that the interior structure was similar to that described for
most later Iroquois houses. It consisted of two parallel rows of large
posts, usually five to eight feet inside the walls, which supported the roof
of the structure, as well as bench-beds.

House 2 actually consists of a complex of two overlapping houses,
one of which shows two building phases. This northernmost dwelling
which we discovered is located entirely outside the original palisade.
The southern wall of the house is almost perfectly aligned with this

stockade line and is hardly distinguishable from it unless one views the complex as a whole. The original construction was oriented west-north-west by east-southeast and measured eighty feet long by twenty-one feet wide. It was constructed essentially as House 1 but lacked the double ends described above. The molds were of the same size and were spaced from two to twelve inches apart as in the former case, and also included the irregularly spaced large support posts. The northern wall of this house was somewhat difficult to locate because of the presence of large crumbling limestone outcrops, but enough molds were discovered to as-certain its existence. At some later time, a forty-foot addition was built at the eastern end of this house bringing the total length to almost 130 feet. The width remained twenty-one to twenty-two feet in this addition, but again limestone outcrops hampered our efforts to locate traces of all the posts which once comprised the northern wall.

Still later, this structure was apparently torn down for some reason and replaced by a still larger structure measuring nearly 210 feet in length and about as wide as the earlier house. That this house postdates the other is indicated by the fact that some of the hearths which pertain to this last construction phase covered post molds which formed the out-lines of the ends of the two earlier construction phases. Although this evidence is not as strong as could be desired, it is consistent with the general pattern of continuous village enlargement and can be accepted with few reservations.

In all three of the above-mentioned building phases of this house, the doors were centrally located at the ends of the houses, and interior con-struction was essentially the same as that found in most houses of this and later periods with large post molds inside the walls which appar-ently supported bench-beds as well as the house roof.

House 3 was located only fifteen feet north of House 1 and ran al-most perfectly parallel with it. Although we uncovered only a small por-tion of one end of this structure, it is safe to say that it probably resembled House 1 very strongly in most respects, apparently lacking only the double ends which were discovered in that structure. House 3 shows every indication, as far as alignment can be trusted, of having been coeval with House 1.

House 4 is located on the southern edge of our main excavation and was only trenched to expose its walls. By this process a dwelling mea-suring seventy-seven feet by twenty-three feet was delimited, with rounded ends, built of posts with dimensions very similar to those de-scribed above—two to four inches in diameter. As in House 3, this structure also lacked the peculiar double ends of House 1. Our method of exposing this house did not reveal much about interior structure, but a small excavation area in the southeast corner revealed two large post molds which probably pertain to structures consistent with other houses at the site. Doors were again located in the center of either end of the house and measured about two and one-half feet in width.

House 5 was located adjacent to House 4 and about eight to twelve feet to the northeast. It was nearly parallel to the previously described structure, hence probably contemporaneous with it. Doors, interior structure, and post mold dimensions were all essentially the same as those described above. There was, however, a concentration of small post molds near the center of the house which do not seem to belong to any definite structure and which cannot be satisfactorily explained.

House 6 was a much smaller structure located between Houses 5 and 2. Although it was out of alignment with the other structures on the site, there are no overlapping post mold patterns and no reason to suppose it was not contemporaneous with them. This house measured forty-five feet by twenty-four feet and was built of posts measuring three to four inches in diameter and again sunk about six to ten inches into the subsoil. A few of the larger posts mentioned as being part of the external walls in the above-described houses were present but not in as great numbers. This house also differed from the others described in the location of the door. A single door was located in the northern side of the house and slightly west of the center (see Figure 3), rather than at either end of the house. This strongly resembles earlier Owasco houses such as that discovered at the Bates site in Chenango County (Ritchie 1965:284–86), at other Owasco stations, and the small House 2 at the Chamberlin site (see p. 30 and Figure 2). Interior structure lacked the large posts of most other houses, but the presence of hearths and a storage pit seem to indicate that this was indeed a dwelling and not some other type of structure. Another early feature of this house is the hearth (Feature 87), located to one side rather than centrally.

House 7 is located on the extreme western border of the site intersecting and presumably post-dating the interior stockade line. It is oriented north-south and so nearly parallels the outer palisade that it looks very much as if that part of the palisade was built specifically to include this structure (see Figure 3). Time did not permit the entire exposure of this structure, but from our limited excavations it can be seen that it exceeds 140 feet in length and is nearly twenty-three feet wide. Construction of the exterior walls differs in no way from the other houses at the site, and interior structure, typical of an Iroquois longhouse, is clearly indicated in the exposed central portion of the house.

House 8 is not as clearly indicated as any of the seven structures described above. It was found at the extreme southern border of the site and does not appear complete, despite our efforts to trace more of it. If it is in fact a house, it seems to measure about thirty-seven feet by twenty-five feet. The southwestern portion of the house, which is missing, may have contained the door for it is not evident elsewhere in the exposed structure (see Figure 3).

Structure A is a small circular structure north of House 2. It measured very close to ten feet in diameter and was evidenced by a circle of small shallow post molds. This is almost an exact duplicate of the structure to be described in the Howlett Hill report. It may have served as an aboveground granary in view of the almost complete lack of other means for food storage.

Structure B is located on the southern edge of the site some twenty-five feet inside the interior stockade and forty feet within the exterior stockade. This feature presents considerable difficulty in interpretation, for no similar structure seems, either historically or archaeologically, to be documented. The structure consisted of two concentric ovals of post molds. The inner oval measured about two and one-half feet east-west by five feet north-south and was composed of post molds about two inches in diameter driven six to nine inches into the subsoil. The outer oval measured about eight feet east-west by ten feet north-south and was comprised of large post molds measuring between twelve and seventeen inches in diameter which extended between twelve and fourteen inches below the surface of the subsoil. This outer row of molds was much less regular than the interior row, and there is some suggestion that some of the molds may pertain to a third, intermediate row of post molds (see Figure 3). Since this is located a good distance from the palisade, it seems unlikely that it represents a bastion or similar defensive structure. The dimensions and arrangement of the posts represented by these molds indicate that they would have supported a platform of considerable weight, but whether such a platform ever existed is a question we may never answer. Whether these molds pertained to a utilitarian structure or a more esoteric purpose is another point which must go unanswered, at least for the present.

Features

Except for feature numbers assigned to refuse-filled tree falls and other natural depressions, the features found at the Furnace Brook site can, with a few exceptions, be described in three major categories. These will be but briefly mentioned here as the individual features are listed and described in some detail in the original report (Tuck n.d.) and variations within a group of features are not great.

The features most frequently encountered were the large post molds left by the support posts which usually lined the center aisles of these and other later Iroquois houses. These range from five or six inches to more than a foot in diameter and range in depth from a few inches to more than eighteen inches. Frequently these posts were placed in holes dug for that purpose rather than forced into the ground as were the smaller pointed posts which comprise the exterior walls of most dwellings.

The second group of features frequently encountered consisted of typical Iroquois hearths, used both for cooking and heating of houses. These features are almost always evidenced by irregular, but occasionally round, patches of fire-reddened subsoil, usually from two to four feet in diameter, and not generally excavated into the subsoil for more than a few inches. They do not often contain any appreciable amount of refuse. All but two of these hearths were found inside of houses and most of these were more or less centrally located in typical Iroquois fashion. Most probably these hearths were shared by two nuclear families, each living on one side of the fire, as was the case among the Iroquois during the earliest period of European contact.

The third type of feature, which is represented by only three examples at Furnace Brook, is the large storage pit so common on sites of the Owasco and Iroquois people who inhabited eastern New York. Briefly, these are circular pits about two feet in diameter and three feet in depth (Plate 11). They are located, in all instances, just inside the walls of houses and most likely were under the beds as was the case at other Iroquois villages. At Garoga (Funk 1967:83), these features literally lined the walls of the houses. In contrast to Garoga, however the pits at Furnace Brook contained almost no refuse. All are shown in Figure 3.

The exceptional features mentioned above included the basal portions of two small probable storage pits not located within the confines of any house structure; a small basin-shaped hearth, fifteen inches in diameter, located more or less centrally in House 1, which contained charcoal, ash, and fishbone, and is more reminiscent of Owasco hearths than those of the Iroquois; and Feature 57, a unique outdoor cooking complex. This feature and its sub-features—designated on the figures as A, B, C, and D—comprised the most interesting feature discovered at Furnace Brook (Plate 12). When first discovered, it appeared to be a large, in some places almost solid, mass of burned stone and other refuse. This mass of rubble was located in an apparently open area near the center of the village surrounded by House 1, 2, 3, 5, and 6 and, from the lack of post molds, had never been covered by any sort of dwellings. As we continued to excavate this rich feature, it became apparent that this was not some sort of collective dump, but actually represented a central out-door cooking area. Ultimately, we discovered the remains of four oval roasting pits between thirty-six and ninety-four inches long and thirty-one to fifty inches wide which had been sunk into the subsoil to depths of between four and seven inches. Doubtless other similar features had once also existed, but had not been dug deep enough by the occupants of the site to escape subsequent cultivation. In every case, these pits had been scooped out of the ground, a fire kindled in the bottom which was then covered with cobbles, generally of granite, to form a platform upon which game or other food could be roasted. These features are not of the dimensions of those apparent ceremonial pits found at the Kelso and Bloody Hill sites and probably served some more mundane purpose.

Artifacts and other refuse were both abundant in Feature 57. Several celts of varying sizes, found throughout the southwestern portion of the feature, almost give the impression of being a lost or discarded set of woodworking tools. We also found several pipe bowls, as well as numerous projectile points and much pottery. Animal bone was particularly well represented and included most species found on the site including elk and bear, which may have been among those carcasses roasted in this feature. Vegetable matter included much corn, especially one portion of a cob of corn in which the kernels had been carbonized and had remained in place while the cob disintegrated. This may offer a clue to food preparation, the whole cob perhaps indicating that corn was roasted along with game on these platforms.

Artifacts

Material remains from the Furnace Brook site constitute one of the most complete samples included in this study. Material from features, small refuse areas within the palisade, and the general scatter of refuse over the village area produced thousands of artifacts including large inventories of potsherds, smoking pipes, points, celts and adzes, other rough stone tools, bone artifacts, and occasional unusual items of personal adornment, all of which are described briefly below.

Post molds, features, and patches of refuse below plow depth preserved over five thousand analyzable potsherds at the Furnace Brook site. Many were extremely small, but nonetheless one or more attributes could be observed on most sherds. The outstanding characteristics of the Furnace Brook site ceramics are (see pp. 227–37 for a description of ceramic attributes): (1) an increase in channeled low collar rim profiles to 51 percent at the expense of plain lips (11 percent) and everted lips (13 percent) and the first significant percentages of Chance rounded (6 percent) and Chance straight (9 percent) lip profiles; (2) three-quarters (76 percent) of all vessel interior edges are plain but decorated examples with either vertical or oblique cord-wrapped paddle impressions occur; (3) over 98 percent of all lips decorated in cord-wrapped stick impressions—over 50 percent with one or two longitudinal lines and the remainder with straight or oblique lines; (4) 15 percent decorated exterior lip edges; (5) a slight decrease from the Castle Creek phase in horizontal bands on collars to 59 percent, 12 percent oblique over horizontal lines, an equal frequency of horizontal over oblique lines, 5 percent oblique lines, the first appearance (4 percent) of opposed lines, and smaller percentages of other motifs executed primarily with a cord-wrapped paddle edge (83 percent) with 10 percent linear punctations, 2 percent interrupted linear, 2 percent incised, and many other techniques; (6) three-quarters (75 percent) of all collar bases decorated with cord-wrapped paddle (77 percent), linear stamp (14 percent), fingernail impressions (4 percent) or corded punctates (4 percent), probably a spillover from collar decorations as at the Cabin site; (7) 67 percent of all sub-collar areas distinctively decorated almost exclusively with oblique lines executed in cord-wrapped paddle (83 percent) or linear stamp (12 percent) impressions; (8) 79 percent of all sub-lip areas decorated usually with oblique lines in either cord-wrapped paddle (72 percent) or linear stamp (23 percent) impressions; (9) a wide variety of neck motifs including horizontal plaits (15 percent), oblique or vertical plats (40 percent), herringbone (22 percent) and opposed lines (7 percent) executed in either cord-wrapped paddle edge impressions (32 percent) or by incising (59 percent); (10) 86 percent decorated sub-neck areas, mostly (83 percent) with cord-wrapped paddle edge impressions but with lesser amounts of linear stamping (10 percent), corded punctates (3 percent), fingernail impressions (1 percent), and incised lines (3 percent); (11) no decorated vessel shoulders; (12) body sherds 98 percent check-stamped and 2 percent corded; and (13) the average collar height was 18.14 mm.

The only other ceramic artifact, exclusive of cooking pots and smoking pipes, found at Furnace Brook is the small ceramic fragment resembling somewhat a clay ear spool fragment about 1 cm. wide, 0.4 cm. thick, originally having had a diameter of about 3 cm. Of this, only about 1 cm. remains. Both ends are flattened, and the object originally resembled a hollow cylinder with expanded ends. The paste is very fine, too fine for any cooking pot handle, resembling more closely the paste typical of smoking pipes. It may very well be a portion of a pipe, perhaps an effigy pipe, which was broken, reground, and used as an ornament.

Fifty-three smoking pipes which could be assigned to one of the varieties described on pp. 239–43 were found at Furnace Brook, by far the largest sample available from any site considered here. The varieties

TABLE 2. Frequencies and Percentages of Smoking Pipe Varieties from the Furnace Brook Site

Variety	Frequency	Percentage
barrel bowl (Plate 14, no. 12)	13	24.5
conical bowl (Plate 14, no. 13)	6	11.3
corn effigy	1	1.9
collared	7	13.2
vasiform (Plate 14, no. 14)	4	7.5
puff-sleeves	6	11.3
vasiform effigy (Plate 14, no. 11)	2	3.8
vertical barred	1	1.9
square bowl (Plate 14, no. 15)	6	11.3
decorated proto-trumpet	6	11.3
other effigy (half moon?)	1	1.9
	53	99.9

and relative percentages are summarized in Table 2. Outstanding characteristics of the pipe sample of Table 2 are the decrease of barrel-shaped bowl forms in comparison to the Cabin site, the corn effigy pipe which is very similar to that from Cabin, and the first appearance of vasiform effigy, puff-sleeves, squared bowl, and proto-trumpet forms, all of which have counterparts in later Iroquois assemblages. Besides these specimens, there are fifteen fragments too small to classify accurately, many apparently pertaining to flaring lip varieties.

Pipestems are quite similar to those from the Cabin site—short, thick, and rather sharply tapered. Thirty-nine examples are round, while two have rounded upper and lower surfaces with flat sides. Most mouthpieces are smooth and rounded, but three specimens have this portion flattened to a plane surface at right angles to the stem. None have bulbous mouthpieces or any other specially made form. The only complete stem measures 8.5 cm. from mouthpiece to the bowl.

Since this is probably the only sample of projectile points (Plate 14, nos. 1–5) from our excavations which has anywhere near enough cases to be statistically significant, it is worthwhile to present here a tabulation of the frequencies and percentages of the various combinations of side and base forms, found in Table 3. It should be noted that straight-sided, concave-based forms have come to predominate at this site with smaller, and about equal, proportions of concave-sided, concave-based forms and straight-sided, straight-based forms. The other variations,

TABLE 3. Frequencies and Percentages of Projectile Point Forms from the Furnace Brook Site

Description	Frequency	Percentage
sides straight, base concave	22	47.83
sides concave, base concave	9	19.57
sides straight, base straight	7	15.22
sides concave, base bifurcate	2	4.34
sides straight, convex, base concave	1	2.17
sides straight, base concave	1	2.17
sides convex, base concave	1	2.17
sides straight, base irregular	1	2.17
sides straight, base bifurcate	1	2.17
sides concave, base straight	1	2.17
	46	99.98

which are more in number than at any of the other sites discussed, can probably be attributed to the relatively large sample, and might be due, in part, to the fact that this is a time of transition in projectile point manufacture between the earlier Owasco or Levanna forms and the Iroquois Madison points (Ritchie 1961a:31–34).

Complete metrical data are given in the original report, but the points average about the same length (3.44 cm.) and width (2.29 cm.) as do those from the Cabin site, hence the length-width ratio is also about the same: 1:50 to 1.

A few words should also be said about the rejects or blanks which were found at the site, at least some of which were presumably discarded by flint knappers during the process of manufacture. It may well be that some of these points were discarded because of some flaw in the raw material, and others because they were broken during the process of manufacture. Others, however, which represent rare variants from the most frequent and therefore probably the most acceptable forms, were probably discarded for that very reason—that they are *not* within the most acceptable forms of projectile points being manufactured at that time.

Five scrapers are also present in the Furnace Brook assemblage, four of them triangular with edges somewhat rounded by use, which were probably made from point blanks or rejects. The fifth is sub-rectangular in shape with similarly worn edges. These artifacts measure between 3.0 and 3.3 cm. long, 2.5 to 2.6 cm. broad, and between 0.7 and 1.2 cm. thick.

Seven retouched flakes are included in the collection from Furnace Brook, all roughly trapezoidal in shape and measuring 2.5 cm. to 3.2 cm. long, by 1.5 to 2.5 cm. wide, and 0.6 to 0.7 cm. in thickness. These are variously retouched on one or two edges, probably frequently through use rather than intentional retouch.

Finally, three large ovate knives were found at Furnace Brook, all bifacially flaked with retouched edges, of the same type as later Iroquois specimens.

Over one hundred artifacts which can be classed as rough or polished stone were recovered at Furnace Brook. Most are hammers, anvils, or combination tools made on flat round cobbles. Four display edge battering indicating use solely as hammers; sixteen show battering on one (twelve examples) or both (four examples) flat faces suggesting use as anvils in flint-knapping; and forty-seven are battered on both the edges and flat surfaces hence are designated hammer/anvils. Many of the latter would ordinarily be called "bipitted hammers," but the sample from Furnace Brook shows continuous variation from slight pitting from use to deep pits in both flat faces which doubtless facilitated gripping the tool. It is impossible to draw a line between the products of long use and those from intentional manufacture.

Two additional hammer/anvils, with one or two narrow grooves worn into the flat surface, were probably used as whetstones for bone awls or needles of bone. Two specialized packing hammers faceted on one end from use complete the stone-working implements from Furnace Brook. A probable pestle, square in cross section with nearly flat surfaces, which seems to have been used against a flat stone mortar, three pebble whetstones, and only one fragmentary probable chipped disc, are the only additional rough stone implements from this site.

Seventeen celts (stone axes or adzes) were recovered from within the village confines, most made from locally available close-grained sandstone, which can be categorized thus: triangular celts, six specimens, three nearly pointed at the poll (the end opposite the bit) and the others with less acutely tapered edges; rectanguloid celts, five examples, all relatively straight-sided, in most cases having the edges carefully ground (see the small example shown on Plate 14, no. 6); and three additional specimens, two unfinished "blanks," the other a fragmentary example.

A lozenge-shaped pendant of greenish schist is the final piece of worked stone from Furnace Brook. It is about 8 cm. long, 2.8 cm. in width, with a peaked top below which is a single perforation drilled from both sides.

Modified bone is quite well represented from the Furnace Brook site owing to the alkaline bedrock and to occasional deep patches of refuse which escaped the plow. Eighteen awls were found—eight with ground bases, sides and points; four with ground sides and points; four with the points only deliberately shaped; and two splinters of bone showing evidence of use as perforators. Most are made from splinters of mammal longbone, including the large specimen shown on Plate 14, no. 16, but several are bird-bone splinter awls (Plate 14, no. 10), and a single specimen is made from wild turkey humerus.

A fragmentary spatulate mat-weaving tool, two smoothed and now-broken antler tines (Plate 14, no. 9), a beaver incisor, a probable bone flesher or scraper of deer longbone, a partially perforated bear canine (Plate 14, no. 8), and two phalanx cones or bangles—one a large specimen made from an elk phalanx decorated in a sloppy herringbone motif with fine incised lines (Plate 14, no. 7), and the other a smaller, deer phalanx with the distal end perforated by scraping or sawing rather than drilling—complete the bone inventory from Furnace Brook.

Food Remains

The only vegetable remains present at Furnace Brook were corn cobs and kernels, beans, and probable hickory nuts, all carbonized.

Faunal remains from Furnace Brook, however, were well represented. They indicate no change in diet from the time of occupation at the Cabin site and probably represent rather more accurately the percentages of birds, fish, amphibians, and shellfish which were utilized by the people of both the Furnace Brook and Cabin sites. Table 4 presents the summary of faunal material prepared by Dr. Waters.

TABLE 4. Faunal Remains from the Furnace Brook Site

Species	No. pieces	Remarks
Mammals		
white-tailed deer (*Odocoileus virginianus*)	860	18 adults: three 1–2 years old, three 2–3 years old, three over 3 years, one adult male
beaver (*Castor canadensis*)	5	one adult
dog (*Canis familiaris*)	3	at least one adult
black bear (*Ursus americanus*)	4	one adult
cottontail rabbit (*Sylvilagus sp.*)	3	one adult
porcupine (*Erethizon dorsatum*)	7	one adult
muskrat (*Ondatra zibethicus*)	5	two adults
woodchuck (*Marmota monax*)	3	one adult
eastern grey squirrel (*Sciurus carolinensis*)	15	four adults
meadow vole (*Microtus pennsylvanicus*)	23	six adults
Birds		
136 pieces including:		
passenger pigeon (*Ectopistes migratorius*) (?)		
mallard duck (*Anas platyrhynchos*)		
blue-winged teal (*Anas discors*)		
ruffed grouse (*Bonasa umbellus*)		at least one adult
Fish		
1500 pieces including:		
fresh water sheepshead (*Aplodinotus grunniens*)		
sucker (*Moxostoma sp.*)		
catfish (*Ictalurus sp.*) (?)		
pike or pickerel (*Esox sp.*) (?)		
largemouth bass (*Micropterus salmoides*) (?)		
sunfish (*Lepomis sp.*)		
Amphibians		
50 plus pieces including:		
bullfrog (*Rana catesbeiana*)		
green frog (*Rana clomitans*)		
Shellfish		
50-plus valves of freshwater clam, species unidentified		

Chronology

Two radiocarbon determinations were made on wood charcoal from the Furnace Brook site. The first of these is derived from material from Feature 1 in House 2 and was associated with a typical sample of pottery from the site. This date was returned at A.D. 1300±60 (Y−1817). The second date was obtained from the wood charcoal taken from post molds in the southwestern portion of the inner stockade. Several post molds were combined to form this sample, but all charcoal came from well into the ground and was often associated with potsherds or other artifacts. The practice of taking charcoal samples from well-buried post molds is desirable because the trees from which these poles were cut could not have been over twenty to thirty years old (probably much younger) and would not, therefore, have heartwood which long ago ceased to absorb radioactive carbon, thereby dating the site earlier than the actual occupation. Also, if all radiocarbon determinations are run on wood samples of equal size and age, this factor of old heartwood would be controlled at all sites. This is especially important during the more recent periods of prehistory, and particularly at sites which may have been occupied for twenty years or less. At any rate, the second date was returned at A.D. 1370±60 (Y−1818).

These dates are not internally consistent with my interpretation of the construction phases at this site. I would have expected them to be returned exactly the reverse of the way they appear here since the interior palisade was presumably built first. Nevertheless, the dates themselves seem to indicate very accurately both the duration and actual time of occupation of the Furnace Brook site.

THE KELSO SITE

The Kelso site (Bwv 12–3), excavated by the New York State Museum and Science Service, has been briefly described in print on two occasions (Ritchie 1965, 1969:303–11; 1967) and a much more extensive analysis is in preparation by Ritchie and Funk. For this reason only a brief description of the settlement data will be presented here. Material remains studied at the New York State Museum through the courtesy of Drs. Ritchie and Funk will be described and compared with that from other sites in somewhat more detail.

Settlement Data

The site is located about one and a half miles southeast of the Chamberlin site (see Figure no. 2) on a ridge of gravelly silt-loam which rises but slightly from the surrounding undulating country. Almost no defensive advantage seems to have been gained from selection of this particular location, a characteristic common of many sites of this period. Excavation of over ten thousand square feet revealed two distinct, overlapping villages which were undoubtedly the product of a single community which Ritchie postulated left the immediate area for a short time to allow firewood and such to become replenished, though the intermediate village has yet to be found. It may be beneath the present village of Elbridge, New York.

A system of slit trenches and the excavation of selected squares near the edges of these settlements revealed one of the most complete patterns of fortifications at any Oak Hill phase village yet excavated. The two oval palisades were composed of double, and in places triple, walls of saplings three to four inches in diameter set from six to eight inches apart. Post molds representing buttress posts are set at an angle which indicates that the palisade must have stood at least fifteen feet above the ground. Also revealed by these excavations were a ditch surrounding at least a portion of the eastern stockade, a door two and a half feet wide in the western palisade, and a probable bastion at a low point in the northeastern corner of the western stockade. Although the site itself presents little defensive advantage, it can easily be seen that defense was a major concern of the community living at the Kelso site.

Houses were of two general types at the Kelso site—small oval houses sixteen by nineteen feet and thirty-two by twenty-six feet and larger true longhouses twenty-two feet wide and ranging in length from 112 to 118 feet. The former are similar in some respects to the smallest houses at the Furnace Brook and Chamberlin sites and the still earlier houses at the Maxon-Derby site. The latter form is Iroquois in every respect, being constructed as were the houses at Furnace Brook, Howlett Hill, and most other stations described in this report. Small poles formed the bulk of the side walls with occasional larger posts irregularly spaced among them. In all, the house types suggest a village in which the transition from Owasco houses to true longhouses was nearly complete.

Features

Features at the Kelso site consisted of two types of hearths and several large roasting pits similar to that found at the Bloody Hill site and described later in this report. The hearths were large and amorphous, typical of most Iroquois villages, centrally located in the houses at Kelso (Ritchie 1965:308) and smaller basin-shape hearths, frequently located outside of the houses, resembling very strongly those found by us at the Chamberlin site (see pp. 31–32). These two types of hearths provide still further evidence of the transitional nature of this site.

The other type feature, the large roasting platforms, are described by Ritchie (1965:308–309) as large, bathtub-shaped features containing a lowermost layer of burned logs and charcoal overlain by a platform of fire-cracked gneissic cobbles and rocks. Each of these features had apparently been used but once, and the presence of bear bones in one feature suggested that these served in some form of bear ceremonialism (see Ritchie 1965:314, Plate 109, for a photograph of one of these features under excavation).

Artifacts

An excellent sample of the "material culture" of the Kelso community was recovered from the village area on the east and an infrequently plowed field on the western part of the site. Because there is little apparent difference in the artifacts from within the two palisades the total sample is described below *as if* it were the product of a single continuously occupied village.

Ritchie and Funk will probably discuss in detail the ceramics from the Kelso site, but particularly noteworthy in the Kelso ceramic series are the following traits: (1) high percentages of channeled low collar (33 percent), Chance rounded (21 percent), and Chance straight (25 percent) rim profiles with much lower percentages of plain (6 percent), everted (5 percent), and characteristic later Iroquois biconcave collar (4 percent) rim profiles; (2) most interiors (64 percent) plain but the remainder decorated with either vertical or oblique cord-wrapped paddle impressions; (3) less than 87 percent of all lips decorated and only slightly more than 40 percent decorated with longitudinal cord-wrapped paddle impressions; (4) less than 4 percent decorated exterior lip edges; (5) collars decorated by horizontal lines (50 percent), oblique lines (19 percent), oblique over horizontal lines (12 percent), horizontal over oblique (4 percent), oblique between horizontal (3 percent), horizontal between oblique (2 percent) and the usual smattering of other motifs executed almost exclusively (97 percent) in the cord-wrapped paddle technique; (6) nearly three-quarters of all collar bases (73 percent) decorated with cord-wrapped paddle (96 percent) or other impressions; (7) 60 percent of all sub-collar areas decorated chiefly with oblique lines in either cord-wrapped paddle (96 percent) or linear stamp (4 percent) impressions; (8) thirteen (or 93 percent) of all sub-lip areas decorated in twelve (92 percent) of the cases by oblique cord-wrapped paddle impressions; (9) a variety of neck decorative motifs not unlike earlier samples (39 percent oblique or vertical plaits, 17 percent herringbone, 14 percent horizontal plaits, etc.) with the addition of 21 percent plain neck sherds, the decorations done either by cord-wrapped paddle impressions (92 percent) or by incising (6 percent); (10) 64 percent of all sub-neck areas specifically decorated (16 percent plain, 20 percent have neck motifs extending to body surface treatment) primarily with cord-wrapped paddle impressions (92 percent), incising (6 percent) and several other techniques with percentages of less than one; (11) no decorated shoulders; (12) body surface treatment consisting of smoothed-over check-stamp (66 percent), check-stamped (25 percent), corded (3 percent), smoothed (3 percent), smoothed-over cord (3 percent), and brushed (?) (.04 percent); and (13) the average collar height was 23.56 mm.

Two miniature vessels of very different quality of workmanship were found at the Kelso site. The first fragment, representing about one-half of the vessel, is an uncollared vessel made around a finger, as are the small pots from Bloody Hill and Cemetery sites. This specimen measures 3.2 cm. high, 2.5 cm. in diameter, and has vessel walls about 2 mm. thick. It is crudely made and decorated, the decoration consisting of two horizontal cord-wrapped paddle impressions immediately below the lip and a short series of similarly executed vertical impressions immediately below these extending to the vessel shoulder.

The second miniature pot, of much better quality clay and workmanship, may actually be a vasiform pipe bowl, though it is fairly complete and shows no sign of a stem. It is similar in size to the previous example, but it was apparently not made over a finger and is collared in rim form. Decoration is similar to that sometimes found on pipes, especially inasmuch as it is over the entire exterior surface of the vessel. The collar is covered with incised horizontal lines interrupted by bands of oblique lines, a motif very common on cooking pots of this phase.

Twenty-seven identifiable smoking pipe fragments from the Kelso site are in the collection of the New York State Museum. Outstanding in this sample are an unusually large conical pipe and a vasiform effigy pipe decorated with mammiform appendages very like a human breast. Motifs and techniques of decoration in the sample listed on Table 5 conform to those described for each variety on pp. 239–43.

Pipestems are primarily round in cross section (seventeen examples), only one specimen being sub-rectangular. Of eight remaining mouthpieces only two have slightly expanding ends, the remaining six being straight with the ends slightly flattened.

Chipped stone from the Kelso site, described below, consists primarily of projectile points with several retouched flakes and probable knife

TABLE 5. Frequencies and Percentages of Smoking
Pipe Varieties from the Kelso Site

Variety	Frequency	Percentage
barrel bowl	7	25.9
conical bowl	7	25.9
vasiform	2	7.4
puff-sleeve	2	7.4
vasiform effigy	3	11.1
squared bowl	6	22.2
	27	99.9

fragments, a sample similar in all respects to most Oak Hill Iroquois sites.

With the exception of a possibly intrusive stemmed point with sloping shoulders and a contracting stem, all projectile points from Kelso are triangular in outline and represent either Levanna, Madison (Ritchie 1961a:31–34), or intermediate forms. This sample, as that from Furnace Brook, is characterized by extreme variability both in form and dimensions, and the average length of completed specimens (3.27 cm.) and width also of completed specimens (2.24 cm.) are very similar to those from previously described sites. Nor is the length-width ratio (1.46 to 1) significantly different.

Three knives are in the New York State Museum collection from the Kelso site. Two are typical Iroquois ovate knives with rounded base and pointed tip (actually there is evidence in the form of a complete specimen recovered by Charles Wray of West Rush, New York, to indicate that these knives were hafted with the point fitted into the haft). The one complete example measures 5.7 by 2.3 by 0.9 cm. The third knife is a flake, irregular in outline, which is retouched on the two longest opposite edges on one face only.

A single small thumbnail end scraper is the only representative of this relatively rare category of artifacts found at Kelso. It measures 2.6 by 1.5 cm. and is 0.7 cm. thick. Retouch is at one end which has been steeply trimmed from only one face.

Rough stone tools include two anvils, thirteen combination hammer/anvils, one hammer/anvil/muller, a small pecking hammer, a cylindrical pestle, and a shallow biconcave mortar, an assemblage not markedly different from that from Furnace Brook. The presence of thirty-five chipped stone discs, presumably hoes, is something of a surprise, however, in view of their virtual absence at Furnace Brook and other stations. Many show wear over nearly the entire edge while others are worn over only about one-half of the surface, suggesting that the former were repeatedly rehafted.

Seven whole or fragmentary celts were found—two thick-polled trianguloid specimens, an ovate example, and four rectanguloid specimens (one doubtful because of breakage)—a single plano-convex adze, and two small probable chisels which form a series of woodworking tools not unlike previously described assemblages.

Modified bone from the Kelso site consists of numerous awls, similar in all respects to the splinter awls from other sites, which will not be described here since Ritchie and Funk will deal with it in detail. Unusual from among the modified bone from this site is a small, spatulate weaving tool, rounded at both ends with a hole near the center probably used for the weaving of rush mats. Also recovered at Kelso was a fragment of a human skull, apparently originally round, with the edges cut and polished smooth. This may have been, or may have been intended to be, a human skull gorget, a type of trophy or ornament usually associated with cannibalism or some other practice connected with warfare.

Food Remains

Ritchie (1965:316) and Ritchie and Funk (n.d.) have discussed food remains from this site in some detail and have arrived at conclusions which indicate dietary patterns no different from those at other sites reported here. Corn and beans comprise the cultigens, while animal bone indicated full exploitation of both terrestrial and riverine fauna.

Chronology

All settlement data and the material remains described above indicate an early Oak Hill placement of this site. The length of occupation, however, is great, and it is not impossible that this site was occupied for nearly the entire Oak Hill phase. The radiocarbon date of A.D. 1390±100 (Y−1380,) originally thought by Ritchie (1965:308) to be a bit too late, is entirely compatible with our dates for all other sites in the area, though it probably does date the latter part of a long occupation.

THE HOWLETT HILL SITE

In a previous article (Tuck 1967) our excavations at the Howlett Hill site (Syr. 12–3) were briefly described but a brief description of the results of this work as well as a somewhat more complete description of the material remains is presented here.

This site was discovered by Robert Ricklis in 1964 and was tested by him and the writer during the fall of that year. At that time we discovered enough material to indicate that this was a village of the Oak Hill phase. We also discovered a line of post molds which seemed to pertain to a house of extraordinary dimensions. During the following spring and summer more extensive excavations were carried out at Howlett Hill, resulting in the recovery of the bulk of the data discussed here.

Settlement Data

The site is located less than a mile west of the Furnace Brook site and about three miles north of the Schoff site (see Figure 1), on a slope of land which drops at a rate of 5 percent to the north. This location offers almost no natural defensive advantage except possibly from a steep, shale-sided ravine some five or six hundred feet west of the site and another small, intermittent stream east of the village area. The former creek is the same small stream upon which the Schoff site is located. The latter stream has been diverted considerably by recent construction in this area which has also, by this time, destroyed almost the entire Howlett Hill site.

The soil in and surrounding the village area is a Palatine silt-loam which overlies a sandy-clay subsoil containing frequent shale outcrops.

Because the site had been extensively plowed for many years and

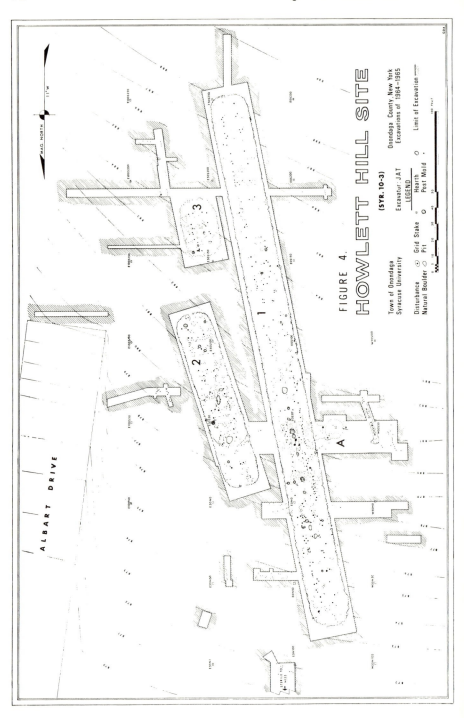

FIGURE 4.

HOWLETT HILL SITE

(SYR. 10-3)

Town of Onondaga   Onondaga County, New York
Syracuse University   Excavations of 1964-1965

Excavator: JAT

LEGEND

Disturbance   Grid Stake   Limit of Excavation
Natural Boulder   Pit   Hearth
                     Post Mold

had been further disturbed more recently by excavating for road beds in the new housing development which now covers the site, much of the eight to ten inch tilth zone was removed with the aid of power machinery. The final few inches of topsoil were removed by hand, however, and the entire exposed area then carefully troweled in a search for post molds and other features. More than thirteen thousand square feet of the village area were completely exposed in this fashion.

As mentioned in the previous report (Tuck 1967) on this site no definite evidence of any defensive structure was found despite test trenches extended in all directions from our main excavations (see Figure 4). Frequently encountered, however, were series of post molds which could be followed for a short distance before they disappeared. It could be that these are actually portions of a stockade, the posts perhaps being set in a low earth ring, since plowed away, leaving no trace of most of the palisade posts. There is also a possible ditch on the western edge of the village which might have pertained to some defensive structure. Even in total this evidence is far from convincing, and it is very likely that the post molds described above actually pertain to houses not completely uncovered.

Houses at Howlett Hill were the most interesting discoveries at the site. While they were extremely varied in length, the techniques of construction differed in no way from other sites of this period. All structures are described below.

House 1 (Figure 4) was partly disclosed by our test excavations of 1964 and was subsequently completely exposed in 1965. This unusual structure measured some 334 feet long by twenty-three feet wide and was, at the time of its discovery, the largest house known in Iroquoia. It had been built in the manner of the houses at most of the other sites reported herein. The exterior walls were made of two to four-inch diameter poles, twisted or otherwise forced into the ground to a depth of between eight and twelve inches. These were spaced from one to twelve inches apart along the walls, and larger posts, up to ten inches in diameter, were distributed among them somewhat randomly. The doors were located in the center of the rounded ends as in most Oak Hill phase structures, but one unusual feature was a side door—undoubtedly necessitated by the extreme length of this house—which was located on the west side of the house exactly in the center—167 feet from either end.

Internal structure was also typically Iroquois, consisting of two parallel rows of large support posts which had been placed in holes dug for them. These posts undoubtedly supported bench-beds as they did in eth-

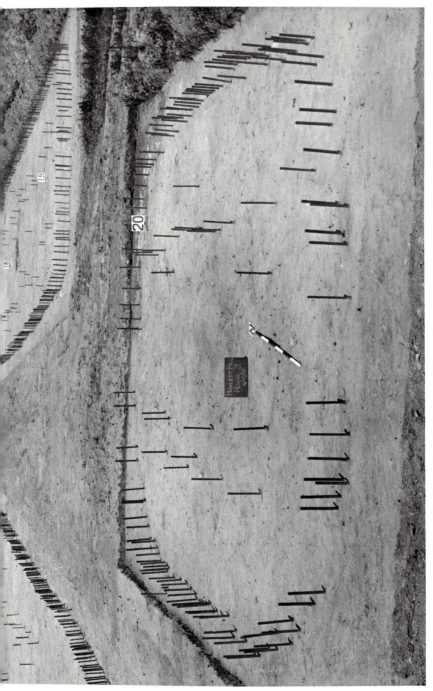

PLATE 16. House 3 at the Howlett Hill site showing exterior structure, bed and roof support post molds, and hearth indicated by number 20.

PLATE 17. Aerial view of excavations at the Howlett Hill site looking south.

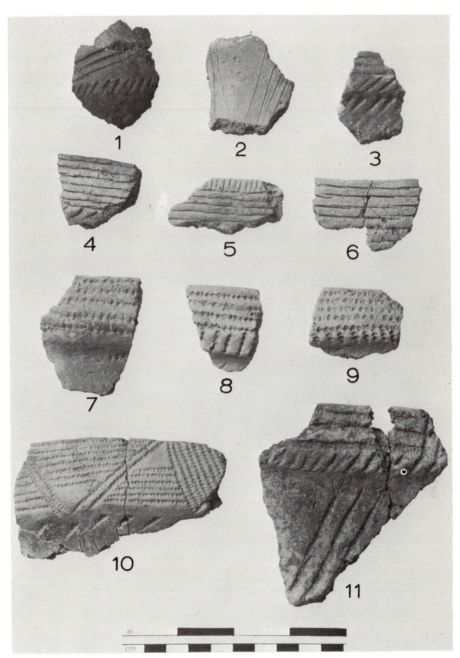

PLATE 18. Ceramics from the Howlett Hill site. 1, neck and shoulder sherd decorated with cord-wrapped paddle impressions; 2, incised neck sherd; 3, rim sherd decorated with linear-stamp impressions; 4–6, incised (possibly with fingernail) rim sherds; 7–9, 11, cord-wrapped paddle impression rim sherds; 10, collar decorated with Iroquois opposed triangle motif executed in early cord-wrapped paddle technique.

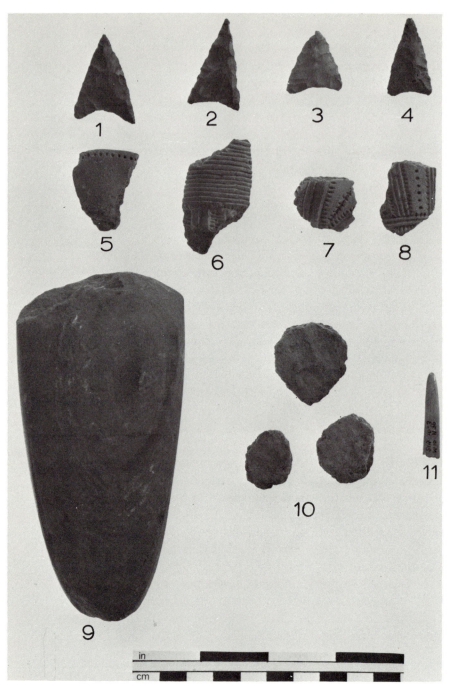

PLATE 19. Artifacts from the Howlett Hill site. 1–4, triangular arrowpoints; 5, fragment of trumpet pipe bowl with single row of fine punctuations near lip; 6 and 7, fragments of vertical-barred pipe bowls; 8, smoking pipe bowl fragment decorated in typical Oak Hill technique of fine incising and pointille work; 9, trianguloid celt of coarse sandstone; 10, chipped pottery gaming discs; 11, fragment of spatulate mat needle.

nographically known structures. Also inside the house were numerous small post molds, difficult to interpret, but which perhaps represent the remains of partitions or cooking structures.

Despite a careful search for additions to this house which might account for its unusual length, none were found. It seems safe, therefore, to assume from this evidence and from the location of the side door, that this was a pre-planned structure perhaps for a predetermined number of families. It further seems likely that this longhouse was occupied, at least in part, by the same group which built House 2 at Furnace Brook (above). This house, as well as the others to be described, are illustrated on Plate 17.

House 2 was located slightly to the east of House 1 and roughly parallel to it. The post mold pattern outlining this structure indicated two building phases. The initial construction resulted in a longhouse measuring eighty-six feet by twenty-three feet and constructed essentially the same as House 1. A subsequent addition of twenty-six feet brought the total length to 112 feet, the width remaining unchanged (Plate 15). Interior and exterior construction were the same as the earlier building phase and House 1.

House 3 (Plate 16), constructed in about the same fashion as the others, differed from them primarily in dimensions. It measured only thirty-five by twenty-two feet and was situated perfectly parallel to House 1 and only ten feet east of it. The east wall is very irregular and was probably almost entirely rebuilt at one time. Interior structure is clearly indicated, at least as far as large support posts are concerned, but numerous smaller post molds present some problems in interpretation.

A final unusual building, designated Structure A, was a small (twelve feet in diameter) circular structure made of posts somewhat smaller than those which comprised the house walls. It stood immediately west of House 1 and was apparently connected with it by what now appear as two rows of small post molds. It was probably a small above-ground granary used to store vegetable products in place of the large storage pits found on some Owasco and Iroquois sites but virtually absent from our Onondaga series.

Features

All features disclosed by our excavations were located within the houses, a fact which probably reflects the salvage nature of our method of excavation at this site more than it reflects strictly any cultural pattern of the occupants. Features aside from large post molds which were given feature numbers if they contained refuse can be classed either as hearths or as small pits of questionable function. Hearths are all centrally located in typical Iroquois fashion with one exception, the small hearth in the northeast corner of House 3. This practice of locating hearths to one side of the house is reminiscent of earlier Owasco practice, and the dimensions of the house itself are likewise consistent more with earlier dwellings than with the Iroquois longhouse. All other hearths are indicated by shallow, generally ovoid, or amorphous patches of fire-reddened earth, almost never containing any appreciable amount of refuse. At the south end of House 1 no hearths were discovered, a situation probably brought about by a combination of plowing which removed the features and caused some soil creep which allowed the plow to dig still deeper, removing more of the features and causing further soil creep.

The second type of feature, the small pits measuring from twelve to twenty inches in diameter and up to twelve inches deep, were distributed irregularly along the house walls, probably beneath the beds. The fill frequently contained flecks of charcoal and occasionally some other refuse, but in no case was there evidence of burning *in situ*. These seem to have been neither hearths nor pits for storage of food, but may be the remains of small pits which the Iroquois are known to have dug in which to store their most valued possessions.

Artifacts

Material remains from the Howlett Hill site are very few in number owing to the much plowed nature of the site and the almost complete lack of productive sub-surface features. There are, however, small samples from nearly every artifact category, all of which are described below.

Although few sherds escaped breakage from cultivation, nearly a thousand ceramic fragments were recovered upon which one or more observations could be made. A summary of these observations follows (see Appendix A for a description of ceramic attributes): (1) only three rim profiles were present—channeled low collar (18 percent), Chance rounded (18 percent), and Chance straight (64 percent); (2) most (88 percent) interiors were plain, but a few were decorated as are previously described ceramics; (3) about the same percentage (87) of decorated lips as Kelso and decorative motifs and techniques also similar but with a somewhat greater frequency of longitudinal decorations (61 percent); (4) less than 3 percent decorated exterior lip edges; (5) collars decorated by horizontal lines (53 percent), oblique over horizontal lines (26 percent), opposed lines (11 percent), horizontal over oblique lines (6 percent), and horizontal between oblique lines (4 percent) executed either by the cord-wrapped paddle (93 percent), linear stamp (4 percent) or one of several other techniques; (6) a decrease in decorated collar bases over earlier Oak Hill phase sites to 32 percent but a continued high percentage (93 percent) of the cord-wrapped paddle impressions; (7) 79 percent of all sub-collar areas decorated, usually with oblique lines executed in the cord-wrapped paddle technique (90 percent) but with lesser frequencies of linear stamping, interrupted linear, and paired crescent punctations; (8) no uncollared vessels were recovered, hence no observations on sub-lip decoration are possible; (9) 23 percent plain vessel necks, 39 percent vertical or oblique plaits, and many other motifs executed either by incising (64 percent) or cord-wrapped paddle impressions (29 percent); (10) 93 percent decorated sub-neck areas, 95 percent with cord-wrapped paddle impressions; (11) no decorated shoulder sherds; (12) body surfaces 92 percent check-stamped, 7 percent smoothed over check-stamped, with corded and smoothed less than 1 percent each; and (13) the average collar height is 25.02 mm.

Several small, check-stamped body sherds found at Howlett Hill are apparently from well-made miniature pots, probably not unlike those from the Cabin site. Unfortunately, all sherds are small and badly broken, and no decorated portions were recovered. Three pottery discs made from sherds of cooking pots (Plate 19, no. 10) represent the first appearance of this Iroquois artifact form. All are nearly round (2.0–2.5 cm. in diameter), and the edges show slight wear or grinding. Similar artifacts, frequently found on later Iroquois sites, are usually interpreted as gaming discs, though whether they were used as counters or as actual equipment in a game of chance (e.g., the deer button or bowl games) is unknown.

Smoking pipe fragments (Plate 19, nos. 5–8) recovered at Howlett Hill were invariably badly broken, hence somewhat difficult to classify. The ten examples which can be classified with some certainty are listed in Table 6. Noticeable, even in the small sample, is the disappearance of early barrel-shaped bowl varieties, the predominance of puff-sleeve and vertical barred varieties typical of the Oak Hill phase, and the single decorated proto-trumpet which approaches very closely the plain proto-trumpet pipes of the later Chance phase. This specimen (Plate 19, no. 5) has a thinned, flaring lip decorated by only two rows of very fine punctations, one surmounting the lip and the other just beneath it on the ex-

TABLE 6. Frequencies and Percentages of Smoking
Pipe Varieties from the Howlett Hill Site

Description	Frequency	Percentage
conical bowl	1	10.0
puff-sleeve	3	30.0
vertical barred	2	20.0
squared bowl	1	10.0
decorated proto-trumpet	3	30.0
	10	100.0

terior surface. Two fragments of pipestems, both badly broken and neither having the mouthpiece, were found. Both are round and, despite their fragmentary nature, can be seen to possess a less pronounced taper than do the specimens from Cabin or Furnace Brook, another trait seemingly trending toward Iroquois styles.

As in the case of most other classes of artifacts from Howlett Hill, the sample of chipped stone is extremely limited. Ten completed, or nearly completed, arrow points were found in addition to five rough blanks too irregular to classify. Despite the limited number of cases, two trends are apparent. The first is an increasing uniformity in the sample with one variety (straight-sided concave-based forms) comprising more than half of the sample. (Compare this with the very heterogeneous sample from the Furnace Brook site.) The second trend, obviously related to the first, is the emergence of these two attributes (straight sides and concave bases) at the expense of all others including most earlier characteristics. Again, over-all dimensions (average length 3.23 cm., average width 2.33 cm.) and the length ratio (1.39 to 1) are not vastly different from the Kelso, Furnace Brook, or Cabin site samples.

Two probable knives, a typical Iroquois ovate knife made of local Onondaga flint and a rectanguloid scraper/knife probably made from a reject of point manufacture, complete the chipped-stone inventory from Howlett Hill.

Thirty-four pieces of rough and polished stone were recovered at Howlett Hill, including five anvils, sixteen hammer/anvils, one hammer/anvil/whetstone, three irregular whetstones made from crystalline rocks, five chipped discs—three of which are questionable specimens—and a single pestle which comprise a fairly typical assemblage of tools in this category.

Four celts or fragments thereof, all typical of the Oak Hill phase, were recovered at Howlett Hill. Two are completed though broken specimens, while the other two are unfinished examples. Three thick-polled trianguloid examples with an ovoid cross section (Plate 19, no. 9) are made from a coarse greywacke which has now become very soft and crumbles easily. The fourth specimen is a rectanguloid specimen with slightly converging sides, a sub-rectangular cross section, and a rounded poll.

Only a single fragment of modified bone was found at this site, owing to the relatively low pH and the intensive cultivation. This fragment, the tip of a small spatulate bone weaving tool is shown on Plate 19, no. 11.

Food Remains

The same factors which prevented the preservation of modified bone also prevented the preservation of any substantial sample of food refuse, especially animal bone. Only two species of vegetable foods are

TABLE 7. FAUNAL REMAINS FROM THE HOWLETT HILL SITE

Species	No. pieces	Remarks
MAMMAL		
white-tailed deer	47	at least one adult
Odocoileus virginianus		
BIRD		
unidentified	4	
FISH		
Probable freshwater sheepshead		
Apoldinotus grunniens	11	
SHELLFISH		
Probable freshwater clam	4	

represented—carbonized corn kernels and beans—though they obviously did not form the entire vegetable diet of the community which dwelt at Howlett Hill (see Table 7).

Chronology

A wood charcoal sample obtained from Feature 3, a large post mold in the center of House 1, was submitted to the Yale Radiocarbon Laboratory for analysis. The material was collected from well below the surface of the subsoil and was nearly sealed off from above by a layer of sherds of a single small vessel decorated with cord-wrapped paddle impressions (Plate 18, no. 1). The date was returned at A.D. 1380±60 (Y−1689) which is very compatible with the dates from the previously occupied Furnace Brook site and is nearly identical with the Kelso date which seems to mark the closing years of a long occupation at that site, as well as with other dates to be discussed later.

THE COYE II SITE

The Coye II site, known primarily from a few specimens in the collection of Dr. Anton Sohrweide of Syracuse, New York, is located on the same small rise of land which was the site of another, later Onondaga hamlet occupied in the 1700s. It is located west of Butternut Creek (see Figure 1) about a mile from the Keough site and two miles from the Bloody Hill site, both of which are described below. It apparently occupied a small, low rise of land which presents no apparent defensive advantage. Despite knowing the exact location of the site, we were unable to locate any remains on the surface which definitely pertain to this occupation. The only objects I have found on this site which may be earlier than the historic occupation are flint chips, part of an ovate or lanceolate knife and a point fragment with concave sides and base, all of which are not typical of mid-eighteenth-century Iroquois. Dr. Sohrweide's collection includes a few sherds from the site, two of which are of collared vessels, one with a Chance phase straight collar, both decorated with horizontal cord-wrapped paddle impressions. Also present are two smoking pipe stem fragments, one round in cross section and the other apparently either square or rectangular. All material is pictured on Plate 20.

While admittedly not much on which to base any conclusions, this sample gives every indication of pertaining to a late Oak Hill phase occupation, perhaps close in time to that at Howlett Hill or Kelso. The possible relationships of this site to other villages will be further explored in Chapter 7.

SUMMARY

From the description of data and material presented in this chapter it is apparent that our excavations do not reveal the distinctiveness of the

PLATE 20. Artifacts from the Coye II site. 1, triangular arrowpoint; 2, ovate knife; 3 and 4, rim sherds from collared vessels decorated with cord-wrapped paddle impressions; 5, square pipestem fragment; 6, round pipestem fragment.

Oak Hill phase. They tend, rather, to point out its continuities with the preceeding Castle Creek Owasco. Clearly indicated too are several later Iroquois traits which will become even more apparent in the chapters which follow. The Oak Hill phase displays exactly the characteristics expected, for it has long been called by archaeologists the transitional stage between Owasco and Iroquois. The specific characteristics which make it so are fortified settlements, longhouses with rounded ends, ceramic and other artifact complexes with elements of both Owasco and Iroquois design.

It is more important to point out some of the differences and similarities among the four Oak Hill phase sites, which offer some further clues to the nature of developing Iroquois social and political organization as well as to changes in "material culture." The geographic separation of the Cabin and Chamberlin communities, first noted in Chapter 2, is continued throughout the Oak Hill phase, and the first glimpse of a third community, is afforded by the data. Specifically, the Kelso site seems to represent a later village of the Chamberlin community, indicated not only by the geographic proximity of the two sites and their relative isolation from other known sites but also by what seems to be a developing ceramic microtradition best displayed by the tendency of the Chamberlin-Kelso potters to decorate the necks of their vessels with cord-wrapped paddle impressions. The second community, which occupied sequentially the Cabin, Furnace Brook, and Howlett Hill sites, preferred to decorate vessel necks with incised lines in an overwhelming percentage of cases. The tight geographic clustering of these sites further illustrates their probable single community affiliation, and we see the first evidence of still another community characteristic—the construction of at least one extremely long longhouse at the Furnace Brook and Howlett Hill villages—which we shall later see persists through several more generations. Finally, if the Coye II site is correctly interpreted as an Oak Hill phase component, it must represent a third community living in Onondaga during the fourteenth century which our C-14 determinations indicate included the entire Oak Hill Iroquois phase.

These distinctive communities, first in evidence during the Oak Hill phase, will be further investigated in the following chapter. The westernmost community disappears from the archaeological record but the presence of the other two communities is increasingly well documented and moreover provides evidence of a territorial fusion which we interpret as the founding of the Onondaga Nation sometime during the mid-fifteenth century.

CHAPTER 4

The Chance Phase

IN THIS CHAPTER we will discuss subsequent developments in Onondaga culture history as evidenced at the Schoff, Bloody Hill, Keough, Burke, and Christopher sites of the Chance phase of the fifteenth century A.D. Some other central New York Iroquois sites—all poorly known—will be briefly described. No settlement data except site locations are available for these latter stations, and material remains are in no case abundant. All indications are, however, that these sites are temporal equivalents of the Chance phase villages described below; hence these enigmatic components are discussed at the conclusion of this chapter on the early Iroquois of central New York.

The Chance level or stage of Mohawk cultural development was early recognized as "the earliest manifest cultural expression which can in all probability be identified as Mohawk by means of a majority of ceramic and other trait correspondences with components, linked in turn by like evidences with protohistoric and later documented Mohawk towns" (Ritchie 1952:6). The type station, and in fact most reported Chance phase sites (as this "horizon" or widespread stage of limited temporal duration, was designated by Ritchie in 1965), are all located in eastern New York, hence the frequent mention of Mohawk affiliations.

In the original report Ritchie wrote that all Chance phase sites in the Mohawk Valley were small, situated upon high, well-drained ground, and at least one site revealed evidence of an Iroquoian longhouse. As is the Oak Hill phase, the Chance phase of the Iroquois tradition or continuum is recognizable primarily as an artifact complex, as the site descriptions which follow will indicate.

It was during this phase that "the artistic quality of Iroquois pottery in the eastern area attained its zenith . . . particularly in the developmental stage represented by the late Oak Hill—early Chance horizon" (Ritchie 1969:312). Incising replaced the long-established cord-impression method of pottery adornment. The continuities with Owasco are nevertheless evident, for incising on vessel necks is characteristic of that culture. Check-stamping and cord malleation were replaced by smoothing of vessel body surfaces (Ritchie 1952:Figure 4). Smoking pipe styles were modified and new forms appeared including many "trumpet varieties and human face and various animal effigies" (Ritchie 1969:313–14).

Chronology of the Chance phase in the Mohawk sub-area rests upon two radiocarbon determinations: A.D. 1325±75 for the early Chance phase Oak Hill No. 7 site and A.D. 1398±150 for the later Getman site, both, it will be seen later, at some variance with our dates from Onondaga.

Our own excavations at Chance phase components were centered at three stations, and data from two additional sites comprise what seem to be most, and very likely all, the Chance phase villages in the mainstream of Onondaga cultural development. Time and financial limitations prohibited our conducting extensive excavations at any single component as we had done at several Oak Hill sites. The material and data recovered, however, and that obtained from other collections, are sufficient to carry our story through the Chance phase, and to add an important piece to the puzzle of Onondaga socio-political development.

THE SCHOFF SITE

The Schoff site (Tly 2–1) is located in the Town of Onondaga, New York, on Abbey Road south of Rte. 173. It is on lands presently owned by Wallace Schoff and Willis Sargent, both of whom kindly allowed us to excavate there during August, 1967. As were the Cabin and Howlett Hill sites, this important site was discovered by Robert Ricklis, then of nearby Onondaga Hill.

Settlement Data

The site is situated on the southern end of a long drumlin which drops off quite sharply to the east and south of the village area. To the north there is a distance of nearly three hundred feet between the apparent limit of the village and the brow of the hill. To the west there is a gentle drop of about fifteen feet at which point the land again begins to rise. This location provides a commanding view of the surrounding area and there can be little doubt that the site was chosen for its obvious defensive advantages. A thousand feet east of the site flows a small stream

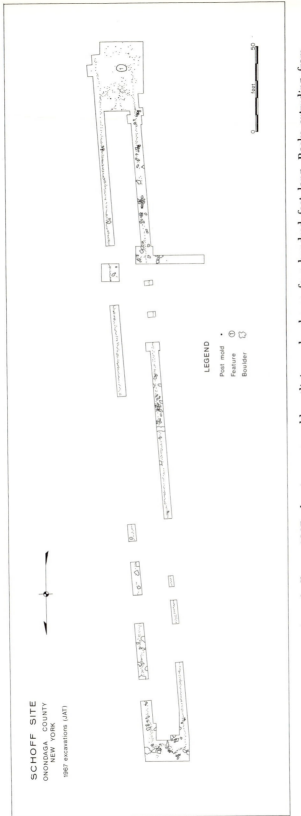

SCHOFF SITE
ONONDAGA COUNTY
NEW YORK

1967 excavations (JAT)

LEGEND

Post mold ·
Feature ⊕
Boulder ♤

50
feet
0

FIGURE 5. Excavations at the Schoff site, 1967, showing post molds outlining a longhouse four hundred feet long. Rocks extruding from the subsoil cause apparent gaps in the house walls. Feature 1 is a large cooking pit located at the south end of House 1.

—the same stream, in fact, near which the Howlett Hill site is located one and three-quarters of a mile to the north (see Figure 1). Although the fields in which the site is located are now overgrown with hay and pasturage it is possible to find small potsherds and other refuse on the surface. By this means it was determined that the village area encompassed about two acres. The soil is similar to that at the Howlett Hill, Furnace Brook, and Cabin sites, a sandy silt-loam overlying a clay subsoil containing numerous shale and limestone fragments which is, in places, almost a pure eroded limestone. Despite this partial handicap our search for data on house types and other structures was rewarded by the disclosure of the large structure described below.

Our concentrated efforts to uncover House I and lack of time and manpower did not permit us to make our usual search for evidences of palisades or other defensive structures. However, the obvious concern for defense evidenced by the choice of this hilltop as a settlement and the palisades found at both earlier and later sites suggest that this site was probably fortified with a system of palisades similar to that at Furnace Brook or the Burke site, though the lack of conclusive evidence for a stockade at the Howlett Hill site makes it possible that the Schoff site was unfortified.

House 1, the only structure discovered at the Schoff site, was first located in a five-foot wide test trench across the hilltop. Two parallel lines of post molds about twenty-two feet apart were followed by slit trenches to expose the perimeter of this house. These excavations resulted in the delimitation of a structure measuring almost exactly four hundred feet long and twenty-two feet wide, the external walls of which were made from posts two to four inches in diameter and set from one inch to over a foot apart. In some instances the posts in these walls were apparently set only a few inches into the ground because of limestone outcrops and have since been obliterated by plowing. In these cases the missing molds cause the post molds in the walls to appear to be located much farther apart than was probably originally the case. Larger posts were found distributed at irregular intervals along the walls as at most other sites described in this report. This unusually long house had rounded ends with doors near the center in typical Iroquois fashion. Interior structure was not clearly indicated as we were unable to expose the entire dwelling which covered close to a quarter of an acre. Near the south end, however, a small portion of the interior was exposed and proved to contain two rows of large post molds about seven feet inside each wall indicating interior structure no different from the houses at Howlett Hill and other sites.

Figure 5 shows the excavations at this site and the post mold patterns uncovered by them. Although the exterior walls were not entirely exposed, nearly the entire west wall was uncovered, both ends completely excavated, and enough of the east wall exposed by slit trenches to indicate not only that it was present but that it was also parallel to, and the same distance (twenty-two feet) from, the west wall wherever it was sought. There can be no doubt, therefore, that this is actually a single house of unusual length. This extraordinary structure is in keeping with the cultural tradition of the people who built it as well as the long houses at Furnace Brook (House 2) and at Howlett Hill (House 1, 334 feet in length).

The only indication of any other structure at this site is a nebulous post mold pattern which seems to suggest some extension built at the south end of the house described above. From the scatter of refuse over the two-acre area mentioned previously it is very likely that this house was not the only dwelling comprising this village. Almost certainly there were other smaller houses similar to those at Howlett Hill.

Features

Only a single feature was disclosed by our excavations at the Schoff site, a large roasting pit located immediately south of House 1 (see Figure 5 for location). This large feature was oval in shape, sixty-three by forty-eight inches at the surface of the subsoil, with curving sides terminating in a flat bottom fourteen inches below the base of the plow zone. The fill was intensely black humus containing burned stones and cobbles (Plate 21), a compact ash layer some six to eight inches thick, and a basal layer of charcoal including some charred logs up to eight inches in diameter. Cultural material in the fill included potsherds, flint chips, an antler bead, a plano-convex adze fragment, carbonized beans, acorns, and a wild plum pit. The charcoal at the base was saved for radiocarbon analysis and provided the date discussed below. From the surface of the subsoil this feature showed clearly several concentric bands of burned earth indicating several fires had been kindled within before its abandonment. Within this feature we found no large mammal bones which might have provided some clue as to its function. Scraps of fish bone and those of small mammals appear to be part of the general camp refuse with which the pit was finally filled.

Burials

The Schoff site is the only station which provides a clue to the mortuary customs of the Chance phase Iroquois in central New York. About

PLATE 21. Feature 1 at the Schoff site with portion of the stone roasting platform exposed.

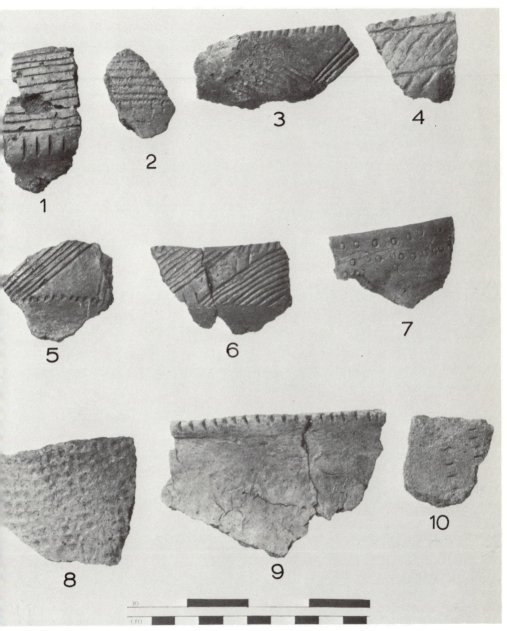

PLATE 22. Ceramics from the Schoff site. 1, collared rim sherd decorated with fingernail incising and fingernail impressions on the collar base; 2, similar motif executed with cord-wrapped paddle; 3, 5, 6, fingernail incised sherds; 4, sherd with unusual underlined motif executed in rough linear-stamp technique; 7, sherd decorated with hollow reed punctuations; 8, check-stamped body sherd; 9, thickened lip type sherd with fine notching on lip edge; 10, neck sherd decorated with fine vertical plaits.

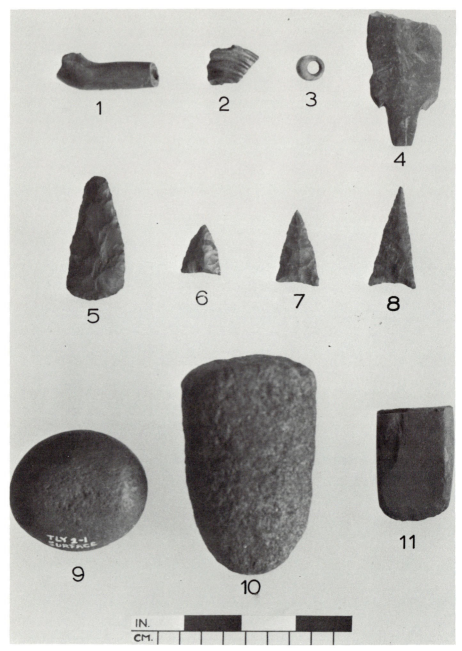

PLATE 23. Artifacts from the Schoff site. 1, stem fragment of a probable trumpet pipe; 2, bowl fragment of a ring-bowl trumpet pipe; 3, discoidal antler bead; 4, ground slate knife or spearpoint from the Archaic period; 5, ovate knife; 6–8, triangular arrowpoints; 9, hammer/anvil stone; 10, poll of a large unfinished celt; 11, bit of a small celt of fine-grained sandstone.

a mile east of this site, slightly over the crest of a long drumlin, the remains of a few human burials were unearthed several years ago. Little remains of them now save a few phalanges which were salvaged from the contractors whose activities disclosed the graves. The residents of the house in whose yard the graves were discovered recall that the skeletons were in shallow graves, apparently flexed, and unaccompanied by any grave goods, all, on the basis of excavations elsewhere, predictable characteristics of Chance phase burials. Intensive survey and test pitting of the area surrounding these graves failed to produce any evidence of occupation, though every level spot was meticulously searched and tested for the slightest bit of occupational debris. The area immediately surrounding the grave site was also test pitted and trenched but no more burials were disclosed. The most likely conclusion, therefore, seems to be that this represented a small cemetery, exact size unknown, which pertained to the Schoff site almost a mile to the west. If this is a normal burial pattern, the distance from the village to these graves probably explains our failure to locate the graves at other sites. Other than its location facing the east there seems no reason for locating a cemetery on this particular hilltop. Soil here is no easier to move than elsewhere in the village area, and the walk to the cemetery must have covered a considerable distance. Perhaps this great distance aided in keeping the spirits of the dead from annoying the living. No other suggestion of early prehistoric Iroquois burial customs were afforded us in three years of investigation.

Artifacts

Material remains from the Schoff site are extremely scarce and no single artifact category provides a very reliable reflection of the "material culture" of the community which dwelt at this site. All artifacts discovered are described below.

The ceramic sample from the Schoff site (Plate 22) is extremely small, hence probably statistically unreliable. Nevertheless several significant characteristics emerge from the analysis (see Appendix A): (1) a majority (10 or 71 percent) of Chance rounded rim profiles with one each of plain, everted, thickened, and Chance straight varieties; (2) nineteen (95 percent) of all vessel interiors undecorated; (3) only eleven (43 percent) lips decorated and these with a wide variety of motifs (longitudinal and oblique lines and wedge-shaped and hollow reed punctations) and techniques; (4) over 22 percent decorated exterior lip edges; (5) collar

motifs so equally divided among seven motifs as to be of almost no ana-
lytical value although collar decorative techniques show profound
change from earlier components to 55 percent incising, 14 percent each of
cord-wrapped paddle and interrupted linear, and 9 percent each of linear stamp and hollow reed punctations; (6) continued low frequencies of
decorated collar bases (three or 38 percent) with the three decorated examples each displaying a different technique; (7) only one (12 percent)
decorated sub-collar area; (8) all sub-lip areas undecorated; (9) 87 percent plain vessel necks and techniques for neck decoration about
equally divided among ten styles with incising (two or 17 percent) and
crescent punctations (also 17 percent) the two most popular; (10) three
(60 percent) decorated sub-neck sherds; (11) a single (12 percent) decorated shoulder sherd with four horizontal corded lines set off by small
triangular punctations on either side; (12) body sherds 78 percent
check-stamped, 13 percent smoothed-over check-stamped, 7 percent
smoothed, 1 percent smoothed-over cord (?); and (13) the average collar
height is 27.00 mm.

Two small fragments from a roughly made miniature vessel were recovered from Feature 1. These were from a relatively thin-walled pot,
probably collared after the fashion of larger ceramics, and having at
least one castellation, which is characteristic of most vessels from all periods included in this study. The rim is rounded, and the portions recovered are undecorated.

Three smoking-pipe fragments were found at the Schoff site, two of
which obviously pertain to Iroquois trumpet pipes, marking the first appearance of this form in the sites so far considered. One specimen is of a
ring-bowl trumpet (see Appendix B for smoking pipe variety descriptions) with a mildly flaring rim and raised bands of incised lines as described for the decorated trumpet variety (Plate 23, no. 2). The second
trumpet (Plate 23, no. 1) is represented by only a portion of the stem,
but its form is indicated by the thin stem with very little taper and a
graceful bend where the stem joins the bowl. The third fragment is also
a stem fragment, this one also thin, having little taper and a flattened
end with unmodified mouthpiece.

Three completed triangular arrowpoints (Plate 23, nos. 6–8), one in
process, and two rough blanks comprise the entire projectile point sample from the Schoff site. Convex-sided, concave-based forms outnumber
straight-sided, concave-based forms by a statistically insignificant two to
one. Formal and metric data indicate the beginning of a trend toward
longer and narrower specimens. Average length is 3.53 cm., and average

width is 2.07 cm., which give an average length-width ratio of 1.71 to 1.

Three ovate knives and a retouched flake knife comprise the relatively abundant sample of knives from the Schoff site. The former class is represented by one complete specimen, somewhat trianguloid in form with rounded corners (see Plate 23, no. 5) which measures 5.8 cm. by 2.6 cm. and is 0.8 cm. thick. The other two fragments seem to conform to this description in all respects. The final probable knife is an irregular flake retouched along the longest edge from but one side. This tool may have served as a scraper as well as a knife.

Rough and polished stone artifacts include a celt blank (Plate 23, no. 10), an adze, (Plate 23, no. 11) and a hammerstone (Plate 23, no. 10) typical of Iroquois and a ground slate knife from a much earlier period. This latter tool is of polished black slate, with a beveled cross section, contracting squared stem, and barbed shoulders (Plate 23, no. 4). Points or knives of this general type have a wide geographical distribution and range in time from the third millennium B.C., far before the advent of Iroquois culture. Most likely this was picked up by an Iroquois inhabitant of the Schoff site, perhaps as a hunting charm, and later broken and discarded or lost in the village. The practice of placing points of earlier cultures within the graves of Iroquois men is common in later times (see Ritchie 1954 on the Dutch Hollow site).

The only bone artifact recovered from this site is the unusual antler bead shown on Plate 23, no. 3. It is a small, discoidal, somewhat asymmetric specimen about 1.5 cm. in diameter and less than 0.5 cm. thick. The edges are ground round and the entire artifact polished to a smooth glossy finish.

Food Remains

Food remains were exceptionally scarce at the Schoff site, but enough were found to indicate that the same type of exploitation prevailed here as at most earlier and later sites. Cultigens were present in the form of beans; wild plants were evidenced by acorns and a plum pit. Animal remains included deer and small scraps of bone from unidentified small mammals, as well as bird, fish bones, and the shells of freshwater mussels.

Chronology

Material cultural remains, although extremely scanty, indicate that this site was occupied during the earliest part of the Chance phase. A radiocarbon determination of 550±80 B.P. or A.D. 1400 (Y-2376) was made on wood charcoal from Feature 1. Revision in the light of Stuiver and Suess' recent article (1966) on fluctuations in the rate of available C-14 suggests this date is not significantly different, being about A.D. 1410. In any event this is in very close agreement with the date from the Howlett Hill site (A.D. 1380) which was occupied immediately prior to the Schoff site.

THE BLOODY HILL SITE

The Bloody Hill site (Tly 5-2) is located in the Town of Pompey, about two miles southeast of the village of Jamesville, New York, on unused pastureland now owned by Verne Moore, of that town, who allowed our party to excavate there during June and July of 1967. The site is mentioned in early records as having been the location of an early battle the relics of which littering the surface were cited as evidence—hence the name "Bloody Hill." The discovery of several historic Iroquois graves on the hilltop, supposedly those of warriors fallen in that battle further reinforced this theory. Parker (1922:642) mentions the site as "primarily a cemetery with recent relics." While studying the collection of Dr. Anton Sohrweide of Syracuse, I observed that there were some discrepancies between Parker's description and the material which had actually been recovered from the site. The Sohrweide collection included almost exclusively pottery and other artifacts typical of the Chance phase some three hundred years older than the historic component indicated by the graves.

Thinking that this site might add to our growing picture of Iroquois development, a survey was conducted at the close of the 1966 field season. Although the area is densely overgrown with hawthorn and other scrub growth, we were able to locate a small area which produced a few potsherds and showed indications of having been excavated sometime in the past. Upon returning to the site after the spring runoff in 1967, we saw that there were marked differences in soil color which readily became apparent when a shovelful of the dampened sod was turned over. By continuing to test in this fashion, a semi-circle of dark soil was defined which enclosed a small rise on the southern end of a larger hill.

Settlement Data

The village area is today cut by a fieldstone wall, to the north of which is a cultivated field in which almost no trace of occupation re-

PLATE 24. Small rise at the southern end of a large hill upon which the Bloody Hill site is located. Excavations were made immediately behind the tree line behind the figures.

PLATE 25. House pattern at the Bloody Hill site outlined by excavated post molds. In the center of the house and left foreground are large roasting pits or hearths. The other two pits in the foreground are historic Iroquois graves from a later village.

PLATE 26. Feature 2 at the Bloody Hill site excavated to expose the cobble and small boulder roasting platform.

PLATE 27. Feature 2 at the Bloody Hill site, roasting pit with broken human bones exposed in place.

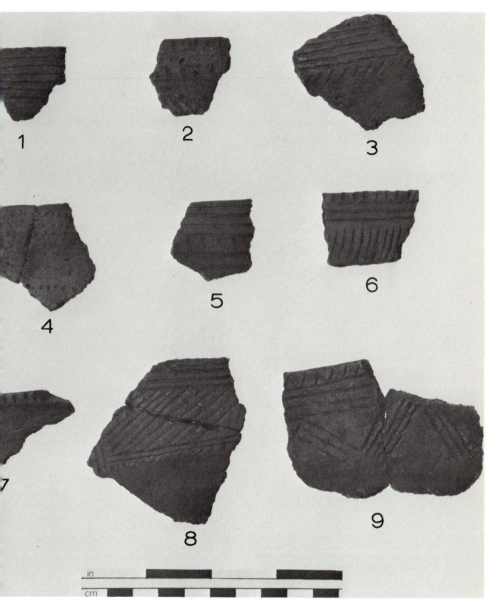

PLATE 28. Ceramics from the Bloody Hill site. 1–4, rim sherds decorated with cord-wrapped paddle impressions; 5, 6, 9, rim sherds decorated with fingernail impressions; 7, thickened lip variety sherd with fine notches on lip edge; 8, rim sherd with incised decoration.

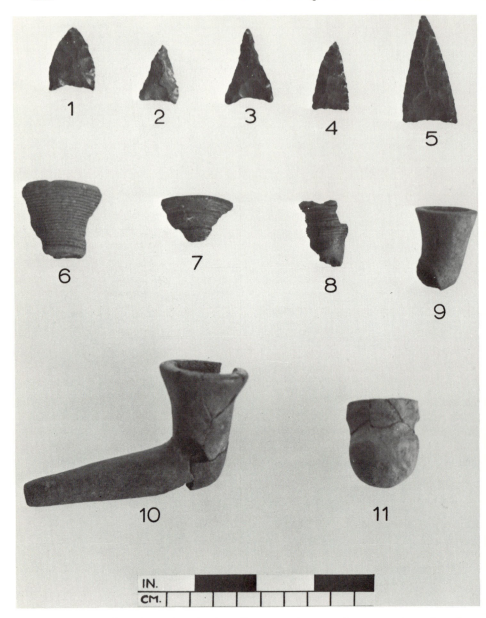

PLATE 29. Artifacts from the Bloody Hill site. 1–5, triangular arrowpoints; 6, early form of trumpet pipe decorated with horizontal lines; 7 and 8, fragments of ring-bowl trumpet pipes; 9 and 10, smoking pipes of the plain proto-trumpet variety; 11, miniature pot.

mains. But if we assume that the midden deposits on the north of this fence bear about the same relation to the topography as they do on the southern, uncultivated portion of the hilltop (which seems a reasonable assumption), we can postulate a village which covered an oval area measuring not more than two hundred and fifty by one hundred feet. This gives a village area of less than one-half acre or about one-third the size of the villages west of the city of Syracuse (Furnace Brook, Howlett Hill, and Schoff).

The defensive advantage offered by the choice of this location was probably considerable as the land slopes away sharply to the east, south, and west, and slightly to the north. To the east flows a small but steady stream which doubtless provided water, as may have several intermittent springs situated nearby. The soil surrounding and within the village area is not especially suited to either farming or archaeology. The topsoil is a very thin, brown, sandy loam interspersed with fragmented limestone derived from the hard yellow clay subsoil which contains numerous limestone outcrops as well as fragmented pieces of this underlying formation. Perhaps the rock helped warm the soil, bringing about earlier fruition of the crops, but it is questionable whether the extra work needed to cultivate such a soil would make this slight advantage worthwhile. Certainly these rocks were of no advantage to the Syracuse University field party which carried out excavations there during the summer of 1967. The numerous outcrops made our search for post molds and other features very difficult though rewarding in many respects. Over thirty-one hundred square feet were excavated, providing the settlement data and the artifact sample described below.

Despite the fact that we trenched both the east and west slopes of the hill on which the village was situated, from above the brow of the hill to well down both slopes, the only trace of a stockade or other defensive structure, other than a few stray post molds in the aforementioned trenches, is a short series of widely spaced post molds which run for about twenty-five feet apparently encompassing the southeast corner of House 1. Two molds directly east of this structure may pertain to this same line of molds which, if it was a stockade, is very different in character from any other palisades discovered during the course of our field work. The possibility that these represent support or buttress posts for a fortification is not supported by the data; the molds are remnants of posts which were set vertically in the ground, rather than at an angle as would be expected of support posts. No trace of any ditch or earth ring was discovered, and it seems likely that if either had ever existed, they would have been mentioned by the early settlers who, as they cleared the land, discovered and named the Bloody Hill site.

The remains of what appears to be a single small house constitute the only evidence of dwellings at the Bloody Hill site. This structure, disclosed by our excavations on the top of the hill, appears to have been oriented roughly east and west and to have measured about thirty-eight by twenty-five feet. The ends were apparently somewhat flattened in the manner of later Iroquois square-ended longhouses but retained the rounded corners of earlier periods. The most probable doorway is located somewhat off center, to the south, in the eastern end. Both natural obstacles and the press of time prevented further excavations on the hill-top which might have disclosed more complete and more regular house patterns. Some of the irregularity in the exterior walls is doubtless due to the uneven and rocky nature of the soil which necessitated deviations from the building plan. Interior structure is not clearly indicated but several large post molds and more numerous smaller ones probably pertain to supports not unlike those found in other Chance phase houses. See Plate 25 for the post mold pattern which defines this structure.

Features

Several types of features were found at Bloody Hill, both within and without the house described above. Those inside the house were all hearths but of two very different types. The first, which includes Features 1, 4, and 5, is the type of shallow, amorphous hearth associated with most Iroquois houses of this period. These were centrally located fireplaces usually defined only by a patch of irregular fire-reddened soil and occasional ash or bits of charcoal. They were probably scooped out of the topsoil to subsoil level where the fires then burned. At most sites these hearths display signs of having been shifted, and those at Bloody Hill are no exception. Features 4 and 5, therefore, are very likely members of the same hearth complex.

The other feature within the house was a bowl-shaped hearth, slightly over three feet in diameter and seventeen inches deep, measured from the base of the plow zone. A similar feature (Feature 6), located to the west of House 1, conformed in most respects to Feature 3, to which it was doubtless functionally related. The latter measured over five feet by four feet in dimensions and was twenty-two inches deep. The fill of both contained dark soil, burned clay, ash, charcoal, fire-broken stone, and little in the way of artifacts. Stone was more common in Feature 6, suggesting its use as a roasting pit.

Feature 2 located on the extreme western edge of the site, in sections W160 and W170 S10, was unquestionably the most interesting feature revealed by our excavations at Bloody Hill. It was first indicated by a slight surface depression which we thought might have been a tree fall hollow in which some refuse had accumulated. To recover any such refuse, the topsoil was carefully removed from the sections which contained the depression. During this process, several fragments of human long bones and two human teeth were discovered, as well as a small amount of other refuse. As the top of this feature was exposed it became clear that it was not a tree fall, but a large pit, which complete exposure disclosed as oval in horizontal profile and measuring ninety-one by fifty-four inches. Upon sectioning this feature, we discovered a solid layer of large fire-cracked granitic rock, not native to the site, which was up to eighteen inches thick at the thickest part. Above this was a twelve-inch mantle of dark soil containing considerable refuse, and beneath the rock layer were the carbonized remains of numerous charred logs and much gray ash covering the pit floor to a depth of three to four inches. The sides and to a lesser extent the bottom of the pit were reddened by the fire which had been kindled there. The maximum depth of this feature, at the center of the flat bottom, was twenty-eight inches. As excavation progressed, more and more human bones were encountered, most frequently lying on or immediately above the stone platform. These were left in place and, since some seemed to bear what looked like knife or butchering marks, were carefully exposed with soft brushes rather than trowels or other metal tools. Mixed with these bones, but generally somewhat higher in the fill, was other refuse including a small projectile point of the Madison type, flint chips, potsherds, and some scraps of mammal, fish, and bird bone.

From these excavations, the following sequence of events involving this feature can be reconstructed: the pit was first dug to its present dimensions, a large and very hot fire was kindled within, large cobbles were used to cover the fire to form a roasting platform atop which game or other food could be roasted.

This feature in all respects is similar to those described by Ritchie (1965:309) at the Kelso site and which he speculated might have served some "esoteric function, as, for instance, a bear ceremonial feast." Our findings at Bloody Hill suggest that at least some of the time the victim of these feasts was not a bear but a human being, the remains found at Bloody Hill being one such unfortunate individual. This suggestion of cannibalism in New York at the beginning of the fifteenth century correlates rather closely with the fourteenth-century appearance of human bones in the refuse of Iroquois sites in Ontario (Wright 1966:60, 64).

An interesting alternative explanation for this unusual feature has been suggested by Elisabeth Tooker as a result of her study (1967:132) of the early historic documents pertaining to the Huron, an Iroquoian people of Ontario. The body of a drowned man was placed near a ditch in the cemetery, the flesh stripped from it and burned and the skeleton thrown into the ditch. This procedure was followed to prevent some misfortune befalling the tribe. Although the circumstances at Bloody Hill are considerably different from those described by Tooker, it is not impossible that this represents an Iroquois version of the ceremony described above. Whether it was cannibalism (which seems more likely) or the latter practice, it is a good example of an Iroquoian trait at a relatively early date.

Another similar feature may have once been located on the extreme eastern edge of the site, about opposite to Feature 2. When we first located the site we found a large hole, obviously the work of some excavator of a few years past, and the ground around this hole was littered with broken stone, dark earth, and a few charcoal chunks.

Feature 7, a large pit west of House 1, was oval at the opening, measuring fifty-seven by thirty-five inches and having a maximum depth of twenty-five inches to the center of the bowl-shaped base. The fill was not at all like that described for other similarly shaped features but was a uniform hard clay only slightly mottled by bits of intrusive topsoil which made determination of the precise limits of this feature somewhat difficult. The only materials found within this feature were a few flint chips and a small fragment of unidentifiable bone. In view of its location and orientation in relation to Feature 8, described below, it seems most likely that this is an early historic grave which had previously been excavated by collectors. A small round depression in the bottom of this pit may well be a shovel hole made during this excavation.

Finally, Feature 8, located next to and parallel with Feature 7, in sections W30 S10 and W40 S10, was apparently also a disturbed historic Iroquois grave, part of the basis for Parker's description of the site as a cemetery. The grave fossa originally measured about seventy by eighteen inches but had been enlarged at the upper portion by the previous excavators, to about eighty-six by forty-six inches. The depth to the floor of the grave was thirty-three inches. The fill was a loose sandy clay mixed with bits of topsoil and containing numerous small fragments of human bone including long bone and cranial fragments as well as teeth.

Also recovered from the fill was the blade of a "sheep's foot" knife, a variety of European iron trade knife very common in the latter half of the seventeenth century. It is not impossible that this grave was anciently disturbed, perhaps for reburial, a practice known among the historic Iroquois, but it seems more likely that the disturbance is the result of much later excavators.

Artifacts

The hillside middens at the Bloody Hill site provided the most complete sample of material remains from any early Chance phase site described from central New York. Almost every artifact category contains enough specimens to facilitate excellent comparisons between this and earlier and later sites.

Bloody Hill site ceramics (Plate 28) comprise one of the most complete collections from any Chance phase settlement in central New York. The distinctive characteristics (see Appendix A) of the more than four thousand sherds recovered are: (1) a preponderance (46 percent) of Chance rounded rim profiles, a revival of everted lip types (28 percent) and lesser numbers of thickened lips (8 percent), channeled low collars (7 percent) and Chance straight collar (9 percent) styles; (2) all vessel interiors undecorated; (3) only 40 percent of lips decorated again displaying a wide variety of motifs (longitudinal lines, oblique lines, rows of punctations, and various combinations of the foregoing) and techniques (cord-wrapped paddle, linear punctations, fingernail impressions, interrupted linear ("push-pull"), incising, round and hollow reed punctations, etc.); (4) slightly over 20 percent decorated exterior lip edges; (5) a great variety of both collar motifs (21 percent oblique over horizontal over opposed, 20 percent opposed, 13 percent oblique over horizontal, 11 percent horizontal between oblique, 9 percent horizontal over opposed, and lesser percentages of nine other motifs) and techniques (42 percent incised, 26 percent fingernail impressed, 20 percent cord-wrapped paddle impressed, 5 percent linear stamped, 4 percent interrupted linear and less than one percent of nine other techniques); (6) decorated collar bases about as common as at the Schoff site (41 percent), though the techniques are by now more distinctively Iroquois (linear punctations 43 percent, fingernail impressions 26 percent, cord-wrapped paddle impressions reduced to 11 percent, and two examples or 4 percent each incising, round punctations, corded punctations, wedge-shaped punctations, and probable paddle corner impressions, the latter few foreshadowing later Iroquois practices; (7) only 9 percent decorated sub-collar areas with fingernail impressions the most popular technique (43 percent) and lesser amounts of cord-wrapped paddle (29 percent), linear stamp (14 percent), and incising (also 14 percent); (8) only two (7 percent) decorated sub-lip areas with the neck decorating reaching to the lip in the remaining twenty-eight instances; (9) 65 percent plain vessel necks with the most common motif being oblique or vertical plaits executed with fingernail (41 percent), linear stamp (16 percent), cord-wrapped paddle (16 percent) impressions, or by incising (9 percent); (10) 89 percent decorated sub-neck areas with techniques consisting of fingernail impressions (46 percent), linear stamping (22 percent), cord-wrapped paddle impressions (13 percent), wedge-shaped punctations (9 percent), and a host of other less frequent techniques; (11) no decorated shoulder sherds; (12) body surface treatment consisting of check-stamping (50 percent), smoothing (44 percent), smoothed-over check-stamping (5 percent) and brushing (.24 percent); and (13) the average collar height is 23.04 mm.

From Feature 6, the large roasting pit described above, the remains of a nearly complete miniature pot were recovered. It is rather crudely made, obviously molded around a finger, and measures 3.8 cm. high by 2.9 cm. in diameter at the mouth. It is a collared pot, as are most of the ceramics from Bloody Hill, but this specimen is undecorated and the exterior surface only roughly smoothed. This is a good example of what has often been called a "child's" or "toy" vessel made, we suppose, by young girls in imitation of their parents, and is in decided contrast to the well-made miniature vessels from the Cabin site. This specimen is illustrated on Plate 29, no. 10.

During the occupation of the Bloody Hill site, the smoking pipes (Plate 29, nos. 6–10) in use were almost exclusively forms of the trumpet variety. These are both early forms (proto-trumpets) and those typical of the late Chance and later phases (decorated trumpets). Two unusual specimens from this site are apparently of the collared variety described on p. 240. This pipe style is most typical of Oak Hill phase sites, and its presence here cannot be satisfactorily explained unless it is a continuation of this early type into later Iroquois times or is a rebirth of a variety no longer in use. The pipe varieties are described on Appendix A and summarized in Table 8.

Of the forty-one pipe stems recovered, forty are round in cross section, and one has rounded upper and lower surfaces and flattened sides. All stems are relatively thinner and less markedly tapered than the specimens from earlier sites. Also in contrast to the earlier pipes, these specimens invariably have carefully finished mouthpieces with the lip squared in relation to the long axis of the stem.

The projectile point sample from Bloody Hill (Plate 29, nos. 1–5) appears to reflect a general trend toward uniformity in point style. Although considerable variation was apparently still permissible, the formal and metric data indicate that straight-sided, concave-based forms or straight-sided, straight-based forms were becoming dominant. The relatively high percentage of straight bases is, however, in contrast to the sites described west of Syracuse (Howlett Hill, Schoff) where concave-based forms predominate. Average length (3.37 cm) and width (2.09 cm.) and the combined ratio (1.61:1) are very similar to the Schoff site averages, demonstrating again the start of a trend toward relatively longer, narrower points.

TABLE 8. Frequencies and Percentages of Smoking Pipe Varieties from the Bloody Hill Site

Variety	Frequency	Percentage
collared pipe	2	9.1
decorate proto-trumpet	3	13.6
plain proto-trumpet	5	22.7
decorated trumpet	12	54.5
	22	99.9

One irregular, bifacially flaked probable knife—roughly triangular in shape with several protrusions along each edge, with one edge retouched along its entire length from one side—and two small utilized flakes complete the chipped-stone inventory from Bloody Hill.

Rough stone artifacts included two cobble anvil stones, one combination hammer-muller, a small pecking hammer made from the reworked poll of a trianguloid celt, a fragment of a cylindrical pestle, five chipped discs, and a roughly made chopper-scraper of soft schist.

A single trianguloid celt, and two rectanguloid specimens are little different from those recovered at earlier stations. A third specimen is represented by the poll of what must have been a long, parallel-sided implement, oval in cross section, not unlike the unfinished example from the Schoff site. Two unfinished celts were also found—one a rectanguloid specimen and the other possibly a small lozenge-shaped celt or chisel like that from the Kelso site.

A large bone inventory was also recovered at Bloody Hill owing both to the alkaline bedrock and lack of intensive cultivation. Included were some twenty-seven whole or fragmentary awls from 5 to 10 cm. long. Fourteen are ground on both sides and the base. One is from a deer cannon bone, three are splinter awls with one edge and the point polished, five are simply sharpened splinters, one is represented by only a small portion of the point, and the final specimen is made from the sharpened and polished bony gill cover of a large fish. A small tubular bird-bone bead, possible conical antler arrowpoint, and a small trapezoidal long-bone fragment with the ends and sides polished and a notch worn in one corner complete the bone assemblage from Bloody Hill.

Food Remains

The only evidence of vegetal remains at the Bloody Hill site were a carbonized corn kernel in Feature 2 and a few small carbonized beans in the western midden in section W160 S20. No remains of wild plant foods were found, though they were undoubtedly utilized by the inhabitants of the Bloody Hill site. Game animals are far better represented, as shown on Table 9.

TABLE 9. FAUNAL REMAINS FROM THE BLOODY HILL SITE

Species	No. pieces	Remarks
MAMMAL		
white tailed deer (*Odocoileus virginianus*)	293	at least six adults, two 1–2 years, two 2–3 years, one over 3 years, one indeterminate
beaver (*Castor canadensis*)	2	one adult
porcupine (*Erethizon dorsatum*)	6	at least one adult
dog (*Canis familiaris*)	9	at least two adults
man (*Homo sapiens*)	3	one adult
BIRDS		
6 pieces including:		
ruffed grouse (*Bonasa umbellus*)	1	one adult
FISH		
12 pieces including:		
freshwater sheepshead (?) (*Aplodinotus grunniens*) bowfin (*Amia calva*)		

Chronology

All material described below indicates a village of the early Chance phase very close in time to the villages described at the Schoff and Keough sites. This is further borne out by the radiocarbon determination from the site which I speculated would be very close to that from Schoff (Tuck 1970:44). This date was run on wood charcoal from near the bottom of Feature 2 and was returned at 430±80 b.p. (Y-2374) which translates to about a.d. 1420±80 by both subtraction from 1950 and as computed by Stuiver and Suess (1966). In any case, the date is within ten years of that from Schoff, further indicating the contemporaneity of these two villages.

The Keough Site

This apparently small site is located in the Town of Pompey, New York, within the village of Jamesville, on the east bank of Jamesville Lake, a body of water created in the nineteenth century as a feeder for the Erie Canal (see Figure 1). It is a little over one mile east of the Bloody Hill site and lies very close to, if not in fact beneath, the Pen site—the Onondaga capital of the late seventeenth century.

In the fall of 1956 and again in the spring of the following year investigations were conducted there under the direction of Ronald Kingsley, then a graduate student in Education at Syracuse University. During the course of these excavations, which were intended to locate the seventeenth-century site, remains of an earlier occupation were also uncovered, though they went unrecognized at the time. From among the many artifacts of European manufacture about two hundred potsherds which pertain to an early Chance phase occupation were culled. Kingsley's field notes and drawings, from which this account is taken, are not specific as to the source of this material, but most of it was apparently surface-derived from a restricted area of the western slope of the hilltop where the Pen site is located. Also exposed by these explorations was a row of post molds presumably pertaining to a stockade of the historic period; the small size of the molds, however, suggests that they may, in fact, have been placed there by the earlier Chance phase occupants of the site.

Artifacts

The Keough site ceramics (Plate 30), though very limited in number, clearly indicate the Chance phase position of the site, as the following summary indicates (see also Appendix A): (1) twelve (75 percent) of the rim sherds of the Chance rounded style with two (12.5 percent) each of the channeled low collar and Chance straight collar types; (2) all vessel interiors plain; (3) 60 percent decorated lips with a variety of motifs and techniques proportionally as great as that from Bloody Hill; (4) 15 percent decorated exterior lip edges; (5) eleven rim sherds divided among six collar motif groups and a similar situation with respect to collar techniques but including 55 percent incised sherds; (6) five (83 percent) plain and one (17 percent) decorated collar bases; (7) four plain and one (20 percent) decorated sub-collar area; (8) no decorated sub-lip areas; (9) 71 percent plain necks, with most of the remainder decorated with oblique or vertical plaits executed with fingernail (58 percent), linear stamp (21 percent), "comma-like" or "tailed" punctation (16 percent), or wedge-shaped punctation (5 percent) impressions, and no incising; (10) all sub-neck areas decorated in a variety of techniques; (11) three (100 percent) decorated shoulders, the only ascertainable motif being horizontal incised lines set off by oblique lines above; (12) body surface treatment 43 percent check-stamped, 52 percent smoothed, 4 percent smoothed-over check-stamped, less than 1 percent each of corded and fabric impressed; (13) collar heights (two only) were 22 and 32 mm.

No smoking pipes were found during Kingsley's excavations, but several stone artifacts were recovered, as described below.

Four uncompleted specimens or blanks comprise the total sample of points. All are between 4 and 5 cm. long, from 3 to 4 cm. wide, and are more than 1 cm. thick. The only specimen even vaguely suggestive of finished form seems to be a convex-sided, concave-based point. Several of these blanks show some wear on the edges which may be attributable to use as a scraper or knife.

The only other chipped-stone implement recovered here is the base of a completed ovate knife. Not enough remains to allow measurements, but there is enough to indicate its conformity to the general Iroquois pattern of this type of tool.

Three probable celt fragments at this site show similarity to sites both earlier and later. The poll of a trianguloid celt with a relatively thick poll and oval cross section is reminiscent of earlier forms. A small

PLATE 30. Ceramics from the Keough site. 1–3, rim sherds decorated with cord-wrapped paddle impressions; 4 and 5, rim sherds decorated with fingernail impressions; 6, rim sherd decorated by incising, probably with a fingernail; 7, sub-neck sherd decorated with a row of fingernail impressions; 8, check-stamped body sherd.

rectanguloid blank, chipped but not polished, was obviously intended to be a small tool similar to those found at Furnace Brook and Burke. The third specimen is a small, nearly round pebble, 3.8 cm. long and only 1.3 cm. thick, with a sharpened edge which suggests a small specialized woodworking tool which had been pecked to shape but not ground or sharpened.

The only scrap of modified bone present in the collection from this site is a small fragment of an awl manufactured from the longbone of some mammal, probably a deer. It is so fragmentary and eroded that it defies further description.

Food Remains

No vegetal remains, either cultivated or wild, were recovered from this site. Identifiable mammal remains include several deer molar teeth, the molar probably of a dog, several deer bone splinters, and the deer bone awl described above. A few probable turkey bone fragments comprise the only bird remains; a few small fish vertebrae of unidentifiable species and single valve from a freshwater mussel shell complete the inventory of dietary information available from this limited sample.

Chronology

No charcoal was present in the sample of material donated by Kingsley to Syracuse University; thus, dating of the site must proceed from a study of the scant cultural remains alone. Ceramics are, in most respects, nearly identical to those previously described from Bloody Hill —similar enough, in fact, to suggest that the Keough site may have been coeval with Bloody Hill. Other material remains, while not so diagnostic as ceramics, also point to a placement in time very close to Bloody Hill.

THE CHRISTOPHER SITE

This important site is located on a low rise of now-wooded land about a mile east of the Bloody Hill site and twice as far from the Keough site (see Figure 1). Excavations have been conducted there on various occasions by several groups including parties from Lowville Academy and a group of students under the direction of Peter Pratt, now of State University of New York at Oswego. These excavations have resulted in the recovery of a good deal of data and material, some of which is described here. The largest collection is now undergoing analysis at Oswego, and is not available for study. This difficulty is somewhat overcome by material obtained from other smaller collections which help to represent the cultural and chronological place of the Christopher site.

Settlement Data

Except for the location of the Christopher site in relation to other sites, its situation on a low, not easily defended rise, and its apparent size of between one and two acres, little settlement data are available. It may well have been fortified, as I believe Pratt's as yet unpublished researches have shown. No data on houses or house types are available.

Artifacts

The small amount of material described here represents the combined collections of Dr. Anton Sohrweide and John Litzenberger, both of Syracuse, Arthur Einhorn, formerly of Lowville, New York, and a photograph supplied by Donald Lenig of St. Johnsville, New York, all of whom are thanked for their cooperation. Because of the limited nature of the sample, only general descriptions and conclusions are permitted.

Only a few characteristics of the ceramics (Plate 31) from this site can be offered here, but they serve to indicate the relative chronological position of this site. These are numbered here to correspond with the more complete data from other sites: (1) collared vessels outnumber everted or thickened lip types by four or five to one; (2) interior lips are decorated on everted lip types; (5) collar motifs consist of 80 percent horizontal lines over opposed lines, 7 percent horizontal lines over oblique lines, and 14 percent opposed lines alone; done in techniques consisting of about 10 percent (four sherds) cord-wrapped paddle, 5 percent fingernail impressed, and 85 percent incised, much of this done with a fingernail and frequently combined with fingernail or small triangular punctations; and (6) plain and decorated collar bases in about equal numbers (four and three respectively). Also of note is the presence of a few decorated shoulders and neck sherds, though too few in number to provide any firm basis for comparison. A final characteristic, not described for most other sites, is the width of incised lines on neck sherds. No attempt will be made to quantify this data precisely, but broad incising (approximately greater than 1 mm.) done with a blunt object, and very fine incising of the Chance phase are each present in about one-quarter of the rim sherds studied, while a seemingly intermediate type of fairly broad incising, slightly less than 1 mm. wide and done with a sharp rather than rounded object, comprises about 50 percent of the cases.

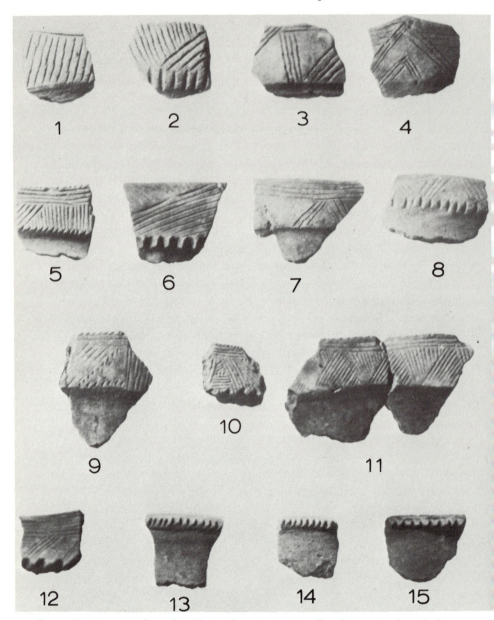

PLATE 31. Ceramics from the Christopher site. 1–3, collared rim sherds with finger-nail-incised decoration; 4–12, collared rim sherds with various styles of incised decoration; 13–15, everted and thickened notched-lip varieties.

Only two smoking pipe fragments were studied from this site both apparently trumpet forms. One is a decorated trumpet pipe, similar to those from the Burke site, while the other is a stem fragment with the gracefully curving stem typical of trumpet forms.

No other material is in the collections studied, but an interesting glimpse at the bone industry of the occupants of the Christopher site is afforded by Beauchamp's description (1902a) and drawings of many beautifully preserved bone tools from this site. Most of the forms are known from later sites in the area (see the Barnes site in this report), but this is the earliest known example of Iroquois bone tools of such quality from central New York.

Chronology

Detailed comparisons will be made later in this report but every indication is, at this point, that this site postdates Bloody Hill and Keough, therefore dating from the middle 1400s and is, perhaps, coeval with the Burke site.

THE BURKE SITE

The Burke site (Tly 6-2) is located in the Town of Pompey, New York, on land belonging to Dr. John Hamel, who lives nearby and allowed us to excavate there during the summer of 1967. The land was formerly owned and farmed by the Burke family, hence the name of the site. Excavations had previously been conducted there by Peter Pratt, but the results of his work are still unpublished. Our excavations, however, provided an adequate sample of artifacts and sufficient settlement data to draw some reasonably accurate conclusions about the cultural and chronological placement of the Burke site.

Settlement Data

The site occupies the top of a long drumlin and apparently covered some two to three acres. The location is very much like that described for the Schoff site. The Bloody Hill site is some two miles northwest, and the Schoff site about ten miles due west of Burke (see Figure 1).

The soil on the hilltop is unusually deep (up to eighteen inches) and rich for an Iroquois site, a fact which suggests an occupation of considerable duration; this suggestion is confirmed by other data to be discussed later. The topsoil, usually a dark brown to greasy black, was underlain over the entire hilltop by a light-colored sandy clay containing very few stones, a fact which greatly facilitated our search for post molds and other features. At the northern end of the site is a midden of considerable depth now covered by a relatively sterile layer of lighter topsoil, apparently washed from the village surface but containing much less refuse than is present in the area of occupation. We excavated five and one-half ten-foot squares in this area where the refuse was most plentiful and where Pratt had also apparently conducted most of his excavations.

On this northern slope the remains of two palisades were encountered. By a stroke of luck our excavations disclosed the exact area where these palisades intersected, indicating without any question two building phases at the site, another evidence of a considerable duration of occupation. The construction methods of the two stockades were essentially the same, consisting of poles measuring from three to five inches in diameter being forced into the ground at distances from a few inches to a foot from one another. Two lines near the village, on the inside, consist of somewhat smaller post molds which are spaced closer together. These two palisades are distinguishable by their angles relative to one another (see Figure 6 and Plate 32) and may be seen to be one stockade of three rows and another of four rows of posts. Outside both palisades we found a small portion of a protective ditch (Feature 2), four to five feet wide, extending into the subsoil slightly more than a foot at the deepest point. The edges were rather irregular, and the dimensions at the time of occupation could have been both broader and deeper owing to the large amount of overburden which the Indians undoubtedly also excavated during the construction of this feature. That the palisades are located in nearly the same position and seem to differ little in both location and style of construction seems to indicate that there was little actual relocation of the village at the time of rebuilding and that the construction was accomplished, in both cases, by the same group.

Other settlement data consist of the somewhat confusing pattern of post molds shown on Figure 6. Because of the limitations of time, and the fact that much of the area of occupation had been reforested with small evergreens, we were forced to use a series of slit trenches to attempt to outline the structures uncovered. This can be very helpful at times (see the Schoff site report), but at other times can be very unsatisfactory. In this case, the results of our trenching were of a mixed nature. What appeared on the ground to be a single house 320 feet long appears on the site map to be portions of two houses, one over eighty feet long and the other over 240 feet long. If this is the case, the smaller of the

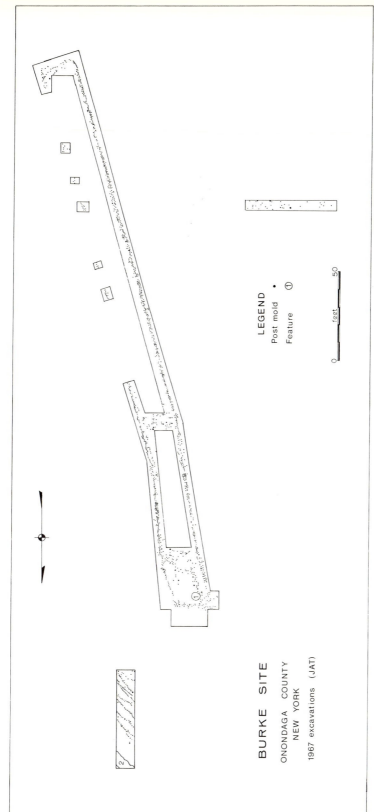

BURKE SITE

ONONDAGA COUNTY
NEW YORK

1967 excavations (JAT)

LEGEND

Post mold •

Feature ①

0   feet   50

FIGURE 6. Excavations at the Burke site, 1967, showing portions of two overlapping longhouses and stockades.

PLATE 32. Post molds of the intersecting stockade lines on the northern edge of the Burke site; scale in feet.

PLATE 33. Ceramics from the Burke site. 1, sherd decorated with fine cord-wrapped paddle impressions; 2 and 3, sherds decorated with fingernail impressions; 4–8, collared sherds decorated with fine incised lines, 7 and 8 with notched collar bases typical of later Onondaga ceramics; 9, everted lip variety with fine notches on lip edge; 10, thickened-lip sherd with decoration similar to 9; 11, sherd decorated with broad incised lines and notched collar base similar to later Onondaga ceramics.

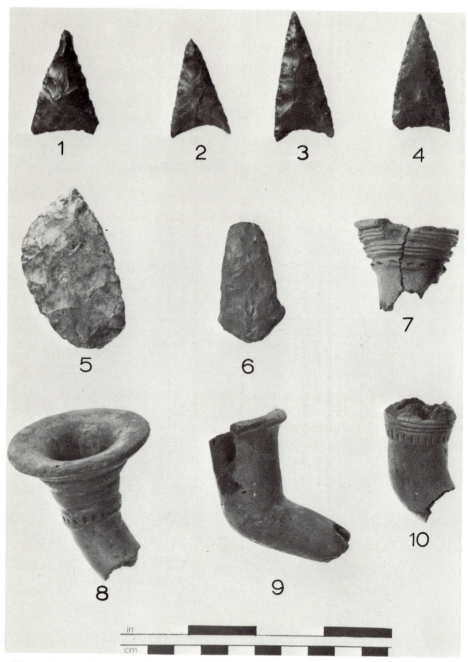

PLATE 34. Artifacts from the Burke site. 1–4, triangular arrowpoints; 5, leaf-shaped knife; 6, chert strike-a-light; 7 and 8, fragments of ring-bowl trumpet pipes; 9, proto-trumpet pipe; 10, stem and bowl fragment of probable trumpet pipe.

two houses is unusual as its walls seem to constrict toward the southern end. The larger house has parallel walls, at least as good as those from other sites excavated, and is unquestionably a single dwelling of unusual length. It is not impossible, but doubtful, that this is a single house which was curved slightly during construction to avoid some natural obstacle or through some accident of planning. Funk (1967:83) mentions houses at the Garoga site, in the Mohawk Valley, which seem to have been built with a slight curve to take advantage of the topography of the site.

Another five-foot trench over the brow of the hill to the southeast of the site failed to produce evidence of the stockade, which was presumably well down the hillside, but did disclose a number of post molds which indicate intensive occupation over the large area mentioned above (see Figure 6).

The house walls were constructed as were those at the Schoff, Howlett Hill, and other sites, of posts averaging three inches in diameter with occasional larger examples reaching eight to ten inches. Interior structure seems typical for Iroquois longhouses, consisting of parallel rows of large support posts which supported bench beds and lined a central corridor within the house. No hearths were found within the structure(s), as our method of excavation exposed a minimum of the interior. Presumably they were centrally located and shared by two families as other archaeological and ethnological data indicate for similar structures.

Within the northern end of the smaller of the two probable houses, we uncovered a small roasting pit, nearly round, and almost exactly four feet in diameter. Its depth, at the center of the rounded bottom, was very close to one foot below the surface of the subsoil. The fill consisted of dark topsoil underlain by a layer of charred wood, some of which was recovered for radiocarbon analysis. Contained within the fill were occasional potsherds typical of the site, as well as chips and a very few fire-broken stones. Several dozen carbonized beans were also recovered from the fill. The relative absence of burned stone suggests that this was not a ceremonial feature of precisely the same type as described at Bloody Hill or Kelso (Ritchie 1965:308–309), but was more similar to that at the Schoff site or possibly Feature 3 at Bloody Hill. As this and the ditch described above were the only features uncovered at the Burke site the usual list of features is omitted.

Artifacts

Material remains were relatively abundant at this site, owing both to the depth of the refuse from a fairly long occupation and also possibly to somewhat less intensive plowing than at other sites nearby. Refuse was located primarily on the northern slope in the midden deposits mentioned previously, but occasional concentrations in the village area were also productive. Points, pipes, ceramics, and modified bone comprise the sample, all of which are described below.

The Burke site ceramic sample, nearly as large as that from Bloody Hill, provides an excellent representation of late Chance phase pottery traits. While space does not permit the presentation of the entire detailed description, the following summary gives a good impression of the Burke site pottery sample (see also Appendix A): (1) a continued plurality (36 percent) of Chance rounded collar lip profiles but with significant increases in everted lip (20 percent), Chance straight collar (18 percent), and late Iroquois biconcave collar (14 percent) styles; (2) nearly all vessel interiors (98.5 percent) undecorated; (3) a further decrease in decorated lips to less than 15 percent but no decrease in the variety of motifs or techniques employed in the decoration of the remaining vessels; (4) over 37 percent decorated exterior lip edges, a fact related to the increased frequency of everted lip type vessels, which frequently have notched, or otherwise decorated, exterior lip edges; (5) a great variety of collar motifs (including 24 percent oblique over horizontal over opposed, 19 percent horizontal over opposed, 16 percent oblique, 14 percent opposed, 13 percent oblique over horizontal over oblique and several lesser motifs) but techniques more stable with incising now 79 percent, fingernail impressions 13 percent, and all other techniques reduced to 2 percent or less; (6) 29 percent decorated collar bases with many techniques employed (linear punctations 36 percent, oval punctations 28 percent, fingernail impressions 18 percent, incising 9 percent, and several lesser techniques) distinctly recognizable as precursors of later Iroquois decorative styles; (7) only 4 percent decorated sub-collar areas, with the eight examples displaying five different techniques; (8) three (23 percent) decorated sub-lip areas with the remainder having the neck decoration extending to the lip; (9) 91 percent plain vessel necks with the remainder decorated in a variety of motifs by incising (40 percent), fingernail impressions (19 percent), and many other less common techniques; (10) 83 percent decorated sub-neck areas, 35 percent fingernail impressed, 29 percent wedge-shaped punctations, 9 percent each of linear and crescent punctation and several other techniques; (11) over 50 percent of decorated shoulders, for the most part bands of horizontal or opposed incised lines set off by rows of various types of punctations; (12) 96 percent smoothed body sherds, 3 percent check-stamped, and 1 percent smoothed-over check-stamped; and (13) the average collar height is 23.11 mm.

No minature pots were found at the Burke site, a situation paralleling that at Schoff, Howlett Hill, and Furnace Brook, although this probably reflects the nature of the sample rather than a cultural tradition.

Smoking pipes from this site are, with one notable exception, rather monotonous in form and decoration (Plate 34, nos. 7–10). Over nine-tenths are variations of trumpet pipes, with the rather late decorated

TABLE 10. Frequencies and Percentages of Smoking
Pipe Varieties from the Burke Site

Variety	Frequency	Percentage
plain proto-trumpet	1	6.25
plain trumpet	5	31.25
decorated trumpet	7	43.25
rimless trumpet	1	6.25
collared pipe	1	6.25
human-face effigy	1	6.25
	16	100.00

trumpet being the most common variety. There is, however, a good representation of earlier forms, including one very early-looking plain proto-trumpet, a small collared pipe fragment, and one specimen decorated with sloppily incised parallel horizontal lines also reminiscent of earlier forms. The exceptional specimen mentioned above is an unusually large human-face effigy pipe of almost portrait quality. This is reminiscent of the pipe from the El Rancho site, an early Mohawk site in the Mohawk Valley (Ritchie 1965:311, Plate 107, No. 3). As does the pottery, the pipes from this site indicate a relatively long occupation during which the trumpet variety, the most common late prehistoric pipe form, reached the apex of its popularity. Pipe variaties are described in Appendix B and summarized in Table 10.

Pipe stems are mostly round (thirty-one examples) but two subrectangular examples are present. Stems are markedly thinner, longer, and have less taper than earlier examples, a trait increasingly evident through time. There are no specially prepared mouthpieces, but this end of the stem is invariably well finished with a flat surface surrounding the bore nearly perpendicular to the long axis of the stem. One unusual specimen is decorated with three fine incised lines parallel to the long axis which are set off by rows of fine punctations on either side.

Chipped stone from the Burke site includes projectile points, knives, retouched flakes, and three artifacts possibly attributable to an earlier occupation or to the Iroquois habit of picking up the relics of earlier cultures, possibly for use as hunting charms (see Ritchie 1954:67–68, Plates 7 and 8; and the Schoff site report in this volume). These latter consisted of a large Adena-like projectile point (Adena culture existed in the Ohio River drainage during the first millennium B.C.) with sloping shoulders and a lobate stem, and two strike-a-lights—thick, bifacially worked flints with extremely battered bases (see Plate 34, no. 6). The edges of these implements could also have served as cutting or scraping tools. Such implements are not typical of Iroquois sites and are, therefore, regarded as belonging to another era. Chipped-stone tools are described and discussed briefly below.

Projectile point data indicate increasing uniformity in projectile point manufacture, both in form and in dimensions. The Burke sample (see Plate 34, nos. 1–4) contains a predominance of straight-sided, concave-based forms (fifteen examples or about 60 percent) a variety which is becoming increasingly popular and which reaches its ultimate expression in the collection of almost identical points from the Barnes site (see pp. 156). Smaller numbers of older forms are present, including convex-sided, concave-based (three examples), concave-sided, concave-based (two examples), and a single specimen with straight sides and straight base. Length continued to increase averaging 3.72 cm. in this sample, while the average width (2.07 cm.) shows no increase over earlier assemblages, yielding a length-width ratio of 1.80 to 1.

A single specimen of a typical Iroquois ovate knife was found at Burke. It is rather leaf-shaped with a rounded base and a sharp point at the other end (see Plate 34, no. 5). The material is a light Onondaga chert not unlike some western New York varieties. A single worked flake completes the chipped-stone assemblage from the Burke site.

Rough stone includes four cobble hammer/anvils, a hammer/anvil/muller, and a large flat mortar perhaps used in conjunction with the muller. Polished stone includes two late Iroquois celts, round in cross section and relatively long, three trianguloid celts with thick polls, two rectanguloid celts, and a roughly worked blank for a large celt or adze.

Only six bone artifacts—four splinter awls, one polished catfish spine and a "cup-and-pin" type deer phalanx cone—were recovered at the Burke site.

Food Remains

Only two species of vegetable food, both cultigens, were found at the Burke site. Corn is represented by a few kernels gathered from post molds, while beans were found in great numbers in over fifty post molds excavated in the walls of the house or houses. Frequently several dozen beans would be found in a series of ten or more post molds along a house wall. This is the earliest site in this study at which large numbers of beans were found, though they are known from earlier sites both in the Onondaga area and in other areas of Iroquoia.

The summary of refuse bone in Table 11, though consisting of a relatively low number of species, indicates patterns little different from those described previously.

TABLE 11. FAUNAL REMAINS FROM THE BURKE SITE

Species	No. pieces	Remarks
MAMMALS		
white-tailed deer (*Odocoileus virginianus*)	136	at least four adults, one adult male (antler), at least one 1–2 years old, one 2–3 years old
black bear (*Ursus americanus*)	3	one adult
dog (*Canis familiaris*)	1	one adult
beaver (*Castor canadensis*)	6	one adult
porcupine (*Erethizon dorsatum*)	17	at least three adults
striped skunk (*Mephitis mephitis*)	4	one adult
BIRD		
ruffed grouse (*Bonasa umbellus*)	3	one adult
FISH		
4 pieces		unidentifiable
SHELLFISH		
freshwater clam	3	unidentified

Chronology

The charcoal sample mentioned above from Feature 1 was submitted to the Yale Radiocarbon Laboratory for analysis and the date returned at 360±80 BP (Y-2375) which gives a standard date of A.D. 1590, far too late for the occupation at Burke. Stuiver and Suess, however, point out in their 1966 article that a single radiocarbon date can represent several actual dates. They also include a table for conversion of age in radiocarbon years to age in calendar years which takes into account the fluctuations in available C-14 over the past two thousand years. Computed by this method, the date at Burke falls close to A.D. 1480±80, still, perhaps slightly late but considerably more satisfactory than the standard reading. Certainly the occupation was well within the deviation of eighty years indicated by the reading obtained from Yale.

OTHER PREHISTORIC IROQUOIS SITES

Several other sites, of which little is known or can even be assumed, should be mentioned here. The first of these is a group of sites located on or near the Seneca River near Baldwinsville, New York, about fifteen miles northeast of the Chamberlin and Kelso sites. Two of these sites, located opposite each other on the Seneca River just west of Baldwinsville, are known as the Crego and Indian Spring sites, both apparently villages in the Chance phase of Iroquois development. A small handful of material collected at the Crego site, including several small rimsherds, flint chips, and a blank for a large celt, is in no way different from material from the Schoff or Bloody Hill sites.

The Hicks Road School Site

The third site in this area is something of an enigma, the pottery quite different from usual Onondaga County Iroquois. Most of the material was given to Peter Pratt, then of the Fort Stanwix Museum in Rome, New York, but a small sample remains at the Hicks Road School, east of Baldwinsville, where the site was located prior to its destruction during the building of the school. The site is obviously prehistoric Iroquois, and from some material appears to be post-Chance phase, but other material suggests a much earlier chronological placement.

Pottery from this site resembles none that I have seen from the Onondaga area, nor does it resemble St. Lawrence Iroquois or Jefferson

County, New York, pottery. In fact, it seems to have no exact counterpart in any published reports or in any collections familiar to the author, although the impression is that of western New York influence. Vessels are both collared and uncollared, the latter types having plain, thickened, or everted lips. On collared specimens, decoration consists of horizontal lines, often interrupted by bands of oblique lines, executed with cord-wrapped paddle impressions, or in one case, by very broad, almost trailed, incised lines. Collars resemble low channeled collars in all attributes except collar height which may reach over 5.0 cm. high. Collarless vessels often have decorated rims and lip edges, usually done with a cord-wrapped paddle. Necks of these vessels are decorated in motifs uncommon to the rest of the ceramics described here, often consisting of horizontal trailed lines or cord-wrapped paddle impressions set off, in one case, by rows of small oval punctations above and below the horizontal lines. Another neck has vertical plaits of small triangular punctations. Body sherds are check-stamped.

Smoking pipes include a probable bear effigy pipe, a decorated trumpet identical in most respects with those from the Burke site, and a proto-trumpet pipe with three short oblique incised lines forming a chevron on the side of the bowl away from the smoker.

A square pestle, nine roughly chipped celts, and four fragments of polished celts comprise the worked stone. Bone implements include a spatulate, bipointed bone weaving tool perforated in the center, a tubular bird-bone bead, and several splinter awls including a very large probable bark perforator.

I am at a loss to explain either the origin of this community, or what became of it. The proximity of the site to Baldwinsville suggests some connection with the two sites on the Seneca River mentioned above, but whether the Hicks Road School site is earlier or later than the others is impossible to say at this point.

The Mountain View Site

Another prehistoric site in central New York which should be mentioned is the Mountain View site now covered by the LeMoyne College campus in the eastern part of the city of Syracuse. Lenig has briefly mentioned this material (1965:74) and has provided several photographs of material collected there by Stanley Gifford. These photographs show a strange mixture of rim profiles and decorative techniques including cord-wrapped paddle impressions on sherds with deeply notched collar bases, some very late looking collared, incised sherds, and numerous notched lip varieties. There are a few decorated neck sherds, and more decorated shoulders. This strange mixture of old and recent attributes somewhat suggests the Hicks Road School site described above, but they are so far removed from each other geographically that any connection is very tenuous. It is possible (and only possible), however, that these two sites represent some community which was "adopted" by the Onondaga or at least allowed to settle in Onondaga territory sometime before European contact. Such a pattern is not unknown in historic Iroquois times.

Summary

From these few data little can be said about the place of these several sites in Onondaga cultural development. The Crego and Indian Spring sites suggest the presence of a fourth community in Onondaga during the nascent Iroquois period, but the Hicks Road School and Mountain View sites seem to reveal a foreign presence in Onondaga, clearly too early and of a different character from anything from Jefferson County or the St. Lawrence Valley, and it may be an early instance of the "adoption" of a village in the manner well known from the historic Iroquois period.

While little can be said of the Crego, Hicks Road School, and Mountainview sites, our excavations at other early prehistoric Iroquois sites have thus far clearly established the continuity of Iroquois villages in Onondaga from the Castle Creek and Oak Hill phases through the Chance Phase of Iroquois development. Artifact types continue the gradual changes seen in earlier assemblages—for instance longer and narrower projectile points, the flourescense of trumpet type smoking pipes, and numerous changes in ceramics including increase in Chance rounded and Chance straight rim profiles, the rise of incising as a predominant decorative technique, the first appearance of typical Iroquois decorated collar bases and decorated vessel shoulders, and smoothed vessel bodies.

Continued evidence for Iroquois warfare is found in easily defended palisaded villages, and the ceremonial cooking pit at Bloody Hill provides additional evidence of warfare, this time in the form of ritual torture and cannibalism.

Settlement characteristics show many similar continuities, but several important changes in settlement pattern are also apparent. First, the Chamberlin-Kelso community disappears, though several sites now beneath the village of Elbridge may represent later villages of these people. Secondly, the community which dwelt consecutively at the Cabin, Furnace Brook, Howlett Hill, disappears from west of the present city of Syracuse. Thirdly, the presence of a third small community east of Syracuse, first suggested by the probable late Oak Hill phase Coye II site (see pp. 90–91), is abundantly confirmed by the early Chance phase Keough and Bloody Hill sites, at least one of which is probably a lineal descendant of that earlier component. Finally, a large community seems to have appeared rather suddenly without nearby antecedents not far from the Bloody Hill site and to have dwelt for many years at the Burke site. Combined with the equally sudden disappearance of the large community responsible for the Cabin-through-Schoff sites this offers the first clue to an unusual village removal in which this community relocated from west to east of Syracuse and to within two miles of another village. Additional data support this unusual relocation, which is interpreted here as evidence of the founding of the Onondaga Nation (see pp. 215–16) and establishment of a two-village settlement pattern which was to characterize the Onondaga until the late seventeenth century.

The "microtraditions" which were developing during the Oak Hill and earlier phases persist into the Chance phase, during which the Cabin-Schoff-Burke site community continued to build at least one extremely long house at each village and to incise the necks of their ceramic vessels (see pp. 219–22 for a further discussion of these "microtraditions").

Whatever the dates of the Chance phase in the Mohawk Valley or elsewhere, our three dates from the Chance phase (A.D. 1400, 1420, and 1480) and those from foregoing stations clearly place the Onondaga expression of the Chance phase in, and in fact during the entire fifteenth century.

In the following chapter we shall see that this two-village pattern established during the Chance phase persisted over the greater part of the following century, with gradual cultural changes similar to those documented since late Owasco times.

CHAPTER 5

The Garoga Phase

DURING THE FINAL STAGE of prehistoric Iroquois culture—the Garoga phase—the local alliance between two villages consummated during the Chance phase was apparently expanded to include larger tribal or "national" groups, which ultimately embraced the Five Nations of New York State.

The term "Garoga phase" is here adopted from Ritchie (1969:317–20) to denote the late prehistoric Iroquois phase in central as well as eastern New York. That this is a legitimate procedure is indicated by our researches which reveal a series of components completely analogous to those in the Mohawk Valley.

Ritchie noted that in that area a few large villages and a greater number of small hamlets are found on tongues or ridges of high land with precipitous slopes on at least two sides, the easily accessible approach being barred by palisades. The chief subsistence for these villages came from hoe tillage, though hunting, fishing, and gathering were still important activities.

The artifact complex typifying this phase included long, narrow, straight-sided triangular arrowpoints of the Madison type, a variety of barbed bone and antler points and harpoons, thick-polled celts, adzes, and chisels and ovate flint knives. Cooking pots were large, globular-bodied, carefully fired, usually collared but often with everted lips, and most commonly decorated with incised oblique lines or chevrons, coarser and more carelessly applied than in earlier Chance phase ceramics. Smoking pipes proliferate in style—human faces and figures and mammal heads, perhaps clan emblems appear—and all are executed with the utmost skill.

All those traits are in evidence in Onondaga, as will be seen in the descriptions which follow. Moreover the two-village settlement pattern

140

developed—probably by a political union—during the Chance phase persists throughout the Garoga phase as an indication of the social and political stability of the Iroquois prior to European contact.

THE CEMETERY SITE

The Cemetery or Century site (Cza 2-1) as it is sometimes known is an early Garoga phase village in the town of Manlius, New York, located on land owned by Louis Broadfield who kindly permitted our excavations there during the summer of 1967. The site is situated only a short distance north of the Indian Hill site, a historic Onondaga town occupied during the latter half of the seventeenth century. The Cemetery site is mentioned in the early literature (Parker 1922:642) as having been a recent site and is usually thought of as a satellite village of this historic site.

During the course of our 1966 field season, Gordon DeAngelo, of Oran, New York, informed us that he had located the Century site and directed us to the exact location. From a small collection made by DeAngelo from material found on the surface during our brief reconnaissance, and from similarities in topography, it was evident that this was the same site represented in the collection of Dr. Anton Sohrweide and known to him as the Cemetery site. Dr. Sohrweide noted that the late Stanley Gifford, also of Syracuse, had named the site "Cemetery" because of the presence of a very early—dating back to the 1790s— European cemetery located on the extreme southern edge of the site. Dr. Sohrweide also remarked that the site has sometimes been known as the "Waterworks site" because the land on which it is located abuts that owned by the Town of Manlius Water Department. The site location is shown on Figure 1 and will be referred to here as the Cemetery site, despite some previous confusion.

Settlement Data

The Cemetery site is located some two miles east of the Christopher site and a slightly greater distance northeast of the Burke site. The village once occupied a roughly triangular peninsula of land which drops off very sharply, in places almost vertically, nearly one hundred feet to the east and a similar distance to the west, though somewhat more gently. To the south, at the tip of the peninsula, a narrow but quite passable footpath leads away from the site. To the north the site offers little defensive advantage save for a slight narrowing of the land and a small drop in the terrain. The spread of refuse over a little more than one acre of the cultivated field suggests that the northern limit of occupation corresponds with this slight constriction, the village possibly having been palisaded at this point. In all, the site gives the impression of having been selected for its defensibility, certainly the best in any of the sites yet described.

The soil within and surrounding the village area is a mixed alluvium which varies from soft sand in many places to areas littered with sizeable limestone cobbles. Most of the nearby fields are a sandy loam which today produce excellent corn crops as they may well have in aboriginal times.

Since the village area is almost constantly under cultivation we were able to recover no data about house types, features, or any other additional occupational characteristics of the site. Presumably, however, the houses and fortifications differed but little from those described from the Burke and Bloody Hill sites and those to be described from other, later sites.

Our excavations were confined to a portion of a much dug over midden on the southeastern edge of the site. The bank in this area is less steep than it is along most of the eastern edge of the site, thus making controlled excavations possible. Fifteen five-foot squares, or 375 square feet, were completely excavated to subsoil, and all material was retained for analysis. The topsoil in this area, as over much of the eastern hillside, ranged from a few inches to over a foot deep and was a black greasy humus—typical "Indian dirt." This soil was underlain by a yellow sandy clay subsoil which contained no cultural material and was similarly devoid of post molds or other features which might have indicated the presence of a stockade in that area.

Artifacts

Although somewhat limited, especially in pipes and modified bone, which were prized by early collectors, the material from the Cemetery sites described below provides an adequate basis for comparison with other sites described in this report.

Despite the fact that the Cemetery site middens had been excavated by others before us, well over six thousand sherds were recovered which provide the most convincing evidence of the temporal provenience of the site and indicate the state of the Onondaga potters' art in the early Garoga phase. The outstanding characteristics of the Cemetery site ceramic sample (Plate 35, nos. 6–10) are (see also Appendix A): (1) The con-

PLATE 35. Artifacts from the Cemetery site. 1, fragment of miniature or toy vessel decorated with fingernail impressions; 2–5, triangular arrowpoints; 6, everted-lip rim sherd with notched lip edge; 7–9, rim sherds from collared vessels decorated with broad incised lines and having deeply notched collar bases.

tinued rise of biconcave collars (40 percent), Chance straight collars (20 percent), and everted lip (29 percent) rim profiles at the expense of the now declining Chance rounded (1.5 percent) type, and a slight increase (to 6 percent) of thickened lip types which are probably related to the everted varieties; (2) nearly all vessel interiors (99 percent) are undecorated; (3) a continuation of the trend toward plain lips, as less than 12 percent are decorated; (4) over 50 percent decorated exterior lip edges; (5) opposed lines forming the bulk of collar decorations, either oblique over horizontal over opposed (40 percent), horizontal over opposed (39 percent), opposed (5 percent), with small percentages of other variations, almost all (99.7 percent) executed by incising; (6) a notable rise in collar base decoration to 98 percent with a large cylindrical object pressed into the collar base accounting for 78 percent of the decorated specimens; (7) no decorated sub-collar areas; (8) two (9 percent) decorated sub-lip areas with the remaining twenty-one examples having the neck decoration extending to the lip; (9) 98 percent plain vessel necks with incising the most popular (93 percent) technique of decorating the remaining sherds; (10) neck decoration extending to body surface treatment in most cases, hence only 6 percent decorated sub-neck areas; (11) fourteen decorated shoulder sherds (about 34 percent), generally with horizontal lines set off by punctations or short opposed lines; (12) almost exclusively smoothed body sherds (99.99 percent) except for five (.01 percent) check-stamped sherds; and (13) the average collar height is 35.0 mm.

A single sherd of a cooking pot with a raised "bead" which may have run horizontally around the entire vessel, near the mouth was also recovered at the Cemetery site. This bead measures about 0.5 cm. wide and is raised an equal distance from the vessel. The edge of the raised portion is flattened and decorated with a series of right oblique linear punctations. This decoration is not, to my knowledge, known from other Onondaga sites, but oblique raised bands somewhat similar to this are frequently found on Cayuga ceramics of about this period.

Two miniature vessels were also found at the Cemetery site, both apparently made around the potter's thumb. One specimen (Plate 35, no. 1) is intact from the shoulder to the base, measuring 3 cm. and 3.7 cm. in diameter at the shoulder. The clay is untempered and averages 6–7 mm. thick. This specimen is undecorated. The second miniature vessel is known only from a small shoulder sherd, similar in size to that described above, very roughly made, and decorated in the same careless or inexpert manner, with rows of round indentations about 3–4 mm. in diameter.

There were but four identifiable smoking-pipe fragments found during our excavations at the Cemetery site, but two others, both the stems of some variety of trumpet pipe, are in the Sohrweide collection in Syracuse. The pipes recovered by us are fragments of two square bowl pipes and two pertaining to plain trumpet pipes.

Pipe stems are invariably thin, with but a slight taper, and are round in cross section. Two examples in the Sohrweide collection have a raised or slightly flaring mouthpiece. These pipes are typical of the early Garoga phase which has been postulated for this site.

Chipped-stone artifacts are relatively rare at the Cemetery site probably because they were carefully gathered by earlier collectors, while pottery and other less exciting relics were cast aside. Eleven points and a single rough scraper or knife are described below.

The trend toward straight-sided, concave-based projectile points of relatively long and narrow proportions continues at the Cemetery site (Plate 35, nos. 2–5). All intact bases except one are concave, and over 50 percent of the points are straight-sided. Summarily, the projectile point data are: average length 3.34 cm.; average width 1.76 cm.; length-width ratio 1.90 to 1, which provides the most relatively long and narrow point sample from any site considered thus far. A single utilized rectangular flake completes the Cemetery site chipped-stone inventory.

Most rough and polished artifacts were recovered from a pile of small cobbles and larger rocks near the eastern edge of the field in which the village was located. Two anvils, one with two pits on the same face, two combination hammer/anvils, and four celts—two long and oval in cross section, one trianguloid, and one partially chipped blank—were found at the edge of the cultivated field where they had obviously been thrown as the field was cleared of rocks.

A single fragmentary red slate discoidal bead, apparently about 2 cm. in diameter and less than 1 mm. thick, was recovered from the surface of a very steep portion of the hillside. This seems to be the earliest occurrence of this typical late prehistoric Iroquois artifact in central New York.

Food Remains

The only vegetable food remains found at the Cemetery site are a number of carbonized beans recovered from a depression in the midden

TABLE 12. FAUNAL REMAINS FROM THE CEMETERY SITE

Species	No. pieces	Remarks
MAMMAL		
white-tailed deer (*Odocoileus virginianus*)	177	at least five adults, one adult male, two 2–3 years old, one over 3 years old
racoon (*Procyon lotor*)	1	one adult
beaver (*Castor canadensis*)	4	one adult
porcupine (*Erethizon dorsatum*)	2	one adult
dog (*Canis familiaris*)	1	one adult
BIRD		
wild turkey (*Meleagris gallopavo*)	3	one adult
FISH		
four pieces not specifically identifiable		
SHELLFISH		
five pieces freshwater clam		

excavated by the Syracuse University field party. Faunal remains, summarized in Table 12, again present a picture of Iroquois hunting and fishing activities which is completely in harmony with our earlier findings.

Chronology

No features were exposed, nor were any reliable charcoal samples obtained from the hillside dump; thus no absolute date is available from the Cemetery site. The relative chronological position of the site can be fairly accurately determined, however, from material remains and the location of the site in relation to other villages, both earlier and later. Both of these lines of evidence indicate an occupation in the early Garoga phase, immediately postdating such Chance phase sites as Christopher and Burke, probably in the first half of the sixteenth century.

THE NURSERY SITE

This important site was discovered recently by Walter Burr of Chenango, New York, who gave a small surface collection made there to

Stanford Gibson, of nearby Norwich, through whose courtesy I was able to study the material thus far recovered. Gibson supplied most of the data presented below.

Settlement Data

The site is located on Rte. 92 on a low rise of land, rather ill-suited for defense, which lies a little more than three and one-half miles northeast of the Burke site and about one and one-half miles in the same direction from the Cemetery site (see Figure 1). While not particularly defensible, the land surrounding this site is all a rich creek-bottom loam which is today, and must have been formerly, quite productive. Nearby also is a small stream which provided a steady supply of water. Considerations other than defensibility must have prevailed in choosing this location, suggesting perhaps a period of relative quiet, or at least security for one reason or another.

Other than the information provided above, there are few settlement data available for this site. No controlled excavations have been carried out, and it is likely that none will ever be accomplished as the site lies partly under Rte. 92, partly under lawns and houses, and partly under the gardens of a plant nursery, from which it takes its name. Gibson reports that the village area is large, but not as large as Barnes, a nearby town which may have covered up to six acres. The low rise on which the Nursery site is situated could easily have supported a settlement of three or more acres. Houses are probably little changed from the Burke site, and it is hard to imagine a time so peaceful that some fortifications would not have been constructed in so vulnerable a location as that occupied by this village.

Artifacts

Aside from its location between Chance phase villages and those of the latest Garoga phase Onondaga sites, the best indicator of the relative chronological position of the Nursery site is the small but significant sample of material remains recovered there. With the exception of several celts similar to that described below, which are in the possession of the landowner, all the material is in Gibson's collection and was recovered by Gibson and Burr.

Only six rim sherds have thus far been recovered from the site, but they, perhaps by some accident, represent about the percentages expected in a site of the early Garoga phase. Five are biconcave collared forms, though too fragmentary to measure collar height, which appear to have been more than 30 mm. high. The remaining rim sherd is of an everted lip type with a notched lip edge which conforms to the Otstungo Notched type described by MacNeish (1952:75–76). Decoration on the former five sherds combines various incised lines to form opposed triangles, usually with horizontal lines above. The incising is in excess of 1.0 mm. wide in four cases, a late Onondaga trait, and slightly less than 1.0 mm. in the remaining cases. No body, shoulder, or neck sherds were recovered.

Three round pipe stems, all relatively thin and with little taper, represent the total pipe sample recovered to date. One stem retains the graceful bend which pertains to a trumpet form, and is certainly characteristic of late prehistoric Iroquois.

Five completed projectile points, one point in process, and nine blanks comprise the entire chipped-stone inventory from the Nursery site. Despite its small size, however, this sample is significant because it indicates several trends in Onondaga projectile point styles. Concave-based forms comprise the total sample, while straight-sided forms were then also on the increase. Significant, too, is the relatively long and narrow proportions of the points. The nine blanks are all too crude to yield reliable data but probably pertain to forms in no way different from the completed specimens. Average length is 3.34 cm., width 1.76 cm., and the length-width ratio is 2.13 to 1.

A single fragment of a long, probable bar-type celt with parallel sides and an oval cross section apparently made from a white-veined black diabase is the only polished-stone implement in Gibson's collection, but he has seen several other, almost identical specimens in the landowner's collection. This artifact is much more common on later Onondaga sites than on Chance phase sites, and is unknown on any sites earlier than the Chance phase.

No modified bone is known from this site.

Chronology

Because of the lack of radiocarbon date or any settlement data, save for its location, the discussion of the chronological position of the Nursery site must be based upon extremely meager data. On the basis of its location between late Chance phase and late prehistoric Onondaga sites its position in the early Garoga phase, or the first half of the sixteenth century, is indicated. This suggestion is attested to by the material remains, though the size and variety of the sample are hardly impressive.

Such, however, are the problems facing anyone attempting to reconstruct the prehistory of the New York Iroquois.

THE BARNES SITE

The Barnes site was discovered in 1929 by Stanford Gibson, who has worked the site off and on since that time. He has amassed a collection of data and prehistoric Onondaga artifacts which is unique in several respects, the most important of which is the fact that his is the only collection extant today which was made at any known Onondaga site before it had been thoroughly looted. All other early collections, which once contained the cream of Onondaga "material culture," have long since been broken up or otherwise destroyed.

Settlement Data

This site is located about three miles east of the Cemetery site and about one and one-half miles from the Nursery site, in the same direction (see Figure 1). It occupies most of what is now a large cultivated field, rather well situated for defense, with a steepsided gorge on one side. Gibson notes, however, that there is no place around the site where one cannot see higher land. The site is a large one—perhaps the largest of any Onondaga site—and may encompass as much as six or eight acres. Whether this represents a single large occupation or a smaller shifting village is uncertain, but Gibson's discovery of a palisade which surrounds much of the village area seems to indicate that the former possibility is more likely.

The palisade mentioned above, which Gibson has traced around three-fourths of the village, was apparently a single row of unusually small posts, some two to three inches in diameter and generally set less than four inches into the subsoil. Outside this stockade there is a suggestion of a shallow ditch which may once have surrounded at least part of the site. This type of construction differs from that found at other late prehistoric sites in other areas (see Funk 1967) but is entirely in keeping with the type of construction at the Burke site.

Because the village area is almost constantly cultivated, and because Gibson's excavations were carried out singlehandedly, hence were limited by the amount of soil he could move, no information on houses or other structures is available. There were, however, many post molds found in the small areas of the site which were excavated, as well as numerous hearths, both of which suggest an occupation of considerable duration. Most likely, houses differed little from those described earlier, except that they may have had square ends, which are recorded from historic Iroquois villages and which replaced the earlier, rounded-ended structures described previously.

Burials

With the exception of the Schoff site, the Barnes site offers us our only glimpse of the burial practices of the prehistoric Onondaga. Gibson reports uncovering (and *re*covering) several burials immediately outside the palisade on the hilltop occupied by this site. In every case the graves were shallow, often scarcely below plow depth; burials were flexed and unaccompanied by any grave offerings. The impression is one of disposal burials rather than the lavish funerals which must have characterized the later Iroquois.

Artifacts

As mentioned above, the collection from this site is the sole surviving example of what prehistoric Onondaga "material culture" actually resembled. Pottery sherds number in the thousands; pipes are numerous; points, rough and polished stone, and modified bone are the most complete representative from any prehistoric Iroquois site in central New York. Although Gibson's report (1968) deals with this material in some detail, he has kindly allowed it to be described briefly here.

While a limited and perhaps not entirely random sample (some sherds in Gibson's collection were on study loan to another individual at the time this analysis was made) the available sample clearly typifies late prehistoric ceramics in central New York (Plate 36). The outstanding characteristics are as follows: (1) the continued increase in popularity of biconcave collar (52 percent) rim profiles with lesser numbers of Chance rounded (14 percent), Chance straight (12 percent), everted lip (12 percent), thickened lip (7 percent) and plain lip (3 percent) styles; (2) all vessel interiors undecorated; (3) an increase in decorated (mostly by incising) vessel lips to over 32 percent, a fact undoubtedly related to the increase in everted lip types, many of which have the everted portion decorated; (4) about equal numbers (48 percent) of decorated and plain exterior lip edges; (5) horizontal over opposed lines (48 percent) and opposed lines (21 percent) forming the majority of collar motifs executed by incising (91 percent) with small percentages of dentate stamp, fingernail impressions, and hollow-reed punctations; (6) 98 percent of all

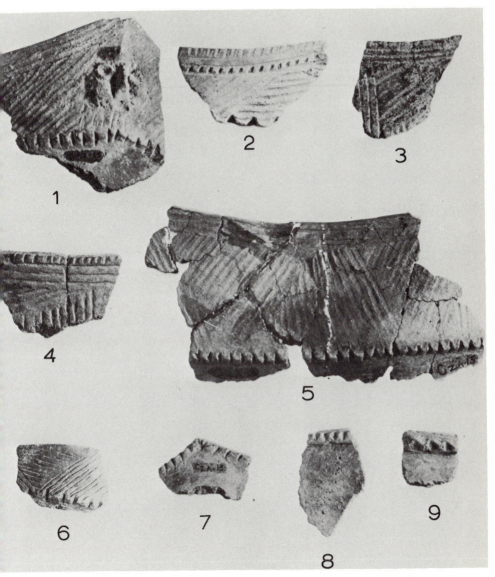

PLATE 36. Ceramics from the Barnes site. 1–5, collared rim sherds with broad incised decoration; 6, collared rim sherd with narrow incising; 7–9, everted or thickened notched-lip variety.

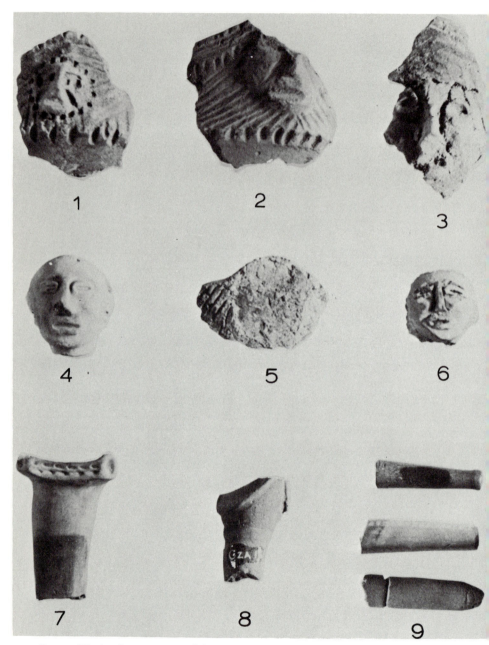

PLATE 37. Smoking pipes and human-face effigies from the Barnes site. 1–3, faces modeled into the clay of vessel collars; 4 and 6, detached faces which were applied to vessel collars; 5, scar caused by the detachment of a human-face effigy; 7, squared-trumpet variety smoking pipe; 8, bird effigy smoking pipe; 9, pipestems, lowermost specimen partially cut, perhaps for use as a bead.

PLATE 38. Stone artifacts from the Barnes site. 1–7, arrowpoints of local Onondaga chert; 8, arrowpoint of white chert; 9 and 11, discoidal shale beads; 10, imperforate shale bead or gaming disc; 12, ovate knife; 13, small celt; 14, bit section of large late Iroquois celt; 15, faceted chipping and/or pecking hammer.

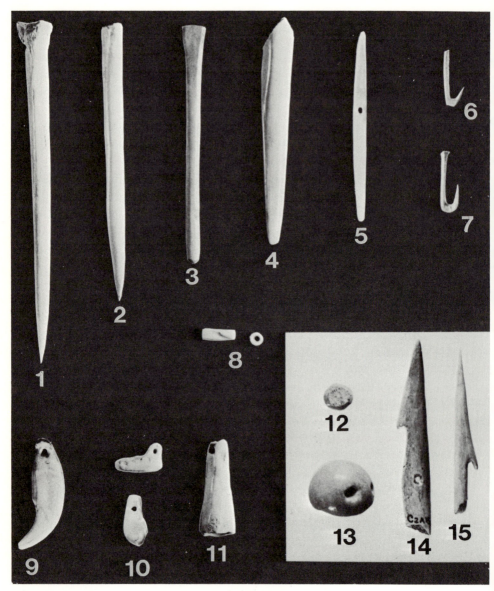

PLATE 39. Bone and shell artifacts from the Barnes site, from the collection of Stanford Gibson. 1 and 2, awls; 3, flaker; 4, perforator with spatulate point; 5, weaving
needle; 6 and 7, bone fishhooks; 8, tubular and discoidal shell beads; 9, bear canine
perforated for suspension; 10, perforated mammal teeth; 11, deer phalanx cone; 12,
probable antler gaming disc; 13 polished and drilled epiphyseal cap of mammal long
bone; 14, barbed bone harpoon; 15, barbed antler point.

collar bases decorated with 73 percent done with the same cylindrical impressions as at the Cemetery site but 16 percent now notched with the fingernail; (7) no decorated sub-collar areas; (8) the neck decoration extending to the lip in all uncollared vessels, hence no decorated sub-lip areas were recorded; (9) 94 percent plain vessel necks; (10) only three sub-neck sherds observed, hence no reliable data; (11) ten decorated and no plain shoulders, even though not a representative sample, a clear indication of the high frequency of decorated shoulders; (12) body surface treatment 99 percent smoothed and 1 percent corded; and (13) the average collar height is 35.54 mm.

One very small fragment of a miniature pot is in the Gibson collection from the Barnes site. It has a thickened lip profile and is completely devoid of any decoration from the interior to the sub-neck area. While little of the shoulder remains, it too seems plain, and the body appears to have been smoothed.

Except for the probable applied human-face effigy from the Cemetery site the Barnes site marks the first appearance of ceramic face effigies in the Onondaga sequence. A total of eighteen human faces, all beautifully molded, are in the Gibson collection and some are illustrated on Plate 37, nos. 1–4, 6. Most measure between 2 cm. and 3 cm. high and proportionally wide. Five of these faces were apparently applied to the still-wet clay of the ceramic vessel, while eleven were molded into the clay near the rim of the pot, apparently always beneath a castellation. The remaining two specimens are too fragmentary to determine whether they were applied or molded. All of those still adhering to the pots are on sherds with broadly incised decoration, usually consisting of opposed lines beneath horizontal lines, or biconcave collars.

Another rare Iroquois trait, a probable "loop" pot handle from this site, is very like an elbow in shape and measures about 3 x 2 cm., having been attached to the collar and some lower point on the vessel.

Gibson recovered nineteen identifiable smoking pipe bowl fragments at the Barnes site. The varieties and percentages are typical of late prehistoric Iroquois, including primarily trumpet forms typical of the Chance and Garoga phases, as well as human face, snake effigy, and the rimless trumpet typical of slightly later sites. Table 13 lists the varieties and relative percentages of smoking pipes from the Barnes site.

Pipe stems include twenty-eight round and three rectangular specimens, one of the latter variety decorated with rows of small round punctations on the rounded edges. All are thin, well-made and have a minimum taper compared to earlier sites. All also show a graceful bend

rather than a pronounced elbow. Five specimens have raised or otherwise specially molded mouthpieces, one apparently round sectioned
specimen with traces of longitudinally incised lines. Several pipes from
this site are shown on Plate 37, nos. 7–9.

TABLE 13. FREQUENCIES AND PERCENTAGES OF SMOKING
PIPE VARIETIES FROM THE BARNES SITE

Variety	Frequency	Percentage
collared	2	10.5
decorated trumpet	3	15.7
square trumpet	7	36.9
rimless trumpet	1	5.3
human-face effigy	3	15.7
other effigy (snake)	3	15.7
	19	99.8

Three knives and forty-one projectile points comprise the chipped-
stone inventory from the Barnes site and also comprise the best example
of chipped stone from any Onondaga site. The points from this site are
by far the most consistent in form and the most finely worked points
from any site considered in this report. They represent the pinnacle of
arrowpoint manufacture among the Onondaga. Thirty have straight
sides and a concave base, seven have slightly concave sides and a concave base, two have slightly convex sides and a concave base, and one
specimen has both straight sides and a straight base. Individual metric
data are not available, but Gibson has provided the following data: average length 4.13 cm., and average width 1.91 cm., which combine to
give the most relatively long and narrow point sample (length to width
ratio 2.15 to 1) seen from any Onondaga site. All are made from local
Onondaga cherts save one which is made of a nearly pure white material resembling a rare piece of western New York Onondaga chert or
something from farther west.

The remarkable uniformity of these points, both in form and dimensions cannot be overemphasized (see Plate 38, nos. 1–8). In comparing
these with points from other sites two things are apparent. The first is
that the Barnes site represents the purest expression of a trend toward
long, narrow points with straight sides and a concave base. The second
is the near identity of the points from Barnes with the bulk of the points

from the Nursery site; the points from these two sites almost appear to have been made by the same hand.

Two typical Iroquois ovate knives, both finely flaked and retouched along both edges, are in the collection from this site (Plate 38, no. 12). A final piece of chipped stone is a small, round, unifacially flaked knife or scraper measuring about 2.5 cm. in diameter.

Rough stone tools include sixteen bipitted hammer/anvils made on nearly round cobbles, three highly polished cobble mullers, and the un- usual pecking hammer illustrated on Plate 38, no. 15. Polished stone celts are considerably more numerous and include a single trianguloid example made of diabase (as are most Barnes site celts)—shown on Plate 38, no. 13—six rectanguloid celts, and six fragments of the large, round, cross section examples (Plate 38, no. 14) identical in every re- spect to those from the Nursery site.

Thirty discoidal beads (Plate 38, nos. 9–11), made of red and black shale, measuring about 1 cm. to 2 cm. in diameter, were found at Barnes. Twenty are perforated in the center with holes up to 0.5 cm. in diameter, and the remaining ten specimens are imperforate, either in process or intended for some purpose other than suspension. All are be- tween 0.1 cm. and 0.2 cm. thick.

The nearly neutral soil at the Barnes site (pH very close to 7.0), and the fact that Gibson has retained practically the entire collection from the site, has resulted in a unique assemblage of bone tools for study. Although the Iroquois have often been thought to have had a small bone industry, the evidence from the Barnes site does not indicate this. This erroneous impression is perhaps best explained by the fact that early collectors quickly removed the choice bone artifacts, leaving be- hind only relatively uninteresting potsherds. Most early sites do not give evidence of a major bone industry, but Beauchamp (1902a) gives a hint of such an industry in the late Chance phase in his description of the now-dispersed original collection from the Christopher site. Undoubt- edly other similar sites—Burke, Cemetery, Nursery—would also have provided evidence of Iroquois skill in working bone had they not been "dug to death" years ago. The bone assemblage from the Barnes site is described below, and many specimens are illustrated on Plate 39.

Fifty-nine bone awls have been recovered from the middens and vil- lage area of the Barnes site. All are of the splinter variety, with the base either a portion of the articulating surface of a longbone or a cut and polished rounded or squared end. Bird, small mammal, deer, bear, and probably elk bones are all represented. Lengths range from about 5 cm.

to over 20 cm. Except for the highly polished surface of these tools, most individual specimens are duplicated from other Iroquois sites. As a group, however, they far surpass the sample from any other component.

Two spatulate awls or chisels, so designated for want of a better name, are included in the Barnes site bone inventory. Both are made from sections of split mammal bone and are similar to those described above except that the point is spatulate or chisel-shaped rather than sharply pointed as are the splinter awls described above. They may well have served either as chisels or some other similar function rather than perforating tools.

Forty-six whole or fragmentary mat needles are known from the Barnes site. All intact specimens are spatulate in form with rounded ends and are perforated near the center. Most are slightly bowed in the manner of the specimen described by Ritchie (1965:310) from the Kelso site. Ribs and occasionally other bones of deer were preferred raw materials for these implements.

Four bone flakers—tentatively identified as flakers despite the absence of signs of wear—were found at Barnes. All are between 13 and 15 cm. long and are bluntly pointed at one end which is round in cross section. The other end, which is expanded, is square or rectangular in cross section, measuring less than 1 cm. in either direction. Ritchie illustrates similar antler specimens from the Dutch Hollow site, a late sixteenth-century Seneca town (Ritchie 1954:Plate 9, nos. 20, 21, 27).

Two bone fish hooks, carved from flat sections of mammal longbone and measuring 3.5 cm. by 1.3 cm. and 3.2 cm. by 1.1 cm. respectively, were also found at Barnes. The former has a slightly expanded shank for line attachment while the latter is not so equipped but has the upper portion of the shank roughened, perhaps also to facilitate line attachment. Neither specimen shows any sign of being barbed. Hooks of this type are known throughout much of the prehistory of New York State but are relatively rare on Iroquois sites, probably for the reasons mentioned above.

A single leister point, round and bipointed, bluntly at one end and sharply at the other, comprises still another type of fishing tackle from the Barnes site. This specimen is not very different from the specimens described from the Cabin site (see p. 43).

The six bone harpoons or barbed bone points from the Barnes site compose the most extensive collection of these weapons from any Onondaga site. All are made from the long bones of large mammals (some identified below), and all have the natural luster which characterizes all bonework from this site. Table 14 provides a summary of the distinguishing attributes of these harpoons.

TABLE 14. Attributes of Bone Harpoons from the Barnes Site

Material	No. barbs	Uni- or Bilaterally	Line hole	Length
bear longbone	2	unilaterally	yes, two	16.4 cm
bear longbone	1	unilaterally	no	23.0 cm
deer (?) metapodial	3	unilaterally	no	18.0 cm
longbone (?)	2 and 3	bilaterally	no	15.2 cm
bear longbone °	1 (?)	unilaterally	?	broken
longbone (?)	1	unilaterally	yes, 1	broken

° This specimen is nearly identical to one from the Dutch Hollow Site pictured in Ritchie 1954, Plate 9, no. 28.

A single small (1.5 cm.) bone or antler disc, lenticular in cross section, about 1 cm. thick and so highly polished as to make identification of the precise material difficult, was found at Barnes. Although there is no discoloration on either side as might be expected in one of a set of gaming discs, this nevertheless is the most likely interpretation of this artifact. The deer button game, a variant of the Bowl Game, was frequently played for amusement among the Iroquois, and such gaming discs are not uncommon on Iroquois sites.

Modified animal teeth, which vary as to species as well as to type and degree of modification. Included are two probable wolf canines, two bear molars carved to represent human feet, two bear molars not so modified, and five small elk teeth. All have in common the very high gloss of all bone from the Barnes site, and all are drilled for suspension.

Four completed phalanx cones and one such artifact in process are also in the Gibson collection. Three of the finished specimens are made from deer phalanges and the fourth of that of an elk. All are of the "cup-and-pin" type and have the proximal articulating surface removed and the edges smoothed and polished. The distal articulating surfaces are ground round and smooth and a hole for suspension drilled through to the hollow interior. The unfinished specimen has the proximal end treated as above, but the distal end was not ground or drilled. Aside from a high polish over the entire artifact these probable bangles are otherwise unmodified.

Two polished and drilled heads of femora, both apparently from bears, one mature and one immature, were probably suspended as items of personal adornment. Although unusual, such specimens are known from other Iroquois sites (see Parker 1922:193, Plate 66, No. 11).

Twenty tubular bird bone beads found at this site range in length from 1 to 7.5 cm. and in diameter from 0.5 to 1.0 cm. All have the ends neatly cut perpendicular to the long axis of the bead and the entire surface of the bead ground and polished to a high gloss.

Another type of bone bead, much less common than those described above, is represented by a single polished entire bone. It is the humerus of a small bird, measuring about 7.6 cm. long which has been drilled transversely through the proximal end for suspension. Except for considerable polishing which has resulted in a high gloss, this specimen is otherwise unmodified.

A unique antler maskette, rather difficult to describe, is 4.5 cm. tall, the face itself measuring about 1 cm. high. Above the face, which is well executed in almost full relief, is a crest which somewhat resembles the Iroquois scalp lock hair style. Below the face the round shaft tapers slightly as though made to fit into a shaft or other receiver. Although this specimen bears no resemblance to any known Iroquois false faces, it nevertheless is consistent with the practice of keeping miniature human-face effigies to ensure good fortune.

Ten shell beads, all native made and white in color, mark the beginning of bead types which doubtless evolved into the "wampum" beads of the historic Iroquois. Seven of these beads are discoidal, measuring 0.6 cm. in diameter by 0.3 cm. thick. The remaining three beads are tubular and measure 1.2 to 1.7 cm. in length and 0.6 cm. in diameter. All are completely perforated near the center, the longer ones apparently from both ends.

A small scrap of copper, which Gibson has had analyzed, and which is *not* native copper, was found by him near a small hearth in the village area. This may indicate the earliest traces of European influence upon the central New York Iroquois. Other trade goods found on or near this site, and which are almost certainly intrusive, include a tubular red glass bead, a dull blue round bead, and a brass button.

Food Remains

Gibson's report (1968) deals extensively with both animal and plant remains from the Barnes site. It is sufficient to note here that almost every mammal, fish, and bird represented at any other central New York Iroquois site has been found at Barnes as well as carbonized corn kernels, beans, and wild plum pits. Undoubtedly the conclusions reached about diet at other sites apply to this site as well.

Chronology

From his study of the material from the Barnes site and other nearby sites, Gibson places this important village in the late Garoga or prehistoric Iroquois phase, a conclusion with which I completely agree. No radiocarbon determination has been made of the age of this site—and such a determination for so recent a site might be meaningless—but an occupation in the middle sixteenth century is suggested by the available data.

THE McNAB SITE

The McNab site is located less than a mile east of the Barnes site on a hill overlooking Cazenovia Lake (see Figure 1). Its precise acreage is unknown, but it is considerably smaller than the Barnes site. The village area of the site is now located in cultivated fields which make recovery of any further settlement data unlikely. Middens along the hillsides have all been dug over many times and are now under lawns and a pine grove which make further excavation impossible. A large collection made some years ago at this site is reported to exist somewhere in New York State, but we have been unable to locate it to date. All that is remembered of this collection by local residents is that it contained many potsherds and that so much carbonized corn was unearthed from the hillsides that one collector was forced to abandon his practice of paying five cents per kernel for its recovery. Perhaps some day this collection will come to light and provide us with a sample of material equal to that from the Barnes site. Until that day, however, we will have to be content with drawing some conclusions from its location relative to other sites and a handful of small potsherds collected by various people from the surface.

The location of the site very near the Barnes site and in the extreme northeast corner of a west to east to south series of village movements suggests an age very close to that of the Barnes site, a fact which is at least not disputed by the material from the site. This included smoothed body sherds and rim (or collar) sherds decorated with broad incised lines typical of late prehistoric Iroquois.

THE TEMPERANCE HOUSE FORT

This site was mentioned as early as 1849 by Clark and was apparently thoroughly looted before Beauchamp's time, since he illustrates few outstanding artifacts from here. Parker apparently visited the site and described it briefly (1922:644). Most collectors of Indian relics in central New York have at one time or another had the opportunity to visit and collect at the Temperance House Fort. The most recent excavations there were conducted by Robert Ricklis who, during 1963 and 1964, excavated portions of two hillside middens and also exposed a portion of the defensive palisade as well as part of a longhouse.

Settlement Data

The site is located about one mile south of the Barnes and McNab sites on the east side of the Limestone Creek valley (see Figure 1). It occupies the top of a steepsided promontory of land which Ricklis (1966) computed as encompassing four and a half acres. The site provides considerable defensive advantage and was doubtless chosen for that reason.

Clark (1849) mentioned that the site was crossed by a "bank and a ditch," and Parker (1922:644) also saw this, though he disagreed with Clark in some details. Most probably this represented a stockade, earthwork, and ditch which defended the peninsula on its most accessible side. Ricklis, while excavating the upper part of two hillside middens, discovered under each the remains of a stockade line which apparently surrounded the entire village. These portions of the palisade were composed of posts from three to eight inches in diameter, in contrast to the much smaller posts at the Barnes site where the largest posts were scarcely three inches in diameter. During this period of Onondaga prehistory the people seem to have been most concerned with defense. The site selected for maximum defensive advantage, the access protected by a ditch, earth wall, and probably a palisade, and the entire site also ringed by at least one row of upright posts presents a picture in marked contrast to the situation at the slightly earlier, but considerably larger, Barnes site which was poorly stockaded. The very size of the Barnes site, however, may have made extensive fortifications seem unnecessary.

During the course of his excavations at this site, Ricklis exposed over 725 square feet of the level hilltop, which disclosed the only house structure known from the site. While time did not permit the excavation of the entire structure, enough was exposed to indicate a house about eighteen feet wide by at least thirty feet long. One end was uncovered, showing clearly that by this time the Onondaga were living in square-ended houses of the type described in early historic accounts of the Iroquois. In the center of this structure we found a small (fourteen-inch diameter) hearth filled with white ash, indicating interior organization quite typical of the Iroquois and probably no different from the sites described previously.

Artifacts

Since this description is taken from Ricklis' brief report of his work at the Temperance House site, a detailed analysis of material remains is not possible at this time. Below is a summary of the material recovered at this site, most of which we have personally inspected.

Ricklis' analysis of Temperance House ceramics was based upon a modification of MacNeish's (1952) typological method. It is somewhat difficult, therefore, to make comparisons between this site and those from which ceramics were analyzed by attributes, but some useful conclusions can be made. Ricklis noted that 60 percent of the Temperance House rim sherds belong to the Onondaga Triangular type, which he defined as "incised chevron or oblique pattern . . . under a band of horizontal lines." This type may or may not have short oblique lines above the band of horizontal lines described by Ricklis. It includes several decorative motifs, defined in Appendix A, which constitute over 70 percent of the Barnes site ceramics. Since this motif, which includes horizontal lines (a carryover from much earlier times), is more common at Barnes than at Temperance it indicates that Temperance is relatively later than the Barnes site. However, Wagoner Incised pottery, characterized by opposed triangles without horizontal lines (a late type), constitutes almost 16 percent of the Temperance House ceramics while it exceeds 23 percent at Barnes, a situation contrary to that expected if the chronological relationship were that suggested above. Other types at the Temperance House site include some sherds decorated with horizontal and oblique lines and several sub-varieties of everted, notched-lip types most of which are so slightly represented as to indicate nothing about relative chronology.

Also noted by Ricklis from this site are four human-face pottery appendages, similar to those from Barnes, a single vertical clay ridge applied to the collar of a pot, and two lug-type pot handles, all suggesting very late prehistoric Iroquois ceramics.

Only two smoking pipe fragments of identifiable form were recovered during the course of Ricklis' excavations, both of which he identified as "barrel-shaped bowls," somewhat surprising in view of the disappearance of this variety from central New York considerably earlier.

Chipped stone includes twenty-six finely-made Madison points, very similar to those from Barnes, as well as two small uniface scrapers and fragments of five ovate knives. Average length of these points is 2.89 cm., average width is 1.74 cm., and the ratio of length to width is 1.65 to 1.

Artifacts of rough and polished stone also indicate a very late prehistoric position for this site. Included are hammerstones, a netsinker, celts similar to those from the Barnes site, discoidal stone beads, and thirty-three stone discs which may be beads in process or, perhaps, counters for some game of chance.

This site would undoubtedly have provided a wealth of bone artifacts had it not been dug over for more than one hundred years. As it is, seven splinter awls were recovered, one awl with the base retaining the articulating surface of the longbone of a small mammal, and an unusual antler maskette which bears unquestionable resemblance to a "blowing" type of Iroquois false face. One trapezoidal shell pendant, in the process of manufacture with the suspension hole only partly drilled, again suggests a very late Iroquois artifact.

No trade goods have been found recently at the Temperance House site, though early records mention such material. Parker (1922:644), when he visited the site, was also unable to find evidence of European contact.

Chronology

Although the evidence is contradictory, the decrease in frequency of sherds with horizontal lines on the collar (Onondaga triangular type), the stone discs, shell pendant, antler maskette, pottery appendages, and the suggestion of trade goods in early records all combine to suggest that the Temperance House site is somewhat later than Barnes, perhaps being the site occupied immediately after the Barnes site. Another factor in favor of this hypothesis is the nearly identical nature of the data and material from this site with that from the Atwell Fort site, discussed next, at which European trade goods have been found in direct association with native material. A further suggestion of this site's position relative to Barnes is its location to the south of Barnes in a pattern of village removals and resettlements which was proceeding from north to south during the years before, during, and after the occupation of the Temperance House site.

No absolute data may be fixed for this site, but all evidence suggests very strongly an occupation dating from the last half, or last quarter, of the sixteenth century.

THE ATWELL FORT SITE

This site (Cza 1-1) occupies the top of a steepsided peninsula located about two and one-half miles south of the Barnes and McNab sites and about a mile south of the Temperance House Fort (see Figure 1). Its location has been known for over a century, and it has, therefore, been almost completely dug over. The only record of most early collections made at this site are contained in Beauchamp's various works describing the artifacts of the New York Indians. More recently the hillside middens have been explored by Robert Ricklis and to a lesser extent by members of the Chenango Chapter of the New York State Archaeological Association. While the results of the excavations of the latter group have not been published, they have generously made the data and material recovered available for study. Ricklis has published two articles (1963, 1966) describing his excavations there. It is from the accounts of Beauchamp, Ricklis' investigations, and those of the many members of the Chenango Chapter that this account is taken.

Settlement Data

Ricklis (1963) described the Atwell site as encompassing about three acres, about two-thirds the size of the Temperance House Fort. The peninsula on which the site is located is this size, but the site could actually have been somewhat smaller. All sides of the peninsula except a narrow neck of land to the east are very steep and would have provided a great measure of security, for which reason this location for the village was probably selected. Several springs are nearby, and level land to the east may have been cultivated by the occupants of the Atwell Fort.

In all probability this site was fortified in much the same manner as

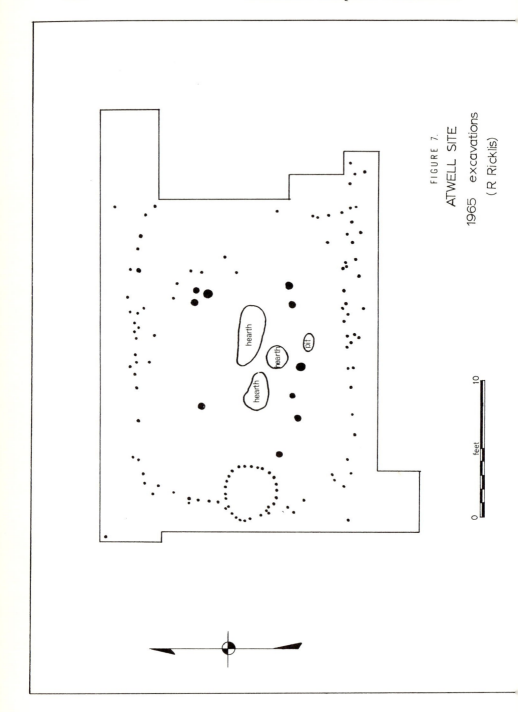

FIGURE 7.
ATWELL SITE
1965 excavations
(R Ricklis)

the previously described Temperance House site. The landowner, Mr. Ingersoll, recalls seeing in the late 1950s the remnants of a ditch which cut off the peninsula from the high ground to the east. This may represent the location of an earth ring, ditch, and probably an allied picket stockade. That the site was also completely surrounded by a wooden stockade is also indicated by Ricklis' discovery of a line of ten post molds, running along the hillside and parallel with the edge of the bank, spanning one of his excavations (Ricklis 1966). These molds ranged in diameter from four to fifteen inches, in depth from eleven to twenty-four inches, and were spaced from eight to thirty-six inches apart.

During August, 1965, Ricklis single-handedly exposed well over five hundred square feet of the hilltop and was rewarded for his efforts by the discovery of a portion of a house very similar to one he had previously excavated at the Temperance House site. This may be a complete dwelling measuring about thirty by eighteen feet, as every effort was made to locate post molds which would indicate that it was longer, with negative results. The width of this structure is consistent with the trend toward narrower houses which had been taking place since the early Chance phase, and the over-all dimensions are consistent with the French practice of referring to houses of a slightly later period as *cabanes* rather than some term more descriptive of long houses. The walls are made from small posts, ends are more square than round, and interior structure is typically Iroquois, consisting of central hearths and large support posts lining a central aisle (see Figure 7). Some breakup of an earlier form of social organization may be indicated by this trend toward smaller houses.

Another small, round, post mold pattern which overlays the west end of the house described above was also disclosed by Ricklis' excavations of 1965, perhaps indicating a small granary similar to those from earlier sites (see pp. 62 and 85) or some other structure of undetermined function.

Features

Features, all of which were located within the house described above, will not be described in detail since they are described in Ricklis' report, but included hearths, large post molds, and a small pit located under the bed lines near the south wall of the structure.

Artifacts

Material remains recovered from this site in recent years generally were those discarded by generations of earlier collectors. Numerous potsherds remain, and occasional artifacts apparently overlooked in years gone by were recovered as well. A brief description of some of the material from this site follows.

I have briefly examined the collection Ricklis made at this site discussed in his 1963 article. While the pottery is of the same monotonous styles as most late Iroquois assemblages, several outstanding features are apparent. The first of these, as determined by Ricklis' modification of MacNeish's typology, is its similarity to that from the Temperance House site. This suggests, as Ricklis has already mentioned, that the two sites were contemporaneous, a conclusion with which I completely agree. By way of illustration, the relative percentages of the pottery types are shown on Table 15. These figures seem to confirm the contemporaneity of the two sites, the other alternative being that they were occupied consecutively during a period in which ceramic styles underwent no change, a very unlikely situation. Interestingly enough, the figures also suggest a slight temporal priority of the Temperance House site, a suggestion reinforced by the recent discovery of a few scraps of trade goods at the apparently slightly later Atwell site (see below).

TABLE 15. CERAMIC TYPE PERCENTAGES FROM THE ATWELL AND TEMPERANCE HOUSE SITES (AFTER RICKLIS 1963)

Type	Atwell %	Temperance House %
Onondaga triangular	54.6	60.3
Wagoner incised	17.5	15.9
Ontario horizontal	5.5	6.5
Roebuck low collar	1.3	0.8
Lawson incised	1.9	0.8
Otstungo notched	3.3	6.3
Collarless rim with notched lip	3.9	3.2
Rice diagonal	6.5	5.5
Fonda incised	1.9	1.6

Also of interest in Ricklis' ceramic sample from this site is the presence of seven human-face effigies, three vertical clay ridges similar to those from Temperance House, and a single lug handle. In Stanford Gibson's collection are three sherds from the Atwell site which are in all respects *identical* to stamped low collar sherds from the St. Lawrence Valley.

Both trumpet pipes and that form which Ricklis has called "barrel bowl" are present at the Atwell site with the latter outnumbering the former. Also known from this site is a human-face effigy pipe (Ricklis 1966).

Sixteen projectile points were found by Ricklis at the Atwell site—fifteen are straight-sided triangles, and one is a lanceolate point. All, however, are thin and finely made, similar in most respects to those from Temperance House and Barnes. Points average 2.76 cm. long, 1.80 cm. wide, and have an average length-width ratio of 1.53 to 1, very close to that from Temperance House. Also recovered from these middens were five scrapers and a small chert drill.

Ricklis reports hammer/anvil stones and several small flat pebbles with scratches on them. While visiting the site with him, we discovered a large biconcave mortar and another stone of similar proportions with a mortar concavity on one side and several ground grooves, perhaps used for rubbing arrowshafts, on the reverse. Celts made of a crystalline rock similar to that from other earlier sites are reported as are imperforate stone gaming discs made from shale and sandstone.

Individual specimens will not be described here as it is sufficient to say that the bone inventory from this site, as recovered by recent excavators and as listed in Beauchamp (1920a) who wrote before the collections were broken up, is nearly identical to that described previously from the Barnes site with the addition of the bone comb, one of which is in Stanford Gibson's collection.

Three pieces of metal, all apparently of European origin, have recently been found at this site by Theodore Whitney of the Chenango Chapter of the New York State Archaeological Association. Gibson, who was also present when these specimens were found, described them as a rolled copper bead, a copper pendant, and an unidentifiable fragment of iron, all typical of the earliest European contact.

Chronology

The chronology of this site has been suggested repeatedly above and will be merely summarized here. Settlement pattern, including location, house type, and defensive structure, is nearly identical to that at Temperance House with the only exception that this site is considerably smaller. This fact—with the pottery and other material remains—points to contemporaneity of the two sites, a conclusion which requires little further documentation. In attempting an absolute date for this site, the first scraps of trade goods in an otherwise prehistoric context suggest very strongly the latter part of the sixteenth century.

SUMMARY

Although the data become increasingly scarce as we approach the historic period—both as a result of our limited excavations on Garoga phase sites and the years of looting on later Onondaga sites—we are still able to follow the Onondaga through the Garoga phase. Changes in "material culture" continue to be of a gradual nature and admit of no profound outside influence as might be expected if, for instance, the Jefferson County Iroquois had moved *en masse* to Onondaga (see pp. 205–207 for further discussion). Ceramics quality may decrease, collar height continues to increase, opposed lines become more popular, vessel bodies are all smoothed, projectile points reach their zenith and begin to decline, perhaps as brass arrowpoints become available.

Settlements are located on high promontories, are heavily palisaded, and give ample evidence of continuing warfare. Houses are smaller, perhaps as a result of some change in the social order, but the two-village pattern persists with the Burke community moving to Nursery-Barnes- and the Temperance House Fort, and the Bloody Hill-Keough-Christopher site community moving to the Cemetery, McNab, and Atwell Fort sites (see pp. 208–19 for further discussion).

Finally, in the middens of the Temperance House site we find the first traces of things to come—scraps of brass brought to the New World by Europeans whose presence in Onondaga is increasingly in evidence during the hundred and fifty years of the Onondaga protohistoric and historic periods described in the next chapter.

CHAPTER 6

The Onondaga, 1600-1795

THIS CHAPTER contains descriptions of Onondaga towns occupied during the protohistoric and historic periods. The former is defined by the presence of European trade goods without actual face to face contact with Europeans while the latter—the historic period—is marked by the first visit of white men to Onondaga.

A few relatively intact collections from six protohistoric stations exist, the site locations are precisely known, and from these data we are able to make some fairly accurate suggestions about the chronological placement and community affiliations of the Chase, Quirk, Dwyer, Sheldon, Pompey Center, and Carley sites.

The dawn of history in Onondaga properly begins on August 5, 1654,° when Father Simon LeMoyne entered the Onondaga capital "singing the ambassador's song and receiving addresses of welcome" (Beauchamp 1905:201). He stayed only about two weeks, but the following year Fathers Dablon and Chaumont returned to Onondaga and on November 17, 1655, built a bark chapel within the confines of the Onondaga town (JR 42:125), naming it St. Jean Baptiste. The following year Fort Ste. Marie de Gannentaa was constructed on the shores of Onondaga Lake (Beauchamp 1905:206–207), but in March, 1658, the French were forced to flee this outpost in fear for their lives.

There is little description of the Onondaga town of the 1650s, though references (JR 42:137; 44:169) to the entrance to the village imply a for-

---

°A possible earlier, less peaceful visit to Onondaga by Champlain and a party of hostile Hurons and Algonkians in 1615 is not considered here because no Onondaga town fitting Champlain's fanciful description has yet been discovered. The Nichol's Pond site in Madison County, supposedly the scene of this battle, dates from the Chance phase, obviously too early to have witnessed Champlain's battle with the Iroquois.

tified settlement. The bark-covered houses were also mentioned, and a large cabin had been prepared for the Jesuits. A fire destroyed some cabins in 1654 during LeMoyne's first visit.

Somewhat later (1677) Onondaga was visited by Wentworth Greenhalgh, who described the town in some detail and mentioned a smaller village south of the main settlement (see pp. 177–78). Finally, a few years later we have a description of the removal of this village (see pp. 3–4) to the capital attacked by Frontenac in 1696. This can be identified with considerable certainty as the Pen site (pp. 188–89).

With this brief background let us now examine the archaeological and documentary evidence from the several protohistoric and historically known Onondaga settlements; then a brief summary of these data will attempt to follow the trail begun in the Chance phase throughout the historic period to the Onondaga Reservation period beginning in the late eighteenth century.

The Chase Site

The Chase site is located about four miles south of the Atwell site (see Figure 1) on a large promontory between two ravines. Parker stated that most of the "lodges" were near the north end, a fact which corroborates Ricklis' observation that the two northern acres of the four-acre site are most productive of camp refuse (Ricklis 1966). Parker also mentioned post molds in a shallow trench which apparently pertained to a defensive stockade. These two facts constituting our entire knowledge of building at this site. Material from the site apparently includes primarily native goods with a scattering of European material. Parker (1922:646) mentioned recent relics, and Ricklis discovered there a tubular brass bead, two iron tools (one an adze blade, the other unidentifiable), and a scrap of sheet copper, which compose 12 percent of all nonpottery artifacts found by him at this site. Native material includes chipped stone points, scrapers, and an ovate knife; a polished stone celt; eight hammerstones; bone awls; two unidentifiable pipe fragments; and ceramics including five human-figure effigies and two vertical raised bars. The percentages of pottery rimsherds, expressed in terms of types rather than attributes, which would require completely reanalyzing Ricklis' collection, are listed on Table 16.

All of the material suggests a chronological position only slightly later than the Atwell and Temperance sites, a fact which was also concluded by Ricklis, particularly on the basis of the decrease in the per-

TABLE 16. CERAMIC TYPES FROM THE CHASE SITE (AFTER RICKLIS 1966)

Type	Percentage
Onondaga triangular	40.5
Wagoner incised	28.9
Ontario horizontal	7.0
Roebuck low collar	3.9
Lawson incised	3.1
Otstungo notched	3.1
Collarless rim with notched lip	3.9
Rice diagonal	9.4

centage of Onondaga triangular ceramics and the corresponding increase in Wagoner incised. Translated into collar motif attributes this can be seen as another step away from the use of older style horizontal lines beneath the lip on collared vessels. Also of considerable importance in assessing the chronological position of this site are the pottery full-figure effigies, the increased frequency of European goods, and the location of this site south of the earlier Atwell and Temperance House sites in a series of village removals which drifted from north to south. That this site is very early in the protohistoric period is suggested by the relatively high percentage of native goods retained by its inhabitants, especially the stone celt and hammerstones which were among the first items to be replaced by European goods. A guess date for this site places it in the late sixteenth or very early seventeenth century.

THE QUIRK SITE

This site is located nearly three miles southwest of the Atwell site (see Figure 1) along the edge of a ravine on a high loaf-shaped hill. Ricklis (1966) computed the area of the village at about two and a half acres. No settlement data, other than location and approximate size, are available as the only controlled excavations carried out at this site were concentrated on a midden area along the steep southern slope.

Material from the site, while not great enough in quantity to provide the basis for any very sound conclusions, nevertheless offers some suggestions about relative chronological position. Trade goods, including three rolled-brass beads and an iron fragment, constitute 16 percent of the non-ceramic artifacts. Native material includes two points and a like number of scrapers, four bone awls, a perforated elk tooth, deer phalanx, and a probable wolf canine, three celts, three hammerstones, and two small unidentifiable smoking pipe fragments. Types and percentages of ceramics, of which only thirty-six sherds are identifiable, are listed on Table 17.

TABLE 17. Ceramic types from the Quirk Site (after Ricklis 1966)

Type	Percentage
Onondaga triangular	52.6
Wagoner incised	27.7
Ontario horizontal	2.7
Roebuck low collar	0
Lawson incised	5.5
Collarless rim with notched lip	2.7
Rice diagonal	5.5

Despite the small sample of material from this site, all indications point to an occupation very close in time to that at the Chase site (see above), in the late sixteenth or very early seventeenth century, a conclusion Ricklis (1966) reached from his excavations and subsequent analyses.

THE DWYER SITE

This site is located in the Town of Fabius and is sometimes known as the "Fabius Fort." It is the southernmost Onondaga town in a series of village removals which by the beginning of the contact period was beginning to assume a northward direction, reversing a previous trend of north to south resettlements along the Limestone Creek Valley. Little is known of the site itself, and the only collection I examined from there was that made several years ago by Robert Hill of Rochester, New York, who permitted me to study and photograph this material and that from several other sites to be described later.

From a grave associated with this site came a large copper or brass knife, perforated near one end and retaining a portion of a thong passing through this hole. The thong was preserved by contact with copper salts. Also in contact with this artifact, hence preserved, are fragments of bark which have been identified as that of the white oak. A copper tube about six inches long and a quarter-inch in diameter also accompanied the skeleton as did a series of discoidal shell beads, both white and purple, which averaged about a quarter-inch in diameter and $\frac{1}{16}$ inch thick. Owing to the acidity of the soil only the tooth crowns remained from the human skeleton.

From the surface of the village area Robert Hill recovered two spirals made from a fine brass or copper tube, some native-made white wampum beads, several barrel-shaped rolled-copper beads, and three triangular projectile points.

The location and relative abundance of early European artifacts place this site within the protohistoric period and most likely in the very early stages of this time, probably slightly later than the Quirk and Chase sites described above.

THE SHELDON FORT SITE

This site is located about midway between the Chase and Quirk sites, about one mile from each (see Figure 1). It occupies what Parker (1922:645) calls the "most commanding situation of any [site] in the county," being on the top of a bluff nearly three hundred feet high with a precipitous drop on the north, sloping abruptly on the east and south, and having the remains of a "depression" (ditch ?) to the west. As described by Parker, the site could have covered over three acres. Undoubtedly drawing on Beauchamp's earlier works, Parker described the occupation as a long one, with recent relics, probably dating about 1630, a conclusion by no means certain, but it will have to suffice until further collections are made or older ones rediscovered.

THE POMPEY CENTER SITE

This well-known village was the only Onondaga site in central New York which MacNeish (1952:56–59) was able to include in his study of Iroquois ceramics, and this from only fifty-three sherds collected years before. He identified it as historic Onondaga and apparently agreed with Beauchamp's date of about 1640.

The site lies about one and one-half miles northwest of the Sheldon site and about half that distance from the Quirk site. Its location seems in line with an apparent northward swing of village removals in the protohistoric period.

Settlement data consist of a record of an oblong stockade enclosing two acres (Parker 1922:644), situated on a triangular rise of land which slopes sharply toward Limestone Creek on the west and drops away more gradually on the remaining sides. Today the site is covered with a thick meadow which permits almost no surface collecting. The hillside dumps remain, especially on the wooded west bank, but they have been so intensively dug over that nothing save discarded animal bone remains.

Parker (1922:644) mentioned European but no French material from the site, and Beauchamp (1902b) illustrated triangular brass points, an iron awl, and an iron spearpoint from the site. Native materials were also rather abundant at this site, though all that remains are the few sherds described by MacNeish, and these have, by now, probably also disappeared. The sherds consisted of about 70 percent collared vessels with horizontal lines above opposed or oblique lines, about 20 percent lacking these horizontal lines. Also present are small percentages of Ontario horizontal, Lawson incised, Roebuck low collar, Thurston horizontal, and, surprisingly, Chance incised pottery types (MacNeish 1952:58). This sample is somewhat suspect, both because of its small size and because the presence of Chance phase sherds casts some doubt on its identification as belonging to the Pompey Center site. Nevertheless, the sample does serve to indicate that there was still a fair percentage of native goods being used at the time of occupation of this site. Parker (1922:644) mentioned that no "council wampum" was present but that shell beads had been found there.

Dates of occupation have been suggested above (around 1640) based upon material remains described by Beauchamp, Parker, and MacNeish. The geographical position of the Pompey Center site north of earlier sites and in line with a general pattern of south to north village removals agrees with these previous estimates of a mid-seventeenth-century occupation.

THE CARLEY SITE

In a previous description of the Carley site (Tuck n.d.:338) the village was described as being located "on a long loaf of land" some distance from the cemetery which apparently pertains to this component. Since that writing the site location has been discussed with Robert Hill, and the collection which he made there some years ago has been studied. Hill reports that the village site is located not on the hill where it was previously thought to have been but in a fairly level field at the junction of Brown's Gulf Road and Hennaberry Road. This puts the town at pre-cisely the same spot as the graves mentioned by Parker (1922:642), and Hill's investigations disclosed that the burials seemed to be located im-mediately outside what must have been the village limits. The village it-self Hill reports, covers a considerable expanse of ground, but the pre-cise area is incalculable as the site is cut by the two roads mentioned above. The village area is marked by soil that is not very heavily stained, suggesting but a brief occupation. Within this stained soil nu-merous trade beads were found, including blue melon beads with black and white stripes, many thin tubular beads, and several chert arrow-points.

From the burials, most of which were dug over years before Hill's ex-cavations took place, were recovered a number of artifacts typical of the protohistoric Onondaga. These include primarily trade beads which were apparently overlooked by earlier collectors. The varieties re-covered consist of a few star beads, melon beads of two-color combinations—blue with black and white stripes and red with white, blue, and white stripes—many red and white tubular beads, faceted yellow beads and a similar form colored green, and seed beads in great profusion, both green and white with blue and red stripes. Other ma-terial recovered from the burials includes tubular beads made from the columella of a whelk or conch shell, a probable beaver effigy in marine shell, conical and triangular brass arrowpoints, several pieces of lead shot which appear to be between .50 and .60 caliber, and four complete smoking pipes, all of native manufacture, of the following varie-ties: two rimless trumpet pipes, one square-bowl trumpet pipe, and an animal-effigy pipe, somewhat damaged, which makes identification of the species depicted uncertain.

Chronology is not precisely indicated by the material remains but they do serve to indicate an occupation in the mid-seventeenth century —a conclusion which is supported by the location of the site in a gen-eral south to north series of village removals. For the precise community affiliations and chronology of the Carley site, see pp. 203, 217.

THE INDIAN HILL SITE

This site is generally regarded as the first Onondaga site to be visited by Europeans, with the possible exception of Champlain's raid on some ethe-real Onondaga or Oneida village in 1615. The best description of the site is provided by Wentworth Greenhalgh, who visited two Onondaga towns in 1677. He described them as follows: "The Onondagoes have butt one towne, butt it is very large; consisting of about 140 houses, nott fenced; it is situate upon a hill thatt is very large, the banke on each side extending itself att least two miles, all cleared land, whereon the corne is planted. They have likewise a small village about two miles beyond thatt, consisting of about 24 houses. They ly to the southward of ye west, about 36 miles from the Onyades. The Onondagoes are said to be about 350 fighting men. They ly about 15 miles from Tshiroqui [Oneida Lake]" (O'Callaghan 1849:11).

Since he apparently approached from Oneida Lake, to the north, the larger of the two sites would appear to be to the north of the smaller, as is the case of the Indian Hill and Indian Castle sites (see Figure 1). The site is also reputed to have been the location of the first Catholic mass said in New York State, and a marker placed there by the Knights of Columbus commemorates that event, though this fact will be called into question later (see p. 217). The site is today maintained as a historic monument by the Onondaga County Parks Commission.

Settlement Data

Since no controlled excavations have ever been conducted at this site, most settlement data are of a general nature and must be taken from old sources. The site does occupy the top of a high north-south oriented hill which could easily have accommodated a town the size of that described by Greenhalgh. On the east and west the land drops quite sharply to a small stream and to the West Branch of Limestone Creek, respectively. The site lies about three and one-half miles north of the Pompey Center site, slightly over two miles northeast of the Carley site, and half as far from Indian Castle.

There is considerable confusion as to whether or not this site was fortified. Greenhalgh stated that it was "nott fenced," but Clark (1849) recorded that settlers arriving there in 1791–93 found a circular earthwork some three hundred to three hundred fifty feet in diameter atop Indian Hill, having one narrow gateway, a fact which was related to Clark by settlers who had actually seen the earthwork. Parker (1922:642) mentioned that the French, who had visited what is generally supposed to have been this site in 1654, described palisades and gates, the latter at least implied on the *Jesuit Relations* (see *JR* 42:137; 44:169; 54:23), if in fact the earliest records do refer to the Indian Hill site. From these data, it seems safe to assume that the site was fortified with a palisade and earthwork, at least in the early period of its occupancy, with

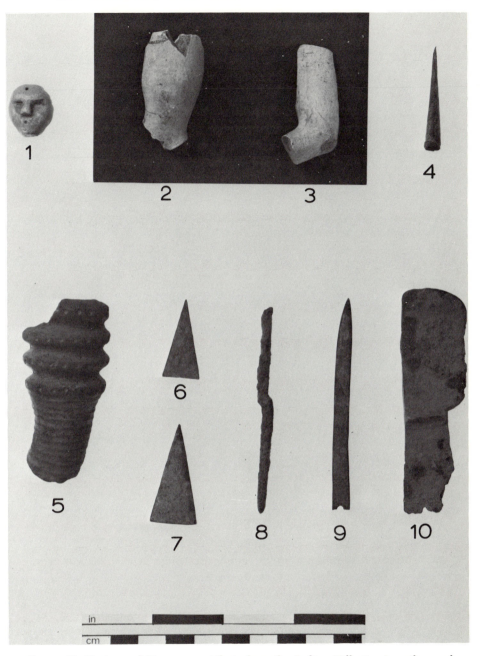

PLATE 40. Native and European artifacts from the Indian Hill site. 1, antler mask-ette; 2 and 3, kaolin trade pipes; 4, conical brass arrowpoint; 5, native-made ring-bowl pipe; 6 and 7, triangular brass arrowpoints; 8, iron awl; 9, brass weaving nee-dle; 10, iron crooked knife.

PLATE 41. Two views of a wooden bowl and ladle from the Indian Hill site, from the collection of Robert Hill.

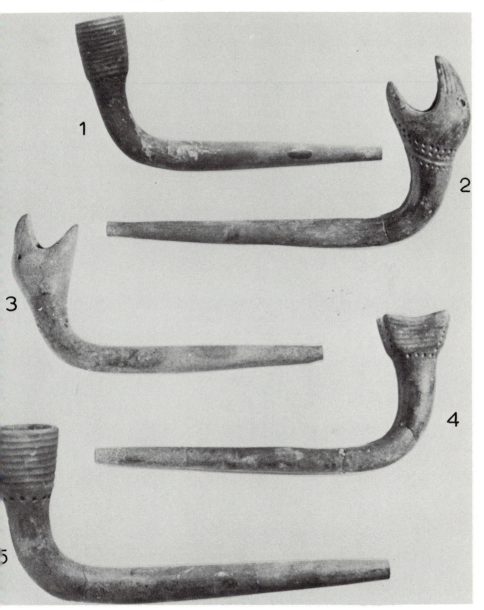

PLATE 42. Smoking pipes from the Indian Hill site, from the collection of Robert Hill. 1 and 5, ring-bowl pipes; 2 and 3, effigy forms; 4, square-bowl pipe.

the wooden palisade perhaps having been removed or fallen into disrepair by the time of Greenhalgh's visit in 1677. Since the Onondaga
moved about four years after Greenhalgh's visit, this seems at least a
remote possibility.

We have nothing better than Greenhalgh's description of the village
to provide data on house types. His mention of 140 houses indicates
that the typical longhouse had been supplanted by smaller dwellings, a
suggestion which fits nicely with the French practice of referring to Iroquois dwellings of this time as *cabanes* which translates as *cabin* but
certainly is difficult to construe as longhouse or any similar structure.
This, with the archaeological record (see the Temperance House and
Atwell sites), indicates a trend toward smaller houses during the late
prehistoric period.

Burials

Burial data from Indian Hill are scanty, but there are early reports
of graves being excavated north and east of the site (Clark 1849), and
Robert Hill reports locating and excavating several graves in what must
have been the same general area. Little information on burial position,
orientation, or precise associations of grave goods, was recovered, but
presumably the interments were in an extended position and the dead
were liberally accoutred with mortuary offerings. From the few graves,
most of which had previously been looted, excavated by Hill, a wooden
bowl and ladle (Plate 41) were recovered, a brass jewel (?) box filled
with vermillion, an iron fire striker, seven ring-bowl pipes, a square
trumpet pipe, and two probable crow effigy pipes (Plate 42), as well as
numerous beads, a whetstone, wood rasp, gun flints, and rings, all typical of those described briefly below.

Artifacts

Material from the Indian Hill site is scattered throughout nearly
every collection of Indian relics in central New York and in many
collections in other parts of the state. Clark (1849) mentioned the early
settlers finding, among other things, "gun barrels, sword blades, hatchets, knives, axes, clay pipes, copper kettles, brass chains, beads of glass,
pewter plates, rings for the fingers and ears, and nose jewels, lead balls,
iron gate hangings, copper coins, tools used for working wood and iron,
and other articles used by civilized men and unknown to savages." He
also reported a brass medal of Louis XIV, found in the year 1821. Beauchamp (1900) and Parker (1922) also described "recent relics" from the
Indian Hill site.

Syracuse University retains a small but well documented collection from this site which will be described briefly here as representing Onondaga "material culture" in the mid- to late-seventeenth century, as well as providing some corroboration for the placement of this site in that time period.

Native material is far outweighed by European trade goods at this site, the only artifacts of Indian origin being a few potsherds, smoking-pipe fragments, some points and knives of chipped stone, and beads and other items of personal adornment, all of which are described below.

About two dozen rimsherds are included in the collection at Syracuse University. Of these, three are everted, notched lip types, while the remainder are collared vessels decorated with bands of opposed lines, often beneath a band of horizontal lines. This site apparently represents the scene of the last native-made Onondaga pottery before earthenware was completely supplanted by European brass kettles.

Native-made pipes, which long outlasted cooking pots before finally being replaced by European kaolin pipes, are fairly numerous in the Indian Hill sample, though most specimens are extremely fragmented. All specimens have the gracefully curved stem characteristic of late Iroquois pipes, and bowl forms include a rimless trumpet, a bowl with three parallel horizontal, raised clay ridges, and a bird effigy in addition to those from the Hill collection mentioned above. Most other fragments apparently pertain to similar forms but are so small as to preclude definite identification.

Projectile points of native manufacture are very scarce from this site, having been almost completely replaced by points cut from sheet brass. Those specimens present are generally small (about 2 cm. by 1 cm.), with straight sides and a straight or slightly concave base. All are relatively thin and well-made, usually of locally available Onondaga chert. Other chipped-stone tools from Indian Hill include a small, round scraper made on a flake, steeply retouched along most of one edge, and a small Brewerton corner-notched point which may have been picked up as a hunting charm.

No rough or polished stone implements are in the Syracuse University collection from Indian Hill as these were apparently among the first tools to be replaced by iron counterparts. Parker (1922:642), however, mentioned a grooved boulder from the site which was used as a whetstone, probably to sharpen iron tools.

A single, small splinter awl, two slightly smoothed deer antler tines, and a small antler maskette (see Plate 40, no. 1) compose the entire collection of worked bone from Indian Hill, though numerous unmodified canines of both bear and other smaller carnivores are also present.

Shell beads and pendants were apparently very popular at this time. Shell was worked extensively, doubtless with the aid of European tools, into a variety of forms including white and purple wampum, small, two-holed crescents, and imitation claws or canine teeth—all forms characteristic of the Dann and Marsh sites, Seneca villages of the 1650–75 period (Wray and Schoff 1953:58).

Items of European manufacture comprise the bulk of the material recovered from the Indian Hill site. Except for objects which might indicate the time and duration of occupation of the site, they will be described only briefly.

No brass kettles from this site are in the Syracuse University collection, but they are in evidence in the form of pieces of flattened brass cut from them and are further suggested by the presence of numerous small brass patches, drilled for riveting, which are very often found on intact brass kettles recovered from Iroquois graves.

Many bowl and stem fragments of white kaolin pipes have been picked up at the Indian Hill site, several of which have a small bowl, somewhat constricted near the mouth, which is typical of the mid-seventeenth century. The only identifiable marks are of the "EB" variety which, while not especially diagnostic, are mentioned by Wray and Schoff (1953:58) as being common on the Dann and Marsh sites. Two examples are illustrated on Plate 40, Nos. 2 and 3.

Twelve triangular brass points, copies of these formerly made of stone (see Plate 40, nos. 6 and 7), and a single conical point of the same material (Plate 40 no. 4) comprise the projectile point sample from Indian Hill. This site seems to represent the last use of stone points in central New York as none to my knowledge were found in the graves excavated at the next-occupied Jamesville Pen or Weston sites.

Cutting and perforating tools are common on most historic Iroquois sites, and the Indian Hill site is no exception. Knives include seven specimens, five of which are too fragmentary to identify. The two remaining specimens are good examples of a "sheepsfoot" knife and a short crooked knife (Plate 40, no. 10). Four awls are in the Syracuse University collection from this site, two of which (one round and one square) are of brass and two of iron. Both iron specimens are square in cross section, and one has a tang which is offset at the middle (Plate 40, no. 8). A large, square, flat-headed nail may also have served as a perforating tool. Finally, the remains of a small pair of iron scissors were also found at the Indian Hill site.

One interesting spatulate weaving tool fragment was found here, a copy in brass of earlier bone forms known from the Barnes site, the Kelso site, and many other prehistoric Iroquois sites. This tool is flat in cross section and sharply pointed at one end with the other end broken but bearing evidence of a perforation (Plate 40, no. 9).

That the Iroquois or someone living at the Indian Hill site were familiar with firearms is indicated by the numerous unused lead balls ranging in diameter from 1.0 cm. to 1.6 cm., a small ball of about #0 buckshot size, the brass ferrule from the forearm of a musket, and a possible decorative sideplate (opposite the lock) from an early pistol.

Two barbed iron fishhooks, one complete, were also found at Indian Hill. The intact specimen has the top of the shaft flattened, rather than eyed, for attaching the line.

Tubular rolled brass beads and conical bangles are in fair abundance from this site. Both forms, however, are quite common throughout much of the historic period and are not especially diagnostic of any short time span.

Glass beads from the Indian Hill site are very numerous, and those in the Syracuse University collection are typical of the mid- to late-seventeenth century. Most common are tubular varieties, in red or occasionally blue or black, and round red beads about the size of a pea. These round red beads are the most common variety from this site in Hill's collection. Less common are older polychrome forms and occasional variations in color of more recent forms. These forms are all common on mid- and late-seventeenth-century Seneca sites (Wray and Schoff 1953).

Jesuit influence on the "material culture" of these people is not as strongly represented in this small sample as might be expected, but there is a small ring showing what seems to be a man kneeling before a crucifix, and a medal with a male holding a child on one side and the bust of another male on the reverse. Unfortunately, the legends on both sides are indecipherable.

Other trade goods from this site include a small brass hinge, ornately wrought, a small brass object which resembles some sort of seal, a large iron key, and an iron ring of unknown function about 2.5 cm. in diameter.

Gordon DeAngelo has called my attention to the following items which indicate something about the date of occupation of the Indian Hill site, all from Beauchamp's (1902b) *Metallic Ornaments of the New York Indians:* a 1656 French laird, once perforated; another 1656

French laird, twice perforated; and a 1640 French coin, which DeAngelo identified as a double tournois, and which Beauchamp inferred also came from Indian Hill.

Chronology

All material remains and the position of the Indian Hill site in the south to north movement of Onondaga villages during the late seventeenth century point to an occupation during the latter half of that century. Clearly the site was abandoned in 1682 in favor of the Pen site village somewhat northwest of Indian Hill. Father Lamberville has left us with a description of this process (*JR* 62:55–57). Lamberville also mentioned that this village was occupied for nineteen years before this resettlement, a statement which is not in accordance with the generally accepted concept that Indian Hill was the scene of the first French visit to Onondaga, since LeMoyne's visit took place in the mid-1650s or about eight years before Indian Hill was occupied. It seems likely, therefore, that one of the villages immediately preceding in time that at Indian Hill was in fact the scene of these historical events.

THE INDIAN CASTLE SITE

This small site occupies the edge of a steep ravine on the opposite side of Limestone Creek from the Indian Hill site and about one mile south of it. Greenhalgh's reference to the site, "a small village . . . consisting of about 24 houses," was quoted at length at the beginning of the description of the Indian Hill site.

Settlement Data

Both the scatter of refuse over the field today and Greenhalgh's description agree in indicating a small site. To the east the ravine provides an excellent measure of defense, while the western part of the site must have been palisaded to provide any protection, though no evidence, historical or archaeological, suggests the presence of any such structure.

The twenty-four houses referred to by Greenhalgh suggest that small bark-covered cabins had replaced the longhouse at this site as well as Indian Hill.

Burials

Several burials were excavated in the 1950s by Robert Hill of Rochester, New York, who kindly allowed me to study the material recovered at that time and supplied the data presented below. The graves were located immediately outside what must have been the limits of the village on a low rise, a practice in keeping with that described for the Carley and Indian Hill sites. Although most of the graves Hill excavated had been anciently looted (one as early as the first half of the nineteenth century, as indicated by the presence of an 1824 U.S. large cent in the refilled grave), many objects of significance were recovered. The burials were apparently extended as indicated by the dimensions of the grave fossae and were equipped with the material described below.

Artifacts

Joshua Clark (1849) described beads, gun barrels, bullets, knives, a brass kettle, and other "trinkets" found at this site, in addition to such atypical and presumably misrepresented material as axes, gouges, arrowheads, pestles, and hatchets of stone—all of which may either be misidentified as to source or, less likely, may represent an earlier occupation at Indian Castle. Fortunately, Hill's excavations, described briefly above, produced the material described here, all of which refers to an occupation in the latter half of the seventeenth century. Glass beads, in order of descending frequency, include tubular red, tubular blue, tubular black and white, tubular black, tubular twisted red, tubular twisted blue, round red with a clear center, round blue, and tubular white. Several shell crescents with two perforations, the head of a duck or swan in shell, several sizes of wampum with large and small perforations, both white and purple; a large rectangular strip of marine shell; many marginella shell beads; and a beautiful owl-effigy pipe with inset brass eyes, one of which is now missing, complete the inventory of artifacts gleaned by Hill from the dug-over graves.

Chronology

Historical data, location, and most material remains combine to indicate an occupation coeval with that at Indian Hill. One bit of contradictory evidence was mentioned by Clark, however, in the presence of a medal of William, Prince of Orange, which he dated at 1689, but which has long since disappeared. One other interesting note concerning the chronology of this site was also provided by Clark. In 1815 a tree cut from the village area was found to have a large chain embedded near its heart which was covered by 178 annual rings. This is taken to indicate an occupation around 1637, and is probably the first use of dendrochronology in New York State.

The Jamesville Pen Site

This site is located southeast of the village of Jamesville in the same field as the Keough site (see Figure 1). It has long been known to local historians and collectors of Indian relics as the site of Frontenac's attack on the Onondaga in 1696, and there is no reason to doubt the authenticity of this conclusion. Indeed, there is considerable evidence to support it. Excavations have been conducted by Mrs. Ethel Fine in the late 1950s, then a graduate student at Syracuse University, and by Peter Pratt, who in 1961 and 1962 excavated an extensive cemetery pertaining to the site and more recently made test excavations within the village area. Unfortunately little of this material has been described in print; Mrs. Fine's work was an M.A. thesis on file at Syracuse University, and Pratt's report has thus far been confined to a paper read at the annual meeting of the Northeastern Anthropological Association at Ithaca, New York, in 1963, and subsequently distributed in mimeograph form.

Settlement Data

The site is situated on a fairly high hill with gently sloping sides. It is about four miles northwest of the Indian Hill site. As Pratt has a detailed description of this site in preparation, it will suffice here to mention a few outstanding features. Early records speak of the site as being surrounded by a nearly square palisade with a bastion in one corner (Parker 1922:641–42), and Pratt (1963) noted that these are still visible, on certain occasions, from the air. What these houses were like is not certain, but there is no reason to think that they were any different from the small cabins which Greenhalgh saw at the Indian Hill site.

Artifacts

From the village area and from the cemetery excavated by Pratt has come the most complete representation of late seventeenth-century material from any Onondaga site, and probably from any Iroquois site. Included in this remarkable inventory are brass kettles, wooden ladles, iron axes, adzes, knives and other tools, firearms and parts of all descriptions, scissors, pipes—both native and kaolin (the native pipes being the only surviving example of Indian ceramic work)—bone combs, and beads by the thousands, to mention but a small part of the artifact inventory.

Chronology

All material and historical data combine to indicate an occupation in the late seventeenth century. Further documentation places the exact dates of occupation between 1682, when Father Lamberville recorded that the Onondaga were moving their village "two leagues distance from their former residence where they had dwelt 19 years" (Beauchamp 1905:102), to at least 1696 when they were forced to leave by Frontenac. They subsequently burned the town, though there is good evidence suggesting that the town was reoccupied during the first two decades of the eighteenth century. This site will not be described further because the material presented here is sufficient to indicate its relative chronological position as well as its absolute dates of occupation.

The Weston Site

This station has suffered from the same type of confusion in designation as did the Cemetery site. It has been known as the Western site, the Bloody Hill II site, and the Oley site. Claude Doxtator, now of Waterloo, New York, who today retains a well catalogued collection from the site, refers to it as the Weston site, after a former owner. Doxtator's collection, made in the late 1920s, and data supplied by him provide the basis for the description which follows.

Settlement Data

The site is located on a rise of land slightly south of the Bloody Hill site and, judging by a thin scatter of refuse over that area, may have encompassed as much as three acres. No defensive structures are mentioned, and no excavations have been made which might have revealed either these or other structures. The sole sample consists of the material recovered by Doxtator which is described below.

Burials

The burials found at the Bloody Hill site (see pp. 114–15) undoubtedly pertain to this village, and a series of burials excavated in 1965 and 1966 at the Jamesville Lake site, to the west of the Weston site are probably also related to this station. The data and material recovered at this site can be duplicated many times over by material from the Pen site indicating a contemporaneous chronological position for the two sites. The glass beads, marine-shell ornaments, rings, religious medals, kettles,

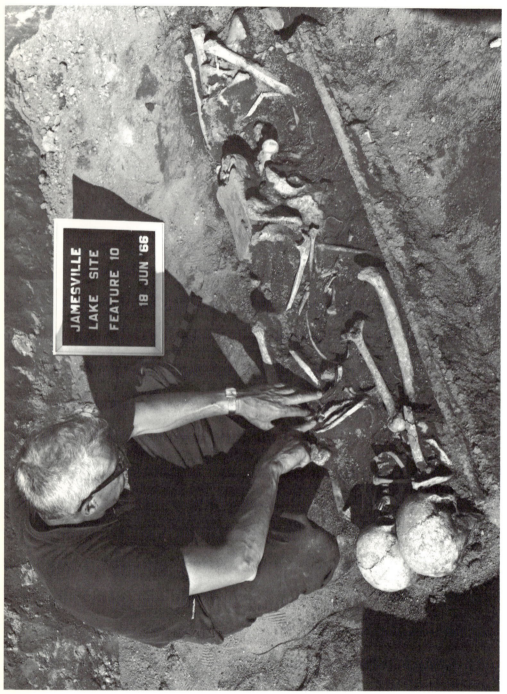

PLATE 43. Excavation of a double reburial at the late sixteenth century Jamesville Lake site. Note the fragmental...

knives, and a late seventeenth-century flintlock musket all present a picture of a people clearly dependent upon European trade for most of their material possessions.

Artifacts

Trade beads constitute the major category of artifacts recovered from this site, and the excellent cataloging of Doxtator's collection allowed a nearly complete summarization of the varieties present. They are listed on Table 18. Other material retained by Doxtator includes catlinite beads in various forms, tubular shell beads, shell crescents and runtees,

TABLE 18. Trade Bead Varieties from the Weston Site

Variety	Frequency	Percentage
round red, pea-size	624	44
round black, pea-size	520	37
seed beads, blue with		
a few white, blue, black	130	9
tubular red	107	8
other	41	2
	1,422	100

discoidal shell beads, triangular brass arrowpoints, several Jesuit rings, a gun spall a large kaolin pipe bowl of European manufacture, and fragments of six native-made pipe bowls: a ring bowl, two bird effigies, a bear effigy, and a human-face effigy.

Chronology

All of the material described above suggests a chronological placement in the late seventeenth century, probably coeval with the larger Pen site. Unfortunately, no firm basis for comparison is yet available, and this conclusion is based upon only an impression gained from a brief inspection of a small portion of the Pen site material.

The Post-1700 Onondaga

The location of the eighteenth-century settlements of the Onondaga from the beginning of that century until the reservation period which began in 1795 is somewhat confusing and may never be completely resolved archaeologically. The records of the Moravian visitors to the area, John Bartram's journal of his visit, and the scant archaeological remains recovered before the area was covered by the growth of the city of Syracuse may be brought together to reconstruct a reasonable picture of the eighteenth-century Onondaga.

The most enigmatic fact supposedly pertaining to an Onondaga village of this period was reported in the Syracuse *Post-Standard*, January 6, 1935. This possible Onondaga village was reported to have been discovered by Stanley Gifford of Syracuse, New York, in an undisclosed area south of the city. Gifford referred to the site as "hitherto unknown" with Dutch, French and English trade goods, and a sixty-year life span which he placed from 1720 to 1780. He mentioned finding "crude pottery [from a previous occupation?], gun parts, the ruins of a smithy," a Jesuit ring, hundreds of bottles which he thought were Dutch in origin, ocean shells, large quantities of catlinite, a little wampum, and a large number of poorly formed flint arrowheads.

This material does not seem to constitute a single eighteenth-century component because it includes such anachronisms as pottery, stone points, and Dutch bottles which are usually confined to much earlier Onondaga components. Further, it is mystifying that the visitors to Onondaga during the time when this site was supposedly occupied did not mention it, though they visited several other Onondaga villages which can be pinpointed with considerable certainty from the archaeological remains and the historic records. It is possible that the village discovered by Gifford was actually the site of Toyadasso, discussed below, though current evidence does not confirm it. Perhaps some day this site will be rediscovered and will provide us with settlement data and artifacts from the early eighteenth-century Onondaga.

Three settlements are described by the mid-eighteenth century visitors to Onondaga—Upper and Lower Onondaga, which were located along the banks of Onondaga Creek, and the village of Toyadasso, which was some distance from the other two settlements. Toyadasso is mentioned by several early travelers, notably the Moravian missionaries to the Onondaga and slightly earlier by John Bartram. David Zeisberger visited "Tue-tah-das-o" in 1745 (Beauchamp 1916:23–24). In 1750, Frederick Cammerhoff and Zeisberger visited a town which Cammerhoff spelled "Tiachton," and Zeisberger mentioned visiting this village again in the mid-1750s, this time spelling the name "Tiojatasche." Despite the varied spellings and vagueness about the precise location of the village, Beauchamp identified this town with the remains located on the Coye farm in the town of Lafayette. Probably this information was gleaned from the writings of Joshua Clark, who noted that John Wilcox, the first settler in the area, spent his nights in the Onondaga castle some three miles distant from his homestead which was located on the site of "Toyadasso." Mr. Wilcox trimmed and pruned the trees which had been abandoned by the Indians when the village (as well as Upper and Lower Onondaga) were destroyed by a force under Colonel Van Schaick in April, 1779 (Clark 1849:241–82; Beauchamp 1905:362–63).

The site apparently occupied a low rise immediately behind the house and outbuildings now comprising the Coye farm not far from where the small Oak Hill phase village described previously was apparently located. From the surface of the site we recovered pieces of heavily oxidized bottle glass, other old, clear glass fragments, scrap brass, unidentified iron fragments, and a honey-colored gun flint, all of which probably pertain to an eighteenth-century occupation. Other collectors have reported finding various items of European manufacture at this site, including glass trade beads in some quantity.

Upper and Lower Onondaga are practically unknown archaeologically, but the records of early European visitors leave little doubt that they were two ends of a settlement which stretched some two or three miles along the banks of Onondaga Creek beneath what is now a residential section known as "Valley Oaks" in the city of Syracuse. Occasionally, construction in the area reveals traces of these former occupations, and William Ennis, of Brewerton, New York, has preserved a typical collection of the mid-eighteenth century which he recovered after one of these accidental discoveries.

The earliest visit to this Onondaga town was in 1743 by John Bartram (1751:42), who described it in this manner: "The town in its present state is about 2 or 3 miles long, yet the scattered cabins on both sides of the water are not above 40 in number; many of them hold 2 families, but all stand single, and rarely above 4 or 5 near one another, so that the whole town is a strange mixture of cabins, interspersed with great patches of high grass, bushes and shrubs some of pease, corn, and squashes."

In 1750, Cammerhoff and Zeisberger counted five clusters of cabins along the creek in addition to occasional scattered huts (Beauchamp 1916:60). At that time Conrad Weiser reported that but one house remained east of the creek, all others by then having moved to the west bank (Beauchamp 1905:294). A few years later Zeisberger and Gottfried Rundt found that the community had polarized somewhat, and they re-

ferred to the two ends of the village as Upper and Lower Onondaga (Beauchamp 1916:124). Throughout this time the population at Onondaga was apparently dwindling for various reasons, especially the Iroquois' involvement in the American Revolution, and in 1793 Zeisberger's Onondaga friends reported to him that only twelve or thirteen families remained at Onondaga, the rest being at Buffalo (Beauchamp 1905:376).

By the treaty between the United States and the Iroquois of January 21, 1795, the Onondaga and other nations were guaranteed their several reservations in central New York. Previous and subsequent land sales by the tribe have reduced greatly their holdings and left them with a small reservation. Little trace remains of these earliest days on the reservation, but a few log buildings (see Plate 44) which doubtless date to at least the early part of the nineteenth century can be seen today.

SUMMARY

Despite the lack of archaeological evidence from the proto- and historic periods, especially after Frontenac's raid of 1696, we are still able to follow the trail of the two villages which became the Onondaga Nation during the Chance phase. The smaller community which was last seen at the Atwell site subsequently underwent a series of village removals evidenced by the Quirk, Dwyer, Pompey Center, Indian Castle, Weston, and Toyadasso (Coye) sites, while the larger Temperance House community successively occupied the Chase, Sheldon, Carley, Indian Hill, Jamesville Pen, and Valley Oaks sites. From Toyadasso and Valley Oaks it was but a short step to the Onondaga Reservation to which many Onondaga returned after the raids resulting from the American Revolution practically depopulated central New York of its Indian inhabitants during the 1780s and 1790s.

CHAPTER 7

Comparisons and Conclusions

In the preceding site descriptions the cultural continuities throughout the Owasco through the historic Iroquois continuum have been repeatedly emphasized. In this chapter we shall briefly review the evidence for an *in situ* development. Summaries are provided of chronological evidence for a continuous series of archaeological components in central New York between the thirteenth and nineteenth centuries, and of the cultural continuities which indicate that these components are the remains of a proto-Iroquois population. Following this, evidence for a migration to Onondaga from Jefferson County or the St. Lawrence Valley will be examined in the light of our findings in Onondaga. Next a reconstruction of Onondaga culture history since the late Owasco period is briefly recounted. Included also are suggestions about some of the social and political forces and events which characterized the formative years of Iroquois culture, especially as revealed by the settlement approach. Other implications of social change, indicated by the development of microtraditions, are also discussed.

Finally the Onondaga and the Five Nations are briefly compared with other peoples—both Iroquoian and Algonkian speaking—and some brief suggestions are made about the course of the Late Woodland period of cultural development throughout the Northeast.

Chronology

Chronological observations are traditionally classed as absolute or relative. The former are measured in calendar years, and in this case are supplied either through radiocarbon determinations or historical records. The latter are based upon comparisons of material remains from various sites and are occasionally augmented by inferences made from the locations of the sites themselves with respect to one another. In the following discussion the absolute dates for sites at both ends of our series are examined, and then an attempt is made to fill the intervening gaps with undated sites based upon the comparisons of material remains and site locations.

Absolute Chronology

Seven radiocarbon determinations from our own investigations and one obtained from the Kelso site by the New York State Museum and Science Service provide the basis for an absolute chronology. The circumstances surrounding the recovery of these samples, and their cultural associations, are all discussed in the preceding site descriptions and need not be repeated here. The dates, however, assembled here for the first time, are as follows: the Chamberlin site (late Owasco) A.D. 1290, plus or minus sixty years; the Furnace Brook site (early Oak Hill phase) A.D. 1300, plus or minus sixty years and A.D. 1370, plus or minus sixty years; the Howlett Hill site (late Oak Hill phase) A.D. 1380, plus or minus sixty years; the Kelso site (late Oak Hill phase) A.D. 1390, plus or minus one hundred years; the Schoff site (early Chance phase) A.D. 1410, plus or minus eighty years; the Bloody Hill site (early Chance phase) A.D. 1420, plus or minus eighty years; and the Burke site (late Chance phase) A.D. 1480, plus or minus eighty years. These determinations, all mutually consistent, indicate beyond the smallest doubt that the transitional Owasco-Iroquois phase, the Oak Hill phase, lasted, in central New York, for very close to one hundred years, between A.D. 1300 and 1400, and further indicate a similar temporal span of one hundred years for the succeeding Chance phase, which apparently flourished between A.D. 1400 and about 1500.

At the upper end of the sequence, historic records indicate that the protohistoric period came to a close in the 1650s when the French Jesuits visited Onondaga, staying for a time at either Indian Hill or some slightly earlier village. Reasonable approximations, also made from the historic record, date the following sites thus: Indian Hill 1663 (?) until 1682; the Indian Castle site (apparently coexistent with Indian Hill) occupied until about 1682; the Jamesville Pen site (burned by Frontenac in 1696) from 1682 until after 1700, perhaps as late as 1720; the Coye site (Toyadasso, a small village) from the early 1700s until 1779 when it was burned by Colonel Van Schaick; the Valley Oaks area (Upper and Lower Onondaga) prior to 1743 until the late eighteenth century; and the reservation period from 1795 to the present.

Relative Chronology

Using the radiocarbon dates and the dates mentioned above from the historic record as anchor dates, it is possible, through a careful consideration of material remains augmented by knowledge of trends in settlement removals and the relation of specific sites to these trends, to construct a reasonably accurate chronological sequence which fills the gap between 1480, our latest radiocarbon date, and the middle seventeenth century, when historic accounts of Onondaga began. Ceramics, smoking pipes, and projectile points were the only classes of artifacts which provided sufficient samples to allow any statistical treatment of the data, and even this was not the case from more than a few sites. By utilizing as much of the available data as seems reliable, some suggestions are possible as to the relative chronological positions of almost all the sites described previously. These suggestions are presented below with the warning that the observations are only as reliable as the material from the various sites allows. Some revision may become necessary should further scientific investigations be carried out on some of the components which are poorly represented in our collections.

Ceramics

To provide a measure of the relative positions of the sites which produced samples of sufficient size to allow statistical treatment the following procedure was followed. First, coefficients of correlation ° were drawn up for each pair of sites for each attribute class (Brainerd 1951). Only those attribute classes with a frequency greater than ten were considered in this procedure. The resulting coefficients of correlation were then averaged providing a rough, but, I think, accurate measure of the temporal relationships among these various sites. A matrix of the various coefficients of correlation is shown in Table 19, suggesting the following

° A coefficient of correlation is a simple statistic designed to test the degree of relatedness between two sets of data. It is derived as follows: (1) the attribute or type percentages from two components are aligned so that attributes of the same class— e.g., rim profile or collar decoration—are next to one another; (2) the difference in percentage for each pair of attributes is then determined, regardless of whether it is positive or negative; (3) these differences are then summed; (4) the sum is subtracted from 200, the total attribute percentage from the two sites. This figure is the coefficient of correlation. The higher the figure the greater the degree of consistency between the two samples; hence a figure of 200 would indicate no difference between any attribute pair or identical samples. The converse is true for a low coefficient of correlation.

chronological ordering of the sites from earliest to latest: (1) Chamberlin, (2) Cabin, (3) Furnace Brook, (4) Howlett Hill, (5) Kelso, (6) Schoff, (7) Bloody Hill, (8) Keough, (9) Burke, (10) Cemetery, (11) Barnes. This matrix is not without discrepancies, especially in the case of the Barnes site, which, as was mentioned previously, may not have provided a representative sample.

Since we are able to understand the stylistic trends practiced by the Onondaga potters and reflected in their products during the period

TABLE 19. Average Coefficients of Correlation
Based on Ceramic Attributes

	Chamberlin	Cabin	Furnace Brook	Howlett Hill	Kelso	Schoff	Bloody Hill	Keough	Burke	Cemetery	Barnes
Chamberlin	x	147	138	135	133	73	73	55	32	11	13
Cabin		x	159	154	146	87	88	82	57	42	41
Furnace Brook			x	158	149	99	93	96	62	58	62
Howlett Hill				x	152	103	98	102	72	59	60
Kelso					x	90	81	91	60	50	59
Schoff						x	144	139	124	109	120
Bloody Hill							x	148	129	109	113
Keough								x	117	99	117
Burke									x	142	134
Cemetery										x	159
Barnes											x

under consideration, we are able to make some suggestions about the chronological placement of various sites which were not included within our attribute analysis. Proceeding from earliest to most recent the following conclusions are suggested by the ceramic remains:

(1) the Coye II site, represented in our collections by two rim sherds —one of the channeled low collar profile and one of the Chance straight profile—both decorated with horizontal cord-wrapped paddle impressions, seems to fall into the late Oak Hill phase, at the end of the fourteenth century where we find ceramics of this type most common (the Howlett Hill site, for example);

(2) the Crego site, on the Seneca River near Baldwinsville, New

York, has produced material in no way different from the Schoff and Bloody Hill sites and hence can safely be attributed to the Chance phase and probably to an early part of that phase;

(3) the Christopher site has numerous ceramic characteristics which are in accordance with a middle to late fifteenth-century date. These include collar motifs consisting of horizontal over opposed lines in four-fifths of the rim sherds examined, a characteristic much more common in late Chance phase and Garoga phase assemblages than in earlier manifestations; 85 percent incised decorations, in contrast to lesser percentages at earlier sites and again much more common in later assemblages; and plain and decorated collar bases in about equal numbers which suggests a chronological position in the same Chance/Garoga phase. All these characteristics suggest a placement in time very close to the Burke site, which has been radiocarbon dated at A.D. 1480;

(4) Nursery site ceramics seem typical of the early Garoga phase, consisting of high collared vessels decorated with opposed triangles beneath horizontal lines, frequently executed in broad incised lines;

(5) the smoothed body sherds from the McNab site suggest a late prehistoric position, but we must rely on its location in the Onondaga village removal sequence for a further suggestion of chronology;

(6) Atwell and Temperance House sites seem, on the basis of ceramic types and the human-face effigies found at them, to be about contemporaneous, with a slight temporal priority possibly going to the former;

(7) Chase and Quirk site ceramics, also analyzed on the basis of types, seem to present a situation analogous to Temperance and Atwell. They appear to be about contemporaneous and slightly later than Temperance and Atwell on the strength of the presence of typological changes as well as the five full-figure human effigies not found in earlier assemblages.

After the Chase and Quirk sites, ceramics become almost worthless in appraising the relative chronological positions of Onondaga villages, primarily because adequate samples are not available by reason of the general decline in production of ceramics at this time and the fact that these sites have been almost completely excavated by early settlers and collectors in Onondaga County. The fact that native-made ceramics are even present in the collections from the Dwyer, Pompey Center, Indian Castle, and Indian Hill sites, however, suggests their placement within the late protohistoric–early historic period. Systematic excavations at both the Carley site and the Sheldon site would probably be rewarded by the recovery of at least minute amounts of native ceramic material, but no such investigations have been carried out to date.

Smoking Pipes

This class of artifacts was treated in somewhat the same fashion as were ceramics, at least to the point of constructing a similar matrix based upon coefficients of correlation using, however, the varieties described on pp. 239–43 as the basis for comparison. Only seven sites produced a sufficient smoking-pipe sample to allow this treatment, which is reproduced in Table 20.

TABLE 20. Coefficients of Correlation between Pairs of Sites Based on Smoking Pipe Varieties

	Cabin	Furnace Brook	Kelso	Howlett Hill	Bloody Hill	Burke	Barnes
Cabin	x	103	82	44	15	24	36
Furnace Brook		x	132	87	x	13	38
Kelso			x	55	0	0	0
Howlett Hill				x	27	0	0
Bloody Hill					x	112	53
Burke						x	72
Barnes							x

Table 20's matrix suggests the following chronological ordering of the sites represented: (1) Cabin, (2) Furnace Brook, (3) Kelso, (4) Howlett Hill, (5) Bloody Hill, (6) Burke, and (7) Barnes, again from oldest to most recent. This agrees essentially with the ordering based upon ceramics, with the exception of the reversal of the Howlett Hill and Kelso sites.

As in the case of ceramics, the pipes from sites not included in the analysis above also offer some suggestions as to their relative chronological positions. They are:

(1) Coye II site squared pipe stem hints at a relatively early placement, perhaps in the late Oak Hill phase, as this variety of stem is somewhat more common in early sites than in later ones;

(2) Schoff site, with a decorated trumpet and another trumpet variety represented by a stem fragment, apparently falls within the early Chance phase;

(3) Cemetery site pipes, four trumpets (at least two plain), and two

square bowl pipes, suggest a chronological placement after the Burke site, probably in the early Garoga phase;

(4) the Nursery site has produced three slender pipe stems, one of which retains the graceful bend of a trumpet form which suggests a relatively late prehistoric settlement, probably also in the early Garoga phase;

(5) Atwell site's several trumpet pipes and a human-face effigy suggest a relatively late date but still within the prehistoric period;

(6) the Carley site has produced a pair of rimless trumpet pipes, a square bowl trumpet pipe, and an animal effigy pipe, all of which suggest that this station postdates any of the components so far mentioned;

(7) Indian Hill site, from which Robert Hill recovered the series of ringbowl and effigy pipes and the single square bowl pipe, seems to fall later in time than does the Carley site; and

(8) the five pipes from the Weston site (described on p. 19) do not clearly indicate its temporal position, but they seem to correspond to many forms from the Jamesville Pen site, though this is only an impression as the Pen site material has not been examined in detail.

In essence, our chronology arrived at by a study of Onondaga pipes bears out almost completely earlier suggestions about the temporal placement of most components.

Chipped Stone

The only artifact class in this category present in sufficient numbers to allow any suggestions about chronology to be based upon it is projectile points. A trend toward longer and narrower varieties seems to have taken place during the course of Onondaga prehistory, with the reverse being true during the historic period. In Table 21 the average lengths, widths, and length/width ratios are compared for sites which have produced projectile points.

Trade Goods

Items of European manufacture suggest the following relative chronological positions within the protohistoric and historic periods of Onondaga culture:

(1) Atwell Fort has temporal priority over all other protohistoric sites for at that station has been found the lowest frequency of European material consisting of a few scraps of copper and iron;

(2) Chase and Quirk sites seem about contemporaneous, as the percentages of non-pottery artifacts of European manufacture are 12 and 16 percent, respectively;

TABLE 21. Average Lengths, Widths, and Length/Width Ratios for Projectile Points from Onondaga Sites

Site	Length	Width	l-w ratio
Cabin	3.48 cm.	2.20 cm.	1.58 to 1
Furnace Brook	3.44 cm.	2.29 cm.	1.50 to 1
Kelso	3.27 cm.	2.24 cm.	1.46 to 1
Howlett Hill	3.23 cm.	2.33 cm.	1.39 to 1
Schoff	3.53 cm.	2.07 cm.	1.71 to 1
Bloody Hill	3.37 cm.	2.09 cm.	1.61 to 1
Burke	3.72 cm.	2.07 cm.	1.80 to 1
Cemetery	3.34 cm.	1.76 cm.	1.90 to 1
Nursery	3.79 cm.	1.78 cm.	2.13 to 1
Barnes	4.13 cm.	1.91 cm.	2.15 to 1
Temperance House	2.89 cm.	1.74 cm.	1.65 to 1
Atwell	2.76 cm.	1.80 cm.	1.53 to 1
Chase	2.27 cm.	2.04 cm.	1.11 to 1

(3) the Sheldon and Dwyer sites are something of unknown quantities, though both appear to have at one time produced considerable European material which Parker and Beauchamp have called "recent";

(4) the Pompey Center site is apparently late protohistoric as indicated by the relatively high frequency of trade goods, though it apparently still retains a fair percentage of native material;

(5) the Carley site seems to be very near in time to Pompey Center on the basis of bead varieties and other European artifacts;

(6) finally, the Weston site is clearly later than any of these sites including Indian Hill and Indian Castle and is probably a contemporary of the Pen site burned by Frontenac in 1696.

These suggestions of relative chronological position, together with the radiocarbon-derived chronology presented earlier, allow the sites described above to be placed with considerable confidence into the following periods:

Castle Creek Owasco—Chamberlin and Cabin sites
Early Oak Hill Phase—Furnace Brook and Kelso sites
Late Oak Hill Phase—Howlett Hill and Coye II sites
Early Chance Phase—Schoff, Bloody Hill, Keough, and Crego sites
Late Chance Phase—Burke and Christopher sites
Early Garoga Phase—Cemetery and Nursery sites
Middle Garoga Phase—Barnes and McNab sites
Late Garoga Phase—Atwell and Temperance House Fort sites
Early Protohistoric—Chase, Quirk, Dwyer, and Sheldon sites

Late Protohistoric—Pompey Center and Carley sites
Historic Onondaga—Indian Castle, Indian Hill, Pen, Weston, Coye (Toyadasso), and Valley Oaks (Upper and Lower Onondaga) sites.

This outline is intended merely to provide a framework upon which to base further discussion of Onondaga cultural development; it is not meant to imply that each of these sites was occupied consecutively by a single community. It does demonstrate clearly that there was an Indian population in residence in what ultimately became Onondaga during the Owasco period and that there are no major gaps or drastic population increases in the sequence which would indicate any major migrations to Onondaga since the thirteenth century. This fact alone is not sufficient to indicate that the residents of the Cabin site, for instance, were proto-Onondaga, but the following discussion adds considerably to this hypothesis for it summarizes some of the cultural continuities, both "material" and "non-material," throughout the sequence.

Owasco and Iroquois—Continuity and Change

By way of illustration, the following cultural continuities between Owasco and Iroquois culture indicate beyond the slightest doubt that Onondaga Iroquois culture was, in fact, the result of a long *in situ* development in central New York.

Villages of both cultures were almost always located away from major waterways, and were often situated upon defensible hilltops frequently defended by earthen or wooden structures as well. From Owasco to Iroquois we see a gradual transition in house construction from small round houses to larger houses which are the prototypes of later Iroquois longhouses. Artifact types also clearly demonstrate cultural correspondences between Owasco and Iroquois cultures far too numerous to be functions of chance, indicating, rather, a direct relationship between the two cultures. Owasco ceramics foreshadow Iroquois vessels in nearly all attributes as a glance at the summaries throughout the preceeding chapters reveals. Rim profiles, for example, clearly show an evolution from uncollared Owasco profiles to late Iroquois collared and everted lip types. Decorative motifs on the interior, interior lip edge, lip, exterior lip edge, collar, and collar base similarly show gradual evolutionary changes from Owasco to Iroquois forms. Decorative techniques of Iroquois potters are likewise foreshadowed in Owasco

times with the appearance of incising, the primary Iroquois design technique, as early as the middle Owasco period when it is frequently found
upon vessel necks. After this point it increases in favor at the expense of
cord-wrapped paddle impressions, the principal Owasco decorative
technique which nonetheless persisted well into the Iroquois period.

Smoking pipes in use among the Owasco culture inhabitants of central New York also display a gradual evolution into Iroquois forms.
Early vasiform pipes with flaring lips seem, through a series of gradual
changes, to evolve into Iroquois trumpet pipes of several varieties. Also
such typical Owasco pipe forms referred to as barrel bowl, corn ear, and
conical pipes are frequently found on early Iroquois sites.

Chipped stone, rough and ground stone, and bone artifacts all demonstrate local evolutions and persistences similar to those mentioned
above.

"Non-material" aspects of Iroquois culture also apparently have their
roots in the Owasco period and include, for example, the same or nearly
identical mixed hunting, gathering, and farming economies (see the very
similar percentages of food remains in the site descriptions); the same or
similar patterns of communal living as suggested by similar house types;
the human-face motif which is found in both cultures and which suggests, perhaps, the rudiments of a masking complex such as is so well-
known among the historic Iroquois; and bear ceremonialism from Kelso
and cannibalism, a possibly related form of ceremonialism, which suggest still another link between the two cultures.

These examples, in addition to the details provided previously by
this writer and others, should lay to rest the notion that the Iroquois
were relatively recent migrants into the Northeast and that they dis-
placed a resident Algonkian population, often thought to be represented
archaeologically by what is now known as the Owasco culture as defined by Ritchie.

The Onondaga and the St. Lawrence Iroquois

Before beginning a reconstruction of Iroquois culture history in central
New York, a few words should be said about the St. Lawrence Iroquois
and their relation, if any, to the Onondaga. We have seen that there is
an essentially unbroken line of artifactual remains in central New York
from at least the middle of the thirteenth century to the present day.
Moreover, these remains reflect a single developing cultural tradition. If,
therefore, the St. Lawrence Iroquois migrated to the Onondaga area

sometime in the sixteenth century, it follows that there should be some
evidence of this movement .in the "material culture" of the Onondaga.

The theory of a northern origin of the Onondaga holds that they
originated near the present-day city of Montreal, moved first to Jefferson
County, New York, and finally occupied central New York. The Jefferson County step can be easily eliminated, as there seem to be no sites
there which have produced any European material—which the Hochelagans, for instance, must have had after Cartier visited them in 1534.
Furthermore, the artifact assemblages of the Jefferson County Iroquois
do not resemble those of the Onondaga, or proto-Onondaga. Some characteristics of these northern people which certainly would have been
brought with them had they moved to central New York include the
following: ° pottery with relatively low collars decorated with several
motifs including crossed lines, two rows of opposed triangles separated
by horizontal lines, and "underlined" decorations which have one or two
horizontal lines lowermost on the collar—all of which are commonly executed in dentate stamping, linear stamping, and apparently, in early
examples, with a cord-wrapped paddle; chipped-stone inventories practically lacking stone projectile points; a bone industry as elaborate as
that of the Onondaga but containing bone points, toggle type worked
deer phalanges, and other forms not characteristic of Onondaga, as is
the case with all the other characteristics described above. It seems
clear, therefore, that the Jefferson County Iroquois did not influence the
development of Onondaga "material culture" to any great extent, if at
all.

The St. Lawrence Iroquois, to whom the Jefferson County people
were much more closely related than to the Onondaga, present a similar artifact complex, also quite unrelated to Onondaga. I have examined material unearthed in the St. Lawrence by Colonel James F.
Pendergast, by the Societé Archeologiè Prehistorique du Quebec, and,
briefly, the collection made at Hochelaga by Dawson in the 1860s.
Traits characteristic of this area, and not typical of the Onondaga include stamped low collar pottery decorated with oblique lines; corn ear
pottery with vertical raised corn ears on the collar; underlined ceramic
motifs; hollow reed punctations forming, among other motifs, stylized
human faces; dentate stamped decoration; pipes not unlike some Onon-

---

° Based on material supplied by Merrill C. Waters of Watertown, New York, Mrs.
Marjorie Berger, a graduate student at Syracuse University engaged in research in
Jefferson County, and my own observations of collections at Syracuse University
made in Jefferson County, New York.

daga examples but many with relatively high bowls and numerous steatite examples, neither of which are known from our studies; again a very
low proportion of chipped-stone points; many toggle-type deer phalanges and discoidal steatite beads. This inventory is similar to that from
Jefferson County and suggests that the people living in these two areas
of the St. Lawrence Valley participated in roughly the same Iroquoian
tradition—a tradition, however, that was markedly different from that
developing in central New York at the same time.

Despite this general lack of similarity between the St. Lawrence Iroquois and the Onondaga, on all but the most general Iroquoian level,
the St. Lawrence Iroquois have long been accepted as the ancestors of
the Onondaga, an assumption now shown to be unwarranted. There is,
however, some evidence of St. Lawrence Iroquois culture in late prehistoric Onondaga assemblages including a few sherds of stamped low collar pottery from the Atwell site which are identical with those from the
Salem site and other St. Lawrence Iroquois manifestations. The sporadic
nature of the appearance of their sherds on the prehistoric-protohistoric
border very strongly suggests the presence of a few people from the
North among the late sixteenth-century Onondaga, probably refugees
from disease or disaster in the St. Lawrence Valley, perhaps occasioned
by the arrival there of the Europeans. These factors may very well have
caused the dispersal of the St. Lawrence Iroquois to many parts of Iroquoia, including Onondaga. Some have suggested a wholesale village
movement, perhaps to Onondaga, in a manner recorded during historic
times, but no evidence of the adoption of a historic foreign village by
the Onondaga has yet been found. The Hicks Road School and Mountain View sites come to mind, but both seem too early to relate to the
Iroquois who were presumably fleeing the Europeans in the St. Lawrence, and neither has produced a typical St. Lawrence Iroquois assemblage. At least for the time being, the evidence from Onondaga indicates
a dispersion of the Hochelagans and other nearby peoples to many parts
of Iroquoia with no appreciable effect on the development of the Onondaga nation.

Reconstruction of Onondaga Culture History

Since all indications from our evidence point to a long *in situ*
development of Onondaga culture in central New York, with no influx of
people from elsewhere in the northeast, it now remains to elucidate
some of the trends and events which characterized Onondaga culture

history, especially during its prehistoric phases. The following discussion is based on the hypothesis that by studying the changes in size and composition of these Onondaga villages and their dispersal over the landscape—revealed by a study of the settlements, dwellings comprising them, and the artifacts found there—we will be able to understand and reconstruct some of the "non-material" aspects of Onondaga culture, especially the development of their well-known political and social systems.

Looking at Figure 1, it is at once apparent that there are three distinct geographically isolated groups of sites. The first is about ten miles west of the city of Syracuse and consists of the Chamberlin and Kelso sites. The second group is some ten to twelve miles east of the first, lies partly within the boundaries of Syracuse, and consists of the Cabin, Furnace Brook, Howlett Hill, and Schoff sites. The third, and by far the largest, group of sites is located east of Syracuse in the Pompey Hills and includes the Coye II, Bloody Hill, Keough, Burke, Christopher, Cemetery, Nursery, Barnes, McNab, Atwell, and Temperance House sites as well as the villages and towns occupied by the proto- and early historic Onondaga. Still another group of sites—the little-known Crego, Indian Spring, and Hicks Road School sites—lies north of the first group on the banks of the Seneca River.

It is obvious that all of these sites were not occupied by the same community as such a situation would have been the result of a series of frequent village removals and resettlements over an area of hundreds of square miles. The most reasonable alternative to a single community is that each of these groups of sites represents the village removals and resettlements of a single small community occupying a restricted geographic area which it probably considered its own. The people who lived at Chamberlin and Kelso, therefore, probably regarded as their territory that area around the present town of Elbridge, New York. A similar situation no doubt prevailed among the community which produced the Cabin, Furnace Brook, Howlett Hill, and Schoff sites, that which left its remains at Coye II, Bloody Hill, and Keough, and presumably at the community which lived at Crego and Indian Spring, near Baldwinsville, New York. The later Chance phase and pre- and protohistoric Onondaga towns are not included in this tentative list of sites occupied by these several communities and their relation to the earlier villages will be discussed later.

Although geographical separation offers the first clue to the presence of several different communities in central New York during the developmental stages of Iroquois culture, other clues suggest that distinctive microtraditions were developing in each of these communities, all of which were participating in the same developing Iroquois tradition. Near Elbridge, at the Chamberlin and Kelso sites, large numbers of chipped-stone discs were found, including several from Chamberlin despite the small size of the sample, and thirty-five nearly intact specimens from the Kelso site. Also distinctive of the artifact assemblage of these people is the high percentage of vessels which were decorated with cord-wrapped paddle impressions on the necks. At the Chamberlin site over 96 percent of the decorated neck sherds were decorated in this fashion, while the Kelso site produced 92 percent of similarly decorated neck sherds. Another probably distinctive characteristic of the ceramics of the Kelso people is the high percentage (70 percent) of smoothed-over check-stamped body sherds, a trait which is not characteristic of fourteenth-century sites in other parts of central New York.

Deviations from the general emerging pattern of Iroquois development are also found among the assemblages of data and material recovered from the Cabin, Furnace Brook, Howlett Hill, and Schoff sites, in that chronological order. Characteristics unique to this community include an almost total absence of chipped-stone discs, represented by only a few questionable specimens from these stations. There is a relatively high percentage of incised vessel necks, consistent within assemblages from these sites and in marked contrast to the percentages of incised neck sherds from the Chamberlin and Kelso sites, including 46 percent from the Cabin site, over 58 percent from Furnace Brook, 63 percent from Howlett Hill, and probably, had the sample been sufficiently large, a similar percentage from the Schoff site. Also, check-stamped body surface treatment persisted through the beginning of the Chance phase, in contrast to the Kelso community where smoothed-over check stamping was predominant by the end of the Oak Hill phase. A final characteristic of the people who left their remains in the Onondaga Hill area is the construction of longhouses which far exceed in dimension anything else discovered in central New York or elsewhere. These houses, measuring 210 feet at Furnace Brook, 334 feet at Howlett Hill, and 400 feet at Schoff, are much longer than houses from any other area of Iroquoia.

Little can be said of the microcultural traditions of the community which lived at Coye II, and presumably at Bloody Hill and Keough as well, for the former site is almost unknown and the latter two date from the early Chance phase at which time, as I plan to discuss more fully

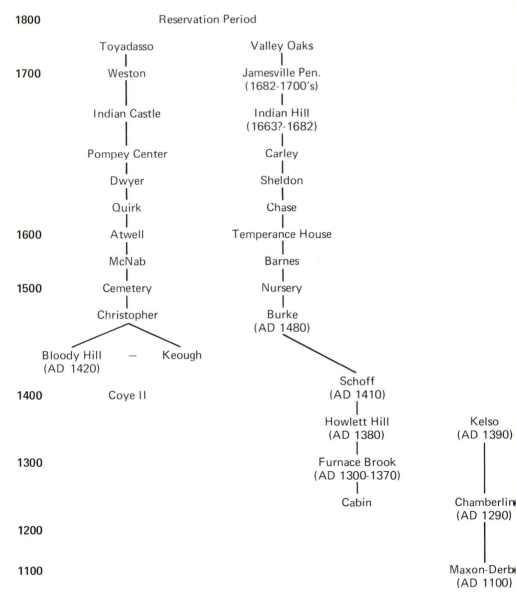

Figure 8. Chronological sequence of Onondaga villages showing suggested community affiliations.

later, some "mixing" of several of these traditions was beginning to take place. The high percentages of collars decorated with fingernail impressions, often combined with triangular punctations, and similarly decorated vessel necks in contrast to the incised or corded decorations of the other two communities, hints at a distinctive tradition among the occupants of these sites. One characteristic of the Bloody Hill site, and perhaps the Keough and Coye II sites as well, which distinguishes them from the two other communities is their relatively small size—for instance about one-half acre at Bloody Hill—which is in marked contrast to the sites of upwards of two acres at Kelso, Furnace Brook, and Howlett Hill.

The community which left its remains on the banks of the Seneca River (the Crego and Indian Spring sites) is so little known from the archaeological record that nothing can be said of the culture of the people other than the fact that at least one site, Crego, is apparently coeval with other early Chance phase sites (Schoff, Keough, and Bloody Hill), suggesting still another distinct community.

Also, little can be said of the Hicks Road School site and the Mountain View sites except that the material from the former is certainly different from anything else in central New York. And the latter, while not certainly related to Hicks Road School, seems to represent a blending of late prehistoric Onondaga with some earlier or foreign tradition which included aberrant vessel forms and combined such unusual characteristics as cord-wrapped paddle impressions (an early trait) with broadly notched collar bases (a late trait) on the same sherd (see pp. 137–38).

Finally, radiocarbon determinations further suggest the presence of several coexistant communities in central New York. The dates from Furnace Brook (A.D. 1300 and 1370), Howlett Hill (A.D. 1380), and Schoff (A.D. 1410), are nearly paralleled by those from the Chamberlin site (A.D. 1290) and Kelso (A.D. 1390) which are cultural equivalents of the former series, as well as by the date from the Bloody Hill site (A.D. 1420) which is very similar to Schoff in most respects.

The data above—geographical isolation, differences in cultural traditions, and carbon-14 analyses—indicate quite clearly that there were at least three and most likely four communities coexisting in central New York between the later Owasco period, at least by A.D. 1250, and the middle of the Chance phase, presumably around A.D. 1450. The data also offer some further suggestions about the nature of these communities and their relations with their neighbors. Internal change is suggested by the presence of several areas of occupation at the Cabin site (see p.

35) and of an outlying concentration of refuse at the Chamberlin site (p. 29). This indicates that in the earliest times settlements were somewhat dispersed, though there probably was a large central village, perhaps fortified. The several successive additions to the village at Furnace Brook suggest a growth in the community larger than that expected from normal population increase, hinting at a possible coming together of these outlying households into a central, heavily fortified town. From this point (the early Oak Hill phase) onward, the villages or towns are invariably nucleated and usually heavily protected by wood and/or earthen fortifications.

Another, somewhat later and different, amalgamation of two small communities is suggested by our data from the series of sites east of the city of Syracuse. Two small sites, Bloody Hill and Keough, have artifact assemblages so similar that the two sites seem to have been occupied simultaneously. No radiocarbon determination is available for the Keogh site to bolster this hypothesis, but the similarities which may be observed by comparing the ceramic characteristics for the two sites as given on pp. 115–16 and 120 clearly indicate the basis for the following conclusion. If these two sites were not occupied simultaneously, it is hard to reconcile the fact that almost no change occurred between them in several rapidly changing facets of the ceramic complex, especially collar motif and technique, neck motif and technique, and body surface treatment, the categories providing the most reliable samples from the Keough site. While this must remain in the realm of speculation, it seems probable that a village merger between these two communities took place sometime in the mid-fifteenth century. Further evidence for this convergence involves the Christopher site, which seems to have been the next town to be inhabited by these combined communities. From limited observations of this site the following speculations can be made. First, the Christopher site seems too large to have been occupied by either the Keough or the Bloody Hill communities alone, though a long occupation is indicated by the amount of refuse which must once have covered the site. Considerable shifting of houses could conceivably have taken place. This, however, would have required the complete rebuilding of the stockade in a different position as well as leveling and perhaps clearing new lands immediately outside the old village where the rebuilding would have taken place, both of which suggest that it is better to build a new village either in precisely the same place (as was done at the Burke site) or to relocate completely, perhaps to a place which offered more defensive advantage than the ground upon which the Christopher site was built. Thus it seems that a fusion of the Keough and Bloody Hill communities is at least a distinct possibility, and is not, in some ways, unlike similar earlier centralizations which apparently took place at the Furnace Brook site and perhaps the Kelso site as well.

One of the reasons for these village convergences or mergers was almost certainly mutual defense. Iroquois legend and archaeology coincide in confirming that a period of internecine warfare existed before the formation of the League. Archaeologically this is indicated by the choice of village locations far from any navigable rivers and very often on hilltop locations which could be easily defended. Defenses were almost always bolstered by the construction of earthworks and palisades of poles and logs.

Finally, the discovery of a worked human skull fragment at the Kelso site and the remains of some cannibalistic ritual at Bloody Hill—both practices generally associated with Iroquois warfare—confirms these legends and other evidence. Other investigators have noted parallels in other parts of Iroquoia, including further evidence of cannibalism in the form of human bones, frequently burned, which appear in the middens of fortified villages or towns. Historic records refer frequently to torture and cannibalism among the Iroquois and clearly connect these practices with warfare (Tooker 1967:31–39, 90).

It was during this time of community convergence that such typically Iroquois institutions as medicine societies, the Eagle, Bear, Buffalo, and Little Water Societies, and the False Face Society (Parker 1913:113–30) might have assumed new importance as socially integrative institutions in the newly formed communities by cutting across traditional kin lines and establishing new patterns of interaction involving members of both smaller communities. Almost no material remains would be expected to indicate the formation or increased importance of these institutions, but it is a rather suggestive fact that human-face motifs, perhaps reflective of the False Face Society, proliferated greatly during and immediately after the Chance phase, only slightly later than many supposed village convergences must have taken place.

While these village mergers undoubtedly resulted in greater safety, they also created some problems in exploitation of the environment which must have occasioned some inconvenience in day-to-day living. For instance, the larger the village the more quickly firewood, local game supplies, and perhaps farmland would become exhausted. Longer and longer distances would have to be covered to procure firewood and other necessities, a factor which would result in more frequent village

removals, perhaps every twenty-five or so years, in comparison to some
earlier towns which were apparently occupied for a much longer time.
Furnace Brook, for instance, was probably occupied for a minimum of
seventy years. The occupation at Kelso may have been of a similar duration, though evidence indicates that the inhabitants left briefly, perhaps to allow the necessities to replenish themselves (Ritchie 1965:304).

For these reasons, the environment and Iroquois ability to exploit it
must have imposed a maximum limit on the size of a town and the number of inhabitants the area immediately surrounding a town could support. A set of conflicting alternatives presented themselves to the central
New York Iroquois during the Chance phase. These were the limited
community size which could be supported in a single village, on the one
hand, and the desire to further amalgamate, for mutual defense, on the
other hand. The solution to this dilemma seems to have been the formation of some sort of socio-political or symbolic alliance between two villages, at least in terms of defense, and perhaps in other respects as well.
Not coincidentally, there is evidence from Onondaga County to suggest
that this is exactly what did take place.

The strongest and most specific evidence for the formation, in prehistoric times, of a socio-political unit larger than the village community
among the central New York Onondaga comes in the form of data which
suggest very strongly that the community which occupied the Schoff and
earlier sites west of Syracuse moved, in the early or middle fifteenth century, to the Pompey Hills east of Syracuse and not far from the Bloody
Hill and Christopher sites. As mentioned above, these sites were occupied by a community distinct from that which lived at Schoff. Besides
the disappearance of the Schoff community from the Onondaga Hill
area, despite long and intensive efforts to locate more remains nearby,
and the appearance of the Burke site in the east at nearly the same
time, which seems to be more than coincidence, there are additional
similarities between the two stations which suggest that a single community occupied both. The size of each site is about two acres, and both
are located on very similar long, high, north-south drumlins. Most important, the community at Burke seems to have had the same tradition
for building very long dwellings as did the community which lived at
Schoff. At the Burke site we discovered a house of undetermined length,
but in excess of 240 feet, probably a continuation of the tradition of
building very long houses well established at the Furnace Brook, Howlett Hill, and Schoff sites. Another interesting and suggestive fact con-

cerning house construction at these sites is the continuation at the Burke site of a trend found at Howlett Hill and Schoff toward somewhat narrower dwellings. At Howlett Hill, House 1 measured twenty-three feet wide, at Schoff the house measured twenty-two feet wide, and at Burke the longest house segment uncovered was twenty-one feet wide. This trend apparently continues through time for excavations at the Atwell and Temperance House sites revealed houses measuring only eighteen feet wide.

Material remains also suggest that these two sites were actually occupied by the same community, though the sample from the Schoff site is far from satisfactory. Ceramics from Schoff have 87 percent plain necks, and Burke ceramics have 91 percent plain necks, both very high, especially when compared with the 65 percent plain neck sherds from Bloody Hill. Incised neck technique, which is the single ceramic trait most distinctive of the Cabin, Furnace Brook, Howlett Hill, and presumably Schoff assemblages, comprises 38 out of 95 decorated neck sherds from the Burke site, or 40 percent of the sample. Other nearby sites—Bloody Hill and Keough—have 9 and 0 percent incised neck sherds, respectively. Projectile points from Schoff present an average length-width ratio much more like those from Burke than do those from any other Chance phase site. Other, perhaps less reliable characteristics—such as the cooking pit near the end of the house at Schoff, the very similar cooking pit located in the same position relative to the longhouse at Burke, and the presence in the Schoff assemblage of a large celt made of a close-grained igneous rock nearly identical to those from later Onondaga sites (especially the Nursery and Barnes sites)—also hint at a connection between the communities which occupied these two sites. It must be pointed out, however, that the percentages of check-stamped and smoothed body sherds from the two sites vary greatly, as noted in individual site reports, but this may simply reflect a rapidly changing ceramic trait rather than any great difference in the tradition in which the occupants of the two sites were participating. In summary, then, the bulk of the evidence indicates that the Burke site was settled by the same community which had formerly dwelt some ten to twelve miles west of the Schoff and earlier sites.

Thus, in the early fifteenth century, a symbolic alliance between two communities was probably consummated for reasons of mutual defense. This can be interpreted as the founding of the Onondaga Nation, at least in an informal way. At what point a feeling of common identity or assumption of a common name came about cannot be said, but these things must not have been far behind the other developments indicated by the archaeological record.

Other communities may also have joined the Onondaga from time to time, either as entire units or by absorption into existing communities. It is also interesting to note, and again it is probably more than coincidence, that the area of central New York claimed by the Onondaga in historic times corresponds almost exactly with the combined territories apparently owned by each of the small comunities existing during the Oak Hill and earlier phases. This approximated the eastern and western boundaries of Onondaga County and extended from near the Pennsylvania state line to Lake Ontario and the St. Lawrence (see p. 1).

The two-village pattern which the evidence indicates was established in Onondaga by the mid-fifteenth century also characterized the Onondaga during the historic period. This is clearly indicated by Wentworth Greenhalgh's statement that there was a large town and a small village in existence in 1677 (see p. 178). These two villages, as suggested above, are almost certainly the Indian Hill and Indian Castle sites which may have been the first Onondaga towns visited by Europeans. This pattern persisted in time through the end of the seventeenth century at the large Jamesville Pen site and the smaller Weston site and into the eighteenth century at the Onondaga village along Onondaga Creek (Valley Oaks site) and the smaller village of Toyadasso, identified as the Coye site.

With this pattern of two Onondaga villages clearly established by the historic record after the mid-seventeenth century and strongly suggested by our archaeological data during the middle Chance phase, it now remains to attempt to fill the two-century gap between the Christopher and Burke sites, which seem to have been coeval Onondaga towns, and the Indian Castle and Indian Hill sites described by Greenhalgh. To bridge this hiatus we have the twelve Onondaga villages described previously.

The evidence cited in the section on chronology suggests that in every instance throughout this time a pair of more or less coeval villages existed. These pairs of villages include, from the earliest to the most recent, the Chance phase towns of Christopher and Burke, the early Garoga phase towns of Cemetery and Nursery, the middle Garoga phase Barnes and McNab sites, the late Garoga phase Atwell and Temperance House sites (the former revealing the first evidence of European contact), the Quirk and Chase sites which have produced the first significant amounts of trade goods, the little-known Dwyer and Sheldon sites which seem to follow in time on the basis of location, a suggestion which is at least not refuted by the material from them, and the Pompey Center and Carley sites which appear to be the pair of villages occupied immediately before the Indian Hill and Indian Castle sites visited by Greenhalgh. Also, if Father Lamberville's statement is true that the Onondaga dwelt at Indian Hill for nineteen years before moving to the Pen site in 1682, the Pompey Center or probably the Carley site may have been that visited by Jesuit missionaries in the 1650s, and therefore the first Onondaga village to appear in the historic record.

Besides this rather general chronology it is possible to offer some suggestions as to which community occupied which of these settlements as they moved throughout the eastern portion of Onondaga County (see Figure 8). The approximate sizes of the various components are given in the site descriptions and need not be repeated here. The larger of the two communities which we first encountered as a small hamlet living at the Cabin site and which we have watched grow in size throughout its sojourns at the Furnace Brook, Howlett Hill, Schoff, and Burke sites, can be traced forward in time through the large Nursery, Barnes, and Temperance House sites of the Garoga phase, into the protohistoric period at the Chase site, then to either Sheldon or Dwyer, then to the reportedly large Carley site where it may have been visited by Europeans, and to the Indian Hill site from which it removed to the Jamesville Pen site, and finally to the Onondaga Valley from where it was but a short step to the reservation where the Onondaga live today.

The second, smaller, community cannot be identified until the early 1400s when we see what appears to be a village union between the communities which lived at the Keough and Bloody Hill sites. Quite possibly the Coye II site, which apparently immediately predated these early Chance phase villages and is located close by, represents an earlier settlement of one of these small communities, though this possibility awaits further investigation before it may be accepted without reservations. From the Christopher site the trial is considerably more lucid and leads through the Cemetery site, the McNab, Atwell, and Quirk sites, then either to Sheldon or Dwyer, to the Pompey Center site, to Indian Castle which was visited by Greenhalgh, to the Weston site, to Toyadasso (Coye) from which the people were driven by American raiders in 1779 when they fled to the Onondaga Creek valley near what is now the Onondaga Reservation.

Other communities which may have been responsible for the additional sites described here do not seem to have made a strong impression on the history of the Onondaga, though this may be as much a reflection of lack of intensive investigation as of the actual situation. The community which lived at the Chamberlin site probably also occupied the Kelso site and may have dwelt at an intermediate site about which we have almost no information but which is located roughly between the two well-known components. There is every indication as well that the community which left its remains at these sites had dwelt previously at the Maxon-Derby site, located a few miles northeast of the Chamberlin site, which is dated at A.D. 1100 (Ritchie 1965:273–74). This fact pushes our history of Iroquois development in central New York well back into the Owasco culture. There are no remains of this early period which can be connected directly with either the large or small Onondaga villages (unless, of course, the Kelso community moved as a unit to the Christopher or some other site), but they may yet be discovered near Syracuse unless they have already been destroyed by the advance of that city into the surrounding countryside.

The Crego and the Hicks Road School sites, though located not far from one another, bear no definite relationship to each other; nor do they seem to have contributed much to Onondaga cultural development. Again, however, this may be because of our limited investigations. The Mountain View site presents another enigma. It seems to fit nowhere in our sequence, and the ceramics found there are not known from other Onondaga sites. These three sites—Crego, Hicks Road, and Mountain View—though the latter is located at some distance from the former two sites—offer some interesting possibilities for speculation. The earliest of the three sites appears to be the Chance phase Crego site which, from the limited sample available, seems to be in no way different from the other developing Iroquois communities studied at the Schoff, Bloody Hill, and Keough sites. The Hicks Road site, however, with its unusual corded pottery, lip profiles, and other attributes which fall outside the range of locally developed Iroquois culture, seems to represent a foreign element in Onondaga territory. Further, the Mountain View material seems to represent an amalgam of ceramic traits which are typically Onondaga and others which *could have* come from the Hicks Road assemblage. Keeping in mind the uncertain nature of these data, it is nevertheless possible to infer that these sites represent a group of people who settled in Onondaga country, were adopted by the Onondaga, and gradually became acculturated and indistinguishable from the Onondaga themselves. These people could not have represented a St. Law-

rence Iroquoian population; nor is the Hicks Road assemblage reminiscent of Jefferson County. It seems most similar to something from western
New York, though I suspect there are no Indians or archaeologists
in that area who will not be somewhat reluctant to claim it. Finally,
it should be pointed out that the adoption of a whole village is known
from historic times when the Mohawk allowed a refugee group of Hurons
to settle in the Mohawk Valley, apparently in a site located not far
from what is now St. Johnsville, New York.

MICROTRADITIONS IN ONONDAGA PREHISTORY

In the following pages a few suggestions as to the origin of the distinctive microtraditions—especially house styles and ceramic attributes—
which characterize the Oak Hill and Chance phase occupants of central
New York will be made. Such minor deviations from the general pattern
of a developing cultural tradition have often been noted by archaeologists, and the insights gained by them offer us a basis for some
speculations about social changes which are reflected in these minor cultural differences.

Dr. Robert Whallon, in an article (1968:234) investigating prehistoric
social organization in New York State, has measured the degree of hom-
ogeneity among the ceramic assemblages from fourteen sites ranging in
time from early Owasco to historic Iroquois. He found that through time
the ceramic assemblage from any one site becomes more and more homogeneous. That is, it has less stylistic variability, which he took to indicate a decreasing rate of village intercommunication through time resulting in the development of local pottery styles which are specific to a
village and are manufactured to the exclusion of most other styles of ceramics.

Our data, however, suggest an alternative explanation for the
phenomenon observed by Whallon which involves not *decreasing*
communication among villages through time but *increasing* village
intercommunication. If, as our data have shown during the Owasco and
Oak Hill phases, there were local microtraditions detectable in the archaeological record, it would seem that there was a class of people who
remained in the village of their birth throughout most of their lives.
These people learned to make pottery, build houses, and use certain
tools in that village and taught the younger generation of that community the same traits which they then passed on. The social isolation of
certain members of a community or of entire communities could be a

function of several factors. Some specific residence regulation such as matri- or uxorilocality (residence of a married couple in the wife's village) could account for the development of some of these microtraditions. Another more probable cause for the maintenance of these distinctive microtraditions during the Castle Creek, Oak Hill, and early Chance phases was the general social isolation of entire communities from one another, a factor directly attributable to the state of internecine warfare which existed prior to the formation of the nations which ultimately composed the League. One expression of this internecine warfare would almost certainly be a decrease in peaceful intercommunication among villages. (By no means, however, would intercommunication cease altogether.) Also, village exogamy ("marrying out") would be unlikely; hence local ways of doing things were perpetuated during the formative stages of Iroquois culture.

Following the Chance phase, however, these microtraditions all but disappeared, and village size remained practically the only distinguishing feature of the two Onondaga towns. The cultures of the two communities, at least so far as they are reflected in the archaeological record, seem to have become nearly identical after the time of the village convergence which we have taken as a political unification. Surely this is no coincidence, for such a political unification must have resulted in a lessening of tensions, hence increased village intercommunication.

This would explain the apparent blending of the several distinct microtraditions which are partially reflected in the archaeological record, to form a more or less homogeneous "pan-Onondaga" tradition at the national level and "pan-Iroquois" (Five Nations) cultural tradition at an even higher level. (The Seneca, however, present an exception to this possibility. See below.) This situation would be reflected not only in an increasingly homogeneous sample from a single component but also from the entire Onondaga nation, or later the entire eastern Iroquois. Beside this lessening of tension there were increased opportunities for people from one village or nation to communicate with those from other villages or nations at the various Iroquois councils and other festivals which Morgan (1901:117) remarked all Iroquois—young and old, men and women—took great pains to attend. This increased contact of a social nature would also have led to a breakdown of village isolation and of local microtraditions.

The other possible causal factor in the maintenance of local microtraditions, especially ceramic traditions, may have been strong village matrilocal residence patterns which Ritchie (1965:296) suggested might have existed during the Owasco period as a result of female-owned and worked horticultural lands. These patterns, if in fact they ever existed, may also have undergone some modification after the formation of the League. Dr. Cara Richards (1967:51), for instance, basing her conclusions upon a study of documentary evidence left by seventeenth-century visitors to Iroquoia and Huronia, found twenty-three cases in which residence rules could be reasonably inferred from these records. Of these, ten were clearly not matrilocal, nine were probably not matrilocal, three probably were matrilocal, and one described a pattern which was neither matri- nor patrilocal. If strong matrilocal residence patterns once existed among the Onondaga and other Iroquois as well, and if, as Richards suggested, this was not the case in the early historic period, several facts observed in the archaeological record might well be explained. First, the breakdown of matrilocality would certainly lead to the breakdown of local ceramic traditions over much of the area in which this breakdown of residence patterns had taken place. In the same manner, we have seen a breakdown in probable patterns of endogamy reflected in the aracheological record. The apparent within-site homogenization of ceramic styles which is taken by Whallon to reflect increasing community corporateness would therefore actually be a reflection of a much wider trend resulting not from *decreasing* communication among potters but actually from *increasing* intervillage and intertribal communication which resulted, perhaps, in women transferring pottery-making styles and techniques from one village to another through intermarriage.

Secondly, this breakup of matrilocal residence groups may help to explain the gradual diminution of Onondaga houses (presumably extended matri-family residences), a decrease in size from the time of League formation until the single-family cabins of the historic period became predominant.

We see then a transition from a state of internecine warfare to nationhood, paralleled by a similar transition from community isolation to peaceful community interaction. These changes are reflected in our data by the blending of ceramic traditions which seems to be the direct result of increased intercommunication among potters which was occasioned by the movement of women among communities. The process appears to parallel that described by Claude Levi-Strauss (1967:79) as "a continuous transition from war to exchange, and from exchange to intermarriage, and the exchange of brides is only the expression of an uninterrupted process of *dons reciproques* which completes the transition from hostility to alliance, from anxiety to confidence, and from fear to friendship."

The Onondaga progression from internecine warfare to alliance to inter-marriage seems not vastly different.

These trends toward increased intercommunication may not in all cases, however, have been pan-Iroquois in nature. While we might expect village endogamy to be broken down nearly universally among the Five Nations, such practices as village matrilocality might have been somewhat more resistant to change. For instance, it is interesting to note that among the Seneca, where Richards found the clearest statement of matrilocal residence, we also find a ceramic tradition maintained which is distinctly different from that of the four more easterly Iroquois na-tions. Whereas the Cayuga, Onondaga, Oneida, and Mohawk had a ma-jority of ceramic styles in common, the Seneca retained such distinct styles as the "Barbed Collar" and "Seneca Notched" types (MacNeish 1952:38–46) which have no counterparts to the East. A definite correla-tion between Richards' suggestion of maintenance of village matrilocal-ity and maintenance of this ceramic tradition is probably not indicated by these few data, but it is certainly suggested.

Also it should be pointed out that at the time of confederation the Five Nations did not give up their practices of warfare but merely turned their attentions from each other to neighboring groups. That there was little peaceful intercourse between the Iroquois and these groups—the Huron, Erie, and the St. Lawrence Iroquois, for instance—is documented both by oral tradition and historic records. Further, we find in comparing the assemblages from these areas with those of the Five Nations that microtraditions seem to have been maintained within these groups. This suggests that many of the traits of the local village community—such as warfare and endogamy—were transferred to the Five Nations in general. That is, the Five Nations, prior to European disruption of their culture, intermarried primarily among themselves and prosecuted their warfare not against each other but against their equally suitable surrounding Iroquoian neighbors—the Huron or Erie—a situa-tion analogous to that which existed among the fourteenth-century vil-lage communities which later became the Onondaga.

The Onondaga and the Northeastern Late Woodland Period

With the history and prehistory of the Onondaga and the suggestions made about social and political changes in mind, let us now very briefly survey other areas of the Northeast during the time that Iroquois culture was developing in New York State.

That the general pattern of cultural development discovered by our researches in Onondaga reflects the history of the Seneca, Cayuga, Oneida, and Mohawk is by no means certain, but the data found suggest that these people also underwent long *in situ* developments in their established areas. Lenig's (1965) Oak Hill through historic Mohawk series probably demonstrated this fact best, and Pratt's Oneida material suggests a similar course of development among that eastern Iroquois nation. To the west Wray and Schoff's (1953) data document a long series of prehistoric and historic Seneca village removals, and the recently discovered typical Oak Hill phase Farrel site * is at least partly ancestral to the communities traced by Wray and Schoff. Finally, our own limited researches indicate a similar pattern for the Cayuga, who seem to have gradually drifted northward along the east bank of the lake bearing their name.

Similar or identical economies, settlement patterns, and artifact complexes suggest that these four groups were subject to the same factors throughout the second millenium A.D. as were the Onondaga. That they met pressure in the same way is indicated by the convergence of settlements, the political unions which account for the formation of nations, and by the formation of the "Great League of Peace" whose objective was to unify all surrounding peoples.

This pattern is not unique to the Five Nations, however, for throughout the Northeast, in the areas where corn agriculture was possible, these same conditions seem to have been present. The Hurons, Eries, Neutrals, Wenro, Western New York Iroquois, Susquehannocks, and the many eastern Algonkian peoples (south of Maine which marks the approximate agricultural limit in the aboriginal Northeast) were farmers whose economy was indistinguishable from that of the Five Nations. Whatever factors occasioned the internecine warfare in New York State were at work elsewhere in this area as well. Most likely these were related to the increased population concomitant with a stable agricultural economic base which in turn resulted in competition for land and hunting territories. John Witthoft's (1959:32–34) intriguing hypothesis concerning the origin of Iroquoian warfare may also pertain, though it is probably not demonstrable. Witthoft postulated that during Late Woodland times, as women horticulturalists became increasingly dominant as food providers, males suffered a corresponding decrease in prestige as their contribution (by hunting) to the larder lessened. They therefore

* Through the courtesy of Charles Hayes III and Lilita Bergs we were able to examine this important material at the Rochester Museum and Science Center.

turned to the deadly game of war to reassert their masculine role in Iroquois society.

The evidence for such conflict includes palisaded villages throughout Huronia, Ontario's Niagara Peninsula, western New York, Pennsylvania, and southern New England, and good historical evidence for one or more characteristics of the Iroquois warfare complex in the same area: head taking, cutting off portions of the enemy's body, scalping, torture and burning of prisoners, running the gauntlet, cannibalism, or adopting prisoners (Flannery 1939:123–128). Moreover, many of these peoples met the danger from warfare by forming confederations. Some, like the Huron (Tooker 1970a), were nearly identical to that of the Five Nations, while others in New England were possibly of a somewhat different internal nature but clearly served the same purpose as the League.

Other similarities throughout the Northeast can also be documented —from projectile point, smoking pipe, and ceramic styles to longhouse type of dwelling construction—further indicating what might be called a northeastern Late Woodland period interaction sphere, a relatively homogeneous ecological zone in which ideas, especially those of major cultural significance (e.g., agriculture, warfare, and confederation), were rather freely diffused, allowing nevertheless for the formation of distinctive traits on a regional or local level (microtraditions).

Summary and General Conclusions

In the preceding pages we have shown that the Onondaga have long held tenure over the lands in central New York where they were first encountered by the Europeans in the seventeenth century. We have extended this tenure back into the twelfth century, if not considerably before. We have been able to trace the development of Onondaga "material culture" and certain other aspects of Onondaga culture back to their Owasco progenitors in central New York and by so doing have laid to rest any theory of Iroquois origins but the *in situ* hypothesis.

The sequence summarized in Figure 8, anchored at one end by a firm series of radiocarbon dates and at the other end by dates based upon historical observations, contains no major gaps either in time or in space and accounts for nearly all the known Iroquois remains in Onondaga County. In forming this sequence, we have, through a consideration of artifact complexes and settlement patterns, been able to trace the history of a single community from its origins as a relatively isolated hamlet in the mid-thirteenth century through a series of village removals and resettlements through which it grew progressively in size. In the fifteenth century this community left its traditional homeland and moved some twelve miles eastward to form a defensive alliance with another, somewhat smaller, community, the two becoming about 1450 what we know as the Onondaga nation. In this political unification we see the seeds of confederation which later sprouted to encompass the entire Iroquois population from the Genesee River to the Mohawk Valley.

We have suggested that our data reflect changes in the social order which occurred at the same time as these major political developments were taking place—the rise of the masking complex, changes in patterns of village communication, in political relationships including warfare, and some of the early ceremonialism which was so richly developed among the Iroquois of New York. Up to this point we have seen Iroquois cultural development as characterized not by the traditional "dendritic-migrationary" or branching model, but rather by a model of village fusion or convergence whereby the historic Iroquois nations crystallized out of a rather evenly dispersed group of earlier communities.

Later we traced a two-village pattern of Onondaga villages, established by the mid-1400s through another series of village removals and resettlements. This was a series of villages in whose middens are mute testimony to the advance of European culture into Iroquoia. Under increasing pressure from explorers and colonists, the Onondaga attempted to maintain a traditional way of life which was shattered forever when they were burned out of their last fortified stronghold before the advance of Frontenac's army in 1696. At that time they retreated to the site of the present reserve where as Morgan (1901) noted, "Their council of fires, so far as they are emblematical of civil jurisdiction, have long since been extinguished, their empire has terminated, and the shades of evening are now gathering thickly over the scattered and feeble remnants of this once powerful League."

Appendix A

Technique of Ceramic Analysis

THE ATTRIBUTE LIST which formed the basis for pottery description and analysis in this report is included here (with little additional comment) for several reasons: first, certain parts explain and illustrate terminology employed in the much-compressed descriptions of ceramics; second, it indicates fully the range and variety (if not the precentages) of decorative motifs and techniques employed by Onondaga potters; and third, it offers a basis for analysis of other ceramics utilizing the same attribute list, thereby providing a standard for description and comparison of other material.

Various Lip Profiles Subsumed in Lip Profile Groups

PLAIN LIP RIM PROFILES

THICKENED LIP RIM PROFILES

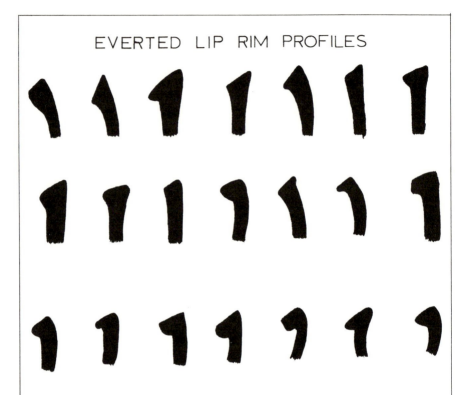

EVERTED LIP RIM PROFILES

BICONCAVE COLLAR RIM PROFILES

BEADED RIM PROFILES

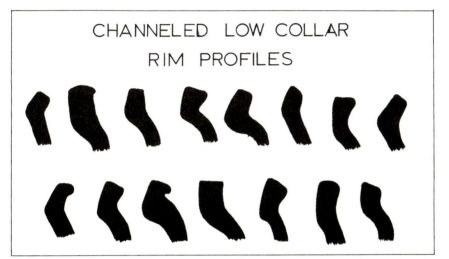

CHANNELED LOW COLLAR
RIM PROFILES

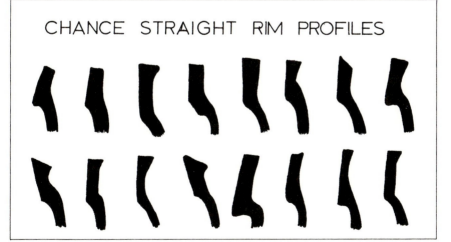

CHANCE STRAIGHT RIM PROFILES

INCIPIENT COLLAR RIM PROFILES

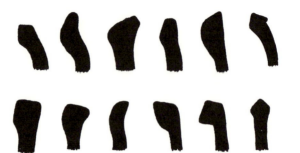

CHANCE ROUNDED RIM PROFILES

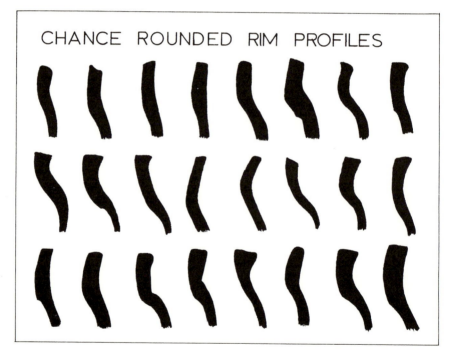

Various Collar Motifs Subsumed
in Collar Motif Groups
Group A Collar Motifs, Horizontal Lines
Group L Plain

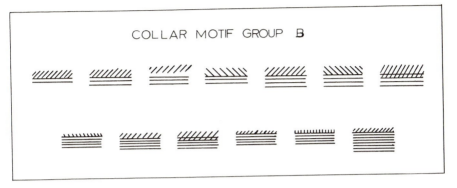

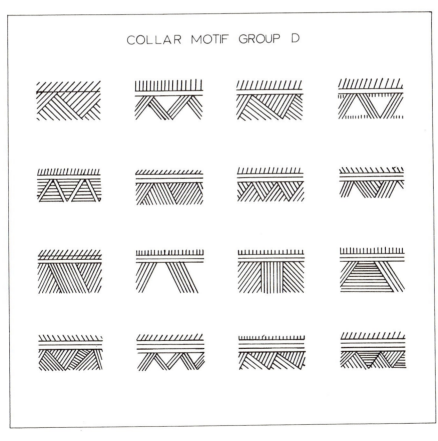

COLLAR   MOTIF GROUP C

COLLAR   MOTIF   GROUP   E

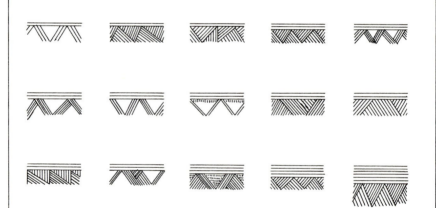

COLLAR   MOTIF   GROUP   G

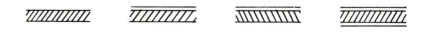

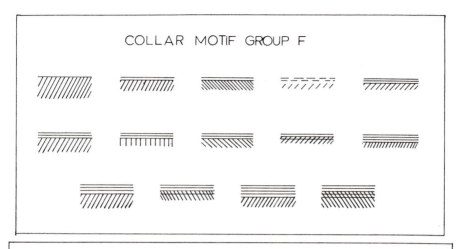

COLLAR MOTIF GROUP F

COLLAR MOTIF GROUP H

COLLAR MOTIF GROUP J

COLLAR MOTIF K

COLLAR MOTIF GROUP M

COLLAR MOTIF GROUP I

COLLAR MOTIF N

COLLAR MOTIF O

Decorative Motifs Employed by Onondaga Potters

Class I—Rim Profiles (see first section for rim profile groups)

Class II—Interior motifs

1. ///////
2. plain
3. ||||||||
4. \\\\\\
5. XXXXXXX
6. ≡≡≡≡≡

Class III—Interior lip edge motifs

1. ||||||||
2. ///////
3. \\\\\\\
4. ▬ ▬ ▬
5. plain
6. • • • • •
7. ● ● ● ●

Class IV—Lip motifs

1. ≡≡≡≡≡
2. ////////
3. \\\\\\\
4. +++++++++
5. ————
6. ||||||||||
7. plain
8. O O O O O
9.
10.
11. XXXXXXX
12. ≡≡≡≡
13. ///////
14.
15.
16. ////////
17. – – – – –
18. -|||– – –|||-
19. //\\//\\//\\
20.
21.
22. ≡≡≡≡≡
23.

Class V—Exterior lip edge motifs

1. |||||||||
2. plain
3. ————
4. ///////
5. \\\\\\\
6.
7. // // //
8. • • • • •
9.
10. pinched

Class VI—Collar motifs (see previous section for collar motif groups)

Class VII—Collar base motifs

1. ////////
2. plain
3. ||||||||||
4. ● ● ● ● ●
5. \\\\\\\
6. || || || || ||
7. // // // // //
8. ● ● ● ●
9. \/\/\/\/
10. ————
11. pinched
12. molded "scallops"

Class VIII—Sub-lip motifs

1. //////////

2. neck motif extends to lip edge

3. \\\\\\\\\\

4. |||||||||||||

5. ⟨⟨⟨⟨⟨⟨⟨⟨⟨

6.   plain

7. ≡≡≡≡≡≡

8. ||||||||||||||||

9. ⫻⫻⫻⫻⫻⫻⫻⫻⫻

10. ————

11. ⟩⟩⟩⟩⟩⟩⟩⟩

12. ┬┬┬┬┬┬┬┬

13. ≡≡≡≡≡≡

Class IX—Sub-collar motifs

1. /////////

2.   plain

3. \\\\\\\\

4. ≡≡≡≡

5. neck motif extends to body surface

6. ≡≡≡≡≡

7. ||||||||||||

8. ⌄⌄⌄⌄⌄⌄⌄

9. ● ● ● ● ●

10. ————

Class X—Neck motifs

1.

2.

3.

4.

5.

6.

7.   plain

8.

9.

14.

15.

16.

17.

18.

19.

20.

21.

22.

27.

28. single horizontal row of any style punctations

29. parallel vertical rows of any style punctations

30. parallel left oblique rows of any style punctations

31.

32.

33.

34.

35.

10.

11.

12.

13.

23.

24.

25.

26.

36.

37.

38.

CLASS XI—SUB-NECK MOTIFS

1.

2. neck motif extends to body surface

3.

4.

5.

6.

7. plain

8.

9.

10.

11. single row of any style punctations

12.

13.

14.

15.

16.

17.

Appendix B

As noted in the site descriptions, smoking pipes were treated in a manner different from the rest of the material remains considered in this study. This was done as a matter of convenience in describing them and partly because of the nature of the pipes themselves. Iroquois smoking pipes seem very susceptible to analysis based upon types rather than attributes. That is, there are numerous consistent and easily recognizable styles of smoking pipes throughout Iroquois prehistory. Ritchie remarked upon this (1965:321,323), and an unpublished dissertation, "Types and Attributes in the Study of Iroquois Pipes" (Harvard University, 1970), has been completed by Cynthia J. Weber. The pipes recovered from our excavations and others studied in collections are therefore, compared on the basis of the varieties described below.

Barrel-shaped Bowl

The bowl of this variety has a bulging midsection and constricted rim and lower section. The rim is generally flattened and perpendicular to the interior and exterior surfaces, which are generally parallel with no flaring on the interior near the lip. In the few cases complete enough to reconstruct, the bowl forms an angle of slightly more than 90 degrees with the stem. Decoration was most often accomplished with a fine cord-wrapped paddle and consists of geometric motifs. Linear punctation, incising, and pointille work are somewhat unusual but not rare on this variety of smoking pipe. This variety of pipe is characteristic of late Owasco and Oak Hill phase sites, apparently disappearing before the beginning of the Chance phase. Pipes of this variety are illustrated on Plate 6, nos. 8, 9.

Corn Effigy

The bowl and other attributes are similar to the barrel-shaped pipes described above. Unique to this variety is the decoration of linear impressions deeply set into the clay, outlining and molding the pipe bowl to resemble an ear of corn. An example is shown on Plate 6, no. 10.

Conical Bowl

The bowl of this variety has straight, or more commonly slightly convex, sides which flare outward to form a cone. The lip is generally slightly flattened, but the interior may flare slightly at the mouth in relation to the exterior surface, perhaps foreshadowing the later trumpet pipes. Decoration most often consists of horizontal bands of lines, either cord-wrapped paddle impressed or incised, often with bands of short vertical lines between these bands. These pipes, as the two previous examples, are characteristic of late Owasco and earliest Iroquois sites. See Plate 14, no. 13 for an illustration of this variety.

Collared Pipes

The form of the lip and the exterior surface immediately below it on these pipes is similar to the collared ceramics which were becoming popular during the early stages of Iroquois cultural development. The bowl form is generally round-bottomed with fairly straight or slightly convex sides. The interior and exterior surfaces are nearly parallel and the lip generally flattened. Immediately below the lip there is a pronounced and sharply defined collar which may be between 5 and 15 mm. high (at least in the small sample available). This collar is usually decorated primarily by horizontal lines, though these may be interrupted by bands of short vertical lines. The remainder of the bowl is most often decorated with vertical lines usually also interrupted by short opposed lines or punctations. The primary technique of decoration is again cording, but incising and pointille work are also known.

Vasiform Pipes

The bowl is round-bottomed with a globular lower portion, constricted neck, and flaring rim. As in all the above examples, the bowl forms nearly a right angle with the stem. Decoration is usually incised or impressed into the clay with a cord-wrapped paddle. Motifs vary greatly, even in the small sample from sites in the Onondaga area, and include vertical bands the entire length of the bowl, often interrupted by short horizontal lines; horizontal lines on the upper portion of the bowl (neck) and vertical lines on the lower, globular portion; and various combinations which include fine pointille work. See Plate 14, no. 14 for an example of this variety.

Puff-sleeve Pipes

This variety is somewhat similar to vasiform pipes and is probably related to them. The bottom of the bowl is globular, though somewhat more flattened than in examples of the vasiform style. The upper portion is flaring and often makes an angle of 90 degrees where it joins the lower part of the bowl. It is always more sharply delineated than in the previous variety. The lip is flaring, the rim flattened and squared in relation to the exterior and interior surfaces which are themselves usually parallel. The bowl again forms an angle slightly greater than 90 degrees with the stem. Decoration is generally, but not exclusively, bands of horizontal lines on the flaring upper part of the bowl and some motif containing vertical lines on the lower part. Both these decorations are most often executed in fine incising, and both are frequently set off by bands of fine pointille work, usually apparently done with the same tool as the incising.

Vasiform Effigy Pipes

These are similar in all formal attributes to the vasiform pipes previously described. The decoration is distinctive, however, in that it consists of effigies, usually of a frog or salamander, either molded in low relief or outlined in fine pointille work or, frequently, defined by both techniques. The decoration over the remainder of the bowl is usually more similar to that found on puff-sleeve pipes than on vasiform pipes. See Plate 14, no. 11 for a fragment of such a pipe.

Vertical Barred Pipes

These are represented only by small fragments in the collections described in this report. Their form seems to be generally similar to the vasiform pipes described above. In this case, however, decoration consists of raised vertical bars of clay molded into the pipe at the time of manufacture. These bars occasionally have vertical incised lines and are frequently set off by rows of fine punctations, apparently done with the same tool as the incising. The upper portion of the bowls are most often decorated with horizontal lines as are other vasiform pipes.

Square Bowl Pipes

The primary feature of this easily distinguishable variety is a square or rectangular (occasionally sub-rectangular) bowl form. Sides are essentially straight, usually converging toward the stem. The bowl forms an angle with the stem of near 100 degrees. Lips are flattened and form nearly a right angle with the sides of the pipe which are parallel. A variety of motifs occur, mostly geometric, and are executed in fine cording, incising and fine punctations. An example of a square bowl pipe will be found on Plate 14, no. 15.

Proto-trumpet Pipes

These pipes seem to be intermediate between the conical pipes of late Owasco and the trumpet pipes typical of the Iroquois. They are first found in the Oak Hill phase but reach their maximum popularity during the early Chance phase. Two sub-varieties are discernible, an earlier decorated form and a later plain variety. They are similarly characterized by slightly flaring rims and a lack of the globular or bulbous base common to the vasiform and puff-sleeve varieties, from which they may also be derived (see Ritchie 1952:48–49). The earlier decorated variety has a flattened lip typical of other early pipe styles and is decorated with various geometric motifs, usually horizontal above vertical lines executed in a combination of fine incising and pointille work. The later plain variety often has a greater flare in the interior surface than in the exterior resulting in a thinned, sharp lip. Decoration is absent on this form, but there are examples fitting this description which have a single row of fine punctations on the lip of the pipe. See Plate 29, no. 10 for an illustration of a proto-trumpet pipe.

Trumpet Pipes

As with the proto-trumpets, several sub-varieties, in this case four, can be distinguished.

Plain trumpets are apparently an early variety developing from the plain proto-trumpet and continuing undecorated. These have considerably more flare than the earlier proto-trumpets, usually with a pronounced rim which flares outward from the bowl to the horizontal. The lip is generally gently rounded, and one specimen has a row of small punctations around the lip, while the bowl remains undecorated. The angle made by the bowl and stem is more obtuse than in any of the varieties described previously and more nearly approaches a gentle bend rather than a sharply defined union between bowl and stem.

Decorated trumpets are similar in form to those described above but usually have an even greater flare in the bowl and a more pronounced rim. Decoration consists of bands of horizontal lines, often grouped on raised ridges of clay, running horizontally around the bowl. Among the pipes considered in this study, such bands are almost always three in number. The lips may have small linear punctations forming a reeded edge or may have a series of round punctations on the lip. The bands of horizontal lines may also be set off by rows of small punctations. There is no clearly defined place at which the bowl joins the stem, the whole being a single gentle curve (see Plate 34, no. 8).

Rimless trumpets are decorated with bands of horizontal lines, often raised, but they lack the flaring rim of the above. White (1961:96 and Plate V, fig. 2) describes this variety from late contexts in western New York. In some respects, these pipes are similar to the collared pipes (see above) but are more likely descended from an earlier trumpet form.

Squared trumpets are probably the easiest of the four to distinguish by virtue of their thicker projecting rim which has been molded into a square surmounting the bowl. This variety, sometimes known as a "coronet" pipe, is also common on later Onondaga sites.

Human-face Effigy Pipes

These pipes seem to range throughout late Owasco and Iroquois assemblages. There are probably several sub-varieties of this pipe style which progress from simply but artistically executed examples in Owasco culture (Ritchie, Lenig, and Miller 1953:73, Plate 8, no. 8) to pipes of almost portrait quality at later sites (Ritchie 1965, Plate 107, fig. 103). Effigies may be either facing the smoker or facing away from him. Most examples are, unfortunately, too fragmentary to determine the direction in which the effigy faces. Occasionally there may be more than one face on a single specimen.

Other Effigy Forms

These include various skillfully molded birds, mammals, and reptiles (especially snakes) found on late Iroquois pipes. The effigy almost always forms part of the bowl rather than being applied to it. These pipes are lumped into a single category because they are most characteristic of sites beyond the temporal range of this study. A detailed study of these various forms, however, will doubtless yield some interesting and valuable information on Iroquois development and trade relations.

Bibliography

Bartram, John, 1751. *Observations on the Inhabitants, Climate, Soil, Rivers, Productions, Animals in his Travels from Pensilvania to Onondago, Oswego and the Lake Ontario.* London.

Beauchamp, William M. 1900. *Aboriginal Occupation of New York.* New York State Museum, Bulletin No. 32, Vol. 7. Albany.

———. 1902a. *Horn and Bone Implements of the New York Indians.* New York State Museum, Bulletin No. 50. Albany.

———. 1902b. *Metallic Implements of the New York Indians.* New York State Museum, Bulletin No. 55. Albany.

———. 1905. *A History of the New York Iroquois.* New York State Museum, Bulletin No. 78. Albany.

———. 1916. *The Moravian Journals Relating to Central New York 1745–66.* Onondaga Historical Association. Syracuse.

Biggar, H. P. 1924. *The Voyage of Jacques Cartier.* Public Archives of Canada, Publication II. Ottawa.

Blair, E. H. 1911. *Indian Tribes of the Upper Mississippi and the Great Lakes Region.* 2 vols. Cleveland.

Blau, Harold. 1967. "Notes on the Onondaga Bowl Game." *In Iroquois Culture, History and Prehistory,* ed. Elisabeth Tooker, pp. 35–49. New York State Museum and Science Service. Albany.

Brainerd, George W. 1951. "A Place of Chronological Ordering in Archaeological Analysis." *American Antiquity,* Vol. 16, No. 4. Salt Lake City.

Chang, K. C. 1967. *Rethinking Archaeology.* New Haven: Yale University Press.

Clark, Joshua. 1849. *Onondaga or Reminiscences of Earlier and Later Times.* Syracuse.

Colden, Cadwallader. 1922. *The History of the Five Nations of Canada.* New York.

Cuoq, Jean-Andre. 1869. "Quels etaient les sauvages que recontre Jacques Cartier sur les rives du Saint-Laurent?" *Annales de Philosophie Chretienne,* Vol. 79, 198–204.

Dawson, Sir J. W. 1860. "Notes on Aboriginal Antiquities Recently Discovered in Montreal." *Canadian Naturalist and Geologist,* Vol. 5, 430–39. Montreal.

———. 1861. "Additional Notes on Aboriginal Antiquities Found in Montreal." *Canadian Naturalist and Geologist,* Vol. 6, 362–73. Montreal.

Fenton, William N. 1940. "Problems Arising from the Historic Northeastern Position of the Iroquois." In *Essays in Historical Anthropology of North America.* Smithsonian Miscellaneous Collections, Volume 100, 159–251. Washington, D.C.

Flannery, Regina. 1939. *An Analysis of Coastal Algonquin Culture.* Catholic University of America, Anthropological Series, No. 7. Washington, D.C.

Funk, Robert E. 1967. "Garoga: A Late Prehistoric Iroquois Village in the Mohawk Valley." In *Iroquois Culture, History and Prehistory,* ed. Elisabeth Tooker. New York State Museum. Albany.

Gibson, Stanford J. 1968. "The Oran-Barnes Site." *Bulletin* of the Chenango Chapter, New York State Archaeological Association, Vol. 10, No. 1, Norwich, New York.

Graham, Robert John, and Charles F. Wray. 1966. *The Boughton Hill Site; Victor, New York.* Mimeographed report distributed at the 1966 Annual Meeting of the New York State Archaeological Association. Rochester, New York.

Griffin, James B. 1943. *The Iroquois in American Prehistory.* Papers of the Michigan Academy of Science, Arts, and Letters, Vol. 29. Norwood.

Hale, Horatio. 1884. *The Iroquois Book of Rites.* Brinton's Library of Aboriginal American Literature, No. 2. Philadelphia.

Jesuit Relations. See Thwaites, Rueben, editor.

Lafitau, J. 1724. *Moeurs des Sauvages Amériquains Comparées aux Moeurs des Premiers Temps.* 2 Vols. Saugrain l'aîné, Paris.

Lenig, Donald. 1965. *The Oak Hill Horizon and its Relation to the Development of Five Nations Iroquois.* Researches and Transactions of the New York State Archaeological Association, Vol. 15, No. 1. Buffalo.

Levi-Strauss, Claude. 1967. *Les Structures Elementaires de la Parente.* 2nd ed. Paris.

Lloyd, Herbert M. 1901. Annotation of the 1901 edition of Lewis Henry Morgan's *League of the Iroquois.* New York.

Lounsbury, Floyd. 1961. "Iroquois-Cherokee Linguistic Relations." In *Symposium on Cherokee and Iroquois Culture,* ed. William Fenton and John Gulick. Smithsonian Institution, Bureau of American Ethnology, Bulletin 180. Washington, D.C.

MacNeish, Richard S. 1952. *Iroquois Pottery Types, A Technique for the Study of Iroquois Prehistory.* National Museum of Canada, Bulletin 124. Ottawa.

Morgan, Lewis Henry. 1901. *League of the Ho-de-no-sau-nee or Iroquois,* ed. Herbert M. Lloyd. New York.

O'Callaghan, E. B. 1849. *The Documentary History of the State of New York,* Volume 1. Albany.

Parker, Arthur C. 1913. *The Code of Handsome Lake, The Seneca Prophet.* New York State Museum, Bulletin 163. Albany.

———. 1916. "The Origin of the Iroquois as suggested by their Archaeology." *American Anthropologist,* Vol. 18, 479–507.

———. 1922. *The Archaeological History of New York*. New York State Museum, Bulletins 235–38. Albany.

Pendergast, James F. 1962. "The Crystal Rock Site, and Early Onondaga-Oneida Site in Eastern Ontario." *Pennsylvania Archaeologist*, Vol. 33, No. 1.

———. 1963. *The Payne Site*. National Museum of Canada, Contributions to Anthropology, Bulletin 193. Ottawa.

———. 1964. "The Waupoos Site: an Iroquois Component in Prince Edward County, Ontario." *Pennsylvania Archaeologist*, Vol. 34, No. 2, 69–89. Gettysburg.

———. 1965. *Three Prehistoric Iroquois Components in Eastern Ontario*. National Museum of Canada, Bulletin No. 208. Ottawa.

Pratt, Peter P. 1963. "The Pen Site: excavations of a cemetery to the Onondaga Iroquois capital attacked by Frontenac in 1696." Paper read at the 1963 Annual Meeting of the Northeastern Anthropological Association, Ithaca, New York. Subsequently distributed in mimeograph form.

Pyke, Elizabeth, and J. H. Manross. 1935. "Indian village found on farm, disclosed by relics dug up on Sentinel Heights." Syracuse *Post-Standard*, January 6, 1935. Syracuse, New York.

Richards, Cara E. 1967. "Huron and Iroquois Residence Patterns 1600–1650." In *Iroquois Culture, History and Prehistory*, ed. Elisabeth Tooker, pp. 51–56. New York State Museum and Science Service. Albany.

Ricklis, Robert. 1963. "Excavations at the Atwell Fort Site, Madison County, New York." New York State Archaeological Association, *Bulletin No. 28*, pp. 2–5. Ossining.

———. 1965. "Preliminary Report on the Cabin Site (Tly 1–1), Syracuse, New York." New York State Archaeological Association, Morgan Chapter, *Newsletter*, Vol. 5, Spring 1965. Rochester.

———. 1966. "A Preliminary Report on some Late Prehistoric and Early Historic Onondaga Sites Near Syracuse, New York." New York State Archaeological Association, Morgan Chapter, *Newsletter*, Vol. 6, pp. 1–11, January, 1966. Rochester.

Ritchie, William A. 1936. *A Prehistoric Fortified Village Site at Canandaigua, Ontario County, New York*. Research Records of the Rochester Museum of Arts and Sciences, No. 3. Rochester.

———. 1944. *The Pre-Iroquoian Occupations of New York State*. Rochester Museum of Arts and Sciences, Memoir No. 1. Rochester.

———. 1952. *The Chance Horizon, an Early Stage in Mohawk Cultural Development*. New York State Museum and Science Service, Circular 29. Albany.

———. 1954. *Dutch Hollow, an Early Historic Period Seneca Site in Livingston County, New York*. Researches and Transactions of the New York State Archaeological Association, Vol. 13, No. 1. Albany.

———. 1961a. *A Typology and Nomenclature for New York Projectile Points*. New York Museum and Science Service Bulletin No. 384. Albany.

———. 1961b. "Iroquois Archaeology and Settlement Patterns." In *Symposium on Iroquois and Cherokee Culture*, ed. William Fenton and John Gulick.

Smithsonian Institution, Bureau of American Ethnology, Bulletin 180, pp. 27–38. Washington, D.C.

———. 1965. *The Archaeology of New York State.* Garden City: Natural History Press.

———. 1967. "The Kelso site: Its Significance for the Problem of Iroquois Origins." In *Iroquois Culture, History and Prehistory,* ed. Elisabeth Tooker. New York State Museum. Albany.

———. 1969. *The Archaeology of New York State.* Revised ed. Garden City: Natural History Press.

Ritchie, William A., and Robert E. Funk. n.d. *Aboriginal Settlement Patterns in New York State.* In preparation.

Ritchie, William A., Donald Lenig, and P. Schuyler Miller. 1953. *An Early Owasco Sequence in Eastern New York.* New York Museum and Science Service, Circular 32. Albany.

Stuiver, Minze, and Hans Suess. 1966. "On the Relationship between Radiocarbon Dates and True Sample Ages." *Radiocarbon,* Vol. 8, 534–40.

Thwaites, Rueben Gold. 1896–1901. *The Jesuit Relations and Allied Documents.* 73 Vols. Cleveland.

Tooker, Elisabeth. 1964. *An Ethnography of the Huron Indians 1615–1649.* Smithsonian Institution, Bureau of American Ethnology, Bulletin 190. Washington, D.C. (Reprinted with the original pagination by the Huronia Historical Development Council and the Ontario Department of Education, 1967. Midland, Ontario).

———. 1967. "Identification of the Contents of the Medicine Bundle from Feature II." In *An Early Historic Niagara Frontier Iroquois Cemetery in Erie County, New York,* by Marian E. White. Researches and Transactions of the New York State Archaeological Association, Vol. 16, No. 1. Rochester.

———. 1970a. "Northern Iroquoian Sociopolitical Organization." *American Anthropologist,* Vol. 72, No. 1, 90–96.

———. 1970b. *The Iroquois Ceremonial of Midwinter.* Syracuse: Syracuse University Press.

Tooker, Elisabeth, and Marian E. White. 1968. "Archaeological Evidence for Seventeenth-Century Iroquoian Dream Fulfillment Rituals." *Pennsylvania Archaeologist,* Vol. 34, No. 3–4, 1–5.

Trigger, Bruce G. 1967a. "Who were the Laurentian Iroquois?" *The Canadian Review of Sociology and Anthropology,* Vol. 3, No. 4.

———. 1967b. "A Fresh Look at the Laurentian Iroquois", paper read at the 1967 Annual Meeting of the New York State Archaeological Association, Saratoga, New York.

———. 1968. "Archaeological and Other Evidence: A Fresh Look at the Laurentian Iroquois." *American Antiquity.* Vol. 33, No. 4, 429–40. Salt Lake City.

Tuck, James A. 1967. "The Howlett Hill Site: An Early Iroquois Village in Central New York." In *Iroquois Culture, History and Prehistory,* ed. Elisabeth Tooker, New York State Museum, Albany.

———. 1970. "Some recent work on the prehistory of the Onondaga Nation." *Pennsylvania Archaeologist,* Vol. 39, Nos. 1–4, 40–52.

———. 1971. "The Iroquois Confederacy," *Scientific American*, Vol. 224, No. 2, 32–49.

———. n.d. "Iroquois Cultural Development in Central New York." Unpublished doctoral dissertation. Syracuse University.

Wallace, Anthony F. C. 1958. "Dreams and Wishes of the Soul: A Type of Psychoanalytic Theory Among the Seventeenth-Century Iroquois." *American Anthropologist*, N.S., Vol. 60, 234–48.

Weber, Cynthia. n.d. "Types and Attributes in the Study of Iroquois Pipes." Unpublished doctoral dissertation. Harvard University.

Whallon, Robert, Jr. 1968. "Investigations of Late Prehistoric Social Organization in New York State." In *New Perspectives in Archaeology*, ed. Sally R. Binford and Lewis R. Binford. Chicago: Aldine.

White, Marian E. 1961. *Iroquois Culture History in the Niagara Frontier Area of New York State.* University of Michigan Anthropological Papers. No. 16, Ann Arbor.

———. 1967. *An Early Historic Niagara Frontier Iroquois Cemetery in Erie County, New York.* Researches and Transactions of the New York State Archaeological Association, Vol. XVI, No. 1. Rochester.

Witthoft, John. 1959. "Ancestry of the Susquehannocks." In *Susquehannock Miscellany*, ed. John Witthoft and W. Fred Kinsey III. Pennsylvania Historical Commission. Harrisburg.

Wray, Charles, and Harry Schoff. 1953. "A Preliminary Report on the Seneca Sequence In Western New York—1550–1687." *Pennsylvania Archaeologist*, Vol. 8, No. 2, 53–63. Milton.

Wright, James V. 1966. *The Ontario Iroquois Tradition.* National Museum of Canada, Bulletin 210. Ottawa.

Index

Abnaki, 10

Adirondacks, 12

"Ad-do'weh," 8

Agriculture, 12, 13. *See also* food remains

Algonkians, 14, 223

Atotarho, 5

Atwell site: discovery and early records, 165; settlement data, 165–67; features, 167; artifacts, 167–69; chronology, 169–70, 200, 202, 203; community affiliations, 217; 19, 170, 172, 173, 195

Bainbridge site, 16

Baldwinsville, N.Y., 136

Barnes site: discovery and naming, 149; settlement data, 149–50; burials, 150; artifacts, 150–60; food remains, 161; chronology, 161, 199, 201, 203; community affiliation, 217

Bartram, John, 9–10, 192, 193

Bates site, 61

Beads, stone. *See* Rough and polished stone

Beads, glass. *See* Trade goods

Bear Society, 213

Beauchamp, William, 175, 192–93

Berger, Marjorie, 206

Bergs, Lilita, 223

Bloody Hill site: discovery and naming, 104; settlement data, 104–12; features, 12–15; artifacts, 115–18; food remains, 118; chronology, 119, 197, 199, 201, 203; community affiliations, 209–11, 217; 19, 93, 119, 122, 125, 132, 170, 212–15

"Bloody Hill II" site, 189

Bone, modified. *See* Modified bone

Bone, refuse. *See* Food remains

Boundaries of Onondaga, description of, 216

Bowl game, 8

"branching model," 17–18

Broadfield, Louis, 141

Buffalo Society, 213

Burials: ethnographic description, 6–7; Schoff, 97–101; Barnes, 150; Dwyer, 174–75; Carley, 177; Indian Hill, 182; Indian Castle, 186–87; Jamesville Pen., 188; Weston, 189–91

Burke site: discovery and naming, 125; settlement data, 125–31; features, 129; artifacts, 132–35; food remains, 135; chronology, 136, 197, 199, 201, 203; community affiliation, 217; 19, 93, 141, 170, 212, 215

Burr, Walter, 146

Cabin site: discovery and naming, 34–35; settlement data, 35–37; artifacts, 37–43; food remains, 43–44; chronology, 45, 199, 201, 203; community affiliation, 208, 210, 217; 19, 48, 92, 94, 209, 215

Calkins Farm site, 16

Cammerhoff, Frederick, 192–93

Canandaigua site, 16

Cannibalism: ethnographic description, 10; at Bloody Hill, 113–14

Carley site: discovery and naming, 176; settlement data, 176–77; burials, 177; artifacts, 177; chronology, 177, 202, 203; community affiliation, 217; 19, 171, 178, 195

Cartier, Jacques, 11, 14

251